IDENTITY IN NORTHERN IRELAND

Identity in Northern Ireland

Communities, Politics and Change

Cathal McCall
Visiting Fellow
University of Ulster
Northern Ireland

First published in Great Britain 1999 by
MACMILLAN PRESS LTD
Houndmills, Basingstoke, Hampshire RG21 6XS and London
Companies and representatives throughout the world

A catalogue record for this book is available from the British Library.

ISBN 0–333–74018–1

First published in the United States of America 1999 by
ST. MARTIN'S PRESS, INC.,
Scholarly and Reference Division,
175 Fifth Avenue, New York, N.Y. 10010

ISBN 0–312–21844–3

Library of Congress Cataloging-in-Publication Data
McCall, Cathal, 1966–
Identity in Northern Ireland : communities, politics and change /
Cathal McCall.
  p.   cm.
Includes bibliographical references (p.) and index.
ISBN 0–312–21844–3 (cloth)
1. Nationalism—Northern Ireland.   2. Northern Ireland—Politics
and government—1944–   3. Northern Ireland—Relations—Europe.
4. Europe—Relations—Northern Ireland.   I. Title.
DA990.U46M432   1999
320.9416'09'049—dc21   98–30879
                                                            CIP

This book is printed on paper suitable for recycling and made from fully managed and
sustained forest sources.

10   9   8   7   6   5   4   3   2   1
08   07   06   05   04   03   02   01   00   99

Printed and bound in Great Britain by
Antony Rowe Ltd, Chippenham, Wiltshire

For Aunt Rose and Nana

Contents

Acknowledgements   x

Introduction   xi

Part One: Intimations of Postmodernity

1 A Postmodernist Approach to Communal Identities in
   Northern Ireland?   3
     Conceptualizing 'the Modern' and 'the Postmodern'
     Towards a Postmodernism of Resistance
     Objectivity versus Intersubjectivity
     Deconstruction and Reconstruction
     Conclusion

2 Interpreting the Development of the Nation, Irish
   Nationalism and Ulster Unionism   19
     The Ethnic Origins of Nations
     The Modern Nation
     The Imagined Community
     (Re)imagining Irish Nationalist and Ulster Unionist
     Identities
     Conclusion

3 The Governance of Northern Ireland: From Modernity
   to Postmodernity?   36
     The Northern Ireland Context: 1921–72
     The End of the Unionist Hegemony: 1963–72
     The UK State Context: 1972–
     After the Anglo-Irish Agreement (1985): Postmodern
       Polity?
     Conclusion

4 Intimations of Postmodernity in the Development of
   the European Union   56
     Integration
     Subsidiarity
     Regionalism

The Committee of the Regions
Citizenship
Conclusion

5 The European Union and the Resources of Communal
 Identities in Northern Ireland 75
 The Economic Resource
 The Territorial Resource
 The Cultural Resource
 Conclusion

Part Two: Dialogues

6 Dialogue with the Social Democratic and Labour Party
 (SDLP) 95
 Introduction
 SDLP Perceptions of Structural Change
 Determining Structural Parameters for Northern
  Ireland
 Structural Change and Nationalist Identities
  Represented by the SDLP

7 Dialogue with Sinn Féin 123
 Introduction
 Sinn Féin Perceptions of Structural Change
 Determining Structural Parameters for Northern
  Ireland
 Structural Change and Nationalist Identities
  Represented by Sinn Féin

8 Dialogue with the Democratic Unionist Party (DUP) 138
 Introduction
 DUP Perceptions of Structural Change
 Determining Structural Parameters for Northern
  Ireland
 Structural Change and Unionist Identities
  Represented by the DUP

9 Dialogue with the Ulster Unionist Party (UUP) 156
 Introduction
 UUP Perceptions of Structural Change

Determining Structural Parameters for Northern Ireland
Structural Change and Unionist Identities Represented by the UUP

10   Dialogue with the Alliance Party of Northern Ireland (APNI)   179
Introduction
APNI Perceptions of Structural Change
Determining Structural Parameters for Northern Ireland
Structural Change and Identities Represented by the APNI

Conclusion   193

Notes   207

Bibliography   213

Index   224

Acknowledgements

The origins of this book lie in postgraduate research conducted in the Department of Government, University of Strathclyde, Glasgow, between October 1992 and June 1997. I would like to thank Professor James Mitchell and Dr Peter Preston, for the advice, criticism and unstinting encouragement that they gave me during the course of my research. Their colleague, Ms Isobel Lindsay, also provided me with helpful advice and criticism. Thanks also to Mr Seán Costello and my father, Mr Charles McCall, for proof-reading the text. They drew my attention to egregious errors, however, those that remain are entirely my responsibility.

I would like to thank my mother Mrs Josephine McCall for typing the interviews and offering expert guidance in the operation of word-processing packages. Ms Jayne Girvin, Miss Sarah-Jane Haston, Mr Seán Macke, Mr Scott McCallum and my sisters, Ms Anne McCall and Ms Marie McCall also helped in various ways. I am grateful to the staff of the National Library of Scotland who dealt with my stream of requests for books during the course of my reading. I would also like to record my gratitude for the assistance that I received in the University Library, the University of Edinburgh; the Andersonian Library, the University of Strathclyde; the Library, the Queen's University of Belfast; and the Linenhall Library, Belfast. Thanks to John Alderdice, Nigel Dodds, Mark Durkan, Reg Empey, Denis Haughey, Mitchel McLaughlin, Francie Molloy, Maurice Morrow and Jim Nicholson, for kindly consenting to be interviewed and giving generously of their time. The book would not have seen the light of day had it not been for the active encouragement and help of Professor Paul Arthur. I am indebted to him.

Chapter 5 is based on an article entitled 'Postmodern Europe and Communal Identities in Northern Ireland' published in the *European Journal of Political Research*, volume 33, number 3.

Introduction

Why is the language of Northern Ireland politics changing? Why do words like 'dialogue', 'rethinking', 'reinterpreting', 'post-nationalism', 'consent', 'parity', 'accommodation' and 'reconciliation' now feature in a political debate once drowned out by the terrible twin epithets of communal conflict in Northern Ireland: 'No Surrender' and 'Tiochfaidh ar Lá'? Norman Porter is busy 'rethinking unionism' with a philosophical verve. John Hume has been 'post'-ing nationalism through a proclivity for repetition unequalled since Martin Luther King Jr went to the mountain top and saw the Promised Land. What has initiated these rumblings of change in the political discourse of Northern Ireland? The answer, this book contends, is to be found in the incremental shift from modernity to postmodernity in the politics of Northern Ireland and the European Union (EU).

Modern politics in Northern Ireland are understood to have as their bedrock 'the outcome of the events of 1912–14 and the Government of Ireland Act (1920)' (Walker, 1994, p. 1). However, the accession of the UK and the Republic of Ireland to the European Economic Community in 1973 may be interpreted as an inconspicuous shift towards a political postmodernity for Northern Ireland. By the act of accession, it was formally recognized by both states that the sovereignty of the modern nation-state[1] could no longer be maintained exclusively. The subsequent development of the European Community (now known as the European Union), as well as the complementary Anglo-Irish approach to Northern Ireland, has initiated change not only in terminology, but also in political concepts and substantive priorities.

The key question addressed in this book is the extent to which Irish Nationalist and Ulster Unionist identities in Northern Ireland are affected by changes in the region's position within wider economic, political, social and cultural structures of power. The substantive concerns are with: (i) the implications of membership of the EU and the process of integration; and (ii) the impact of the Anglo-Irish political process after 1985. This book attempts to detail the development of opportunities for communal identities in Northern Ireland as they pass through the prism of postmodern structural change in the EU. Possibilities for the uptake of such opportunities through change in the perceptions of individuals and subsequent change in the identities of communities are then examined in dialogues with the political representatives of communal identities. It is here, in the politics of Northern Ireland and in the economic, territorial and cultural resources of Ulster Unionist and northern Irish Nationalist identities, that evidence of change is sought.

INTIMATIONS OF POSTMODERNITY

Postmodernity is used to identify the contemporary world in which the sovereignty of the nation-state is being subverted by transnational economic, social, political and cultural forces. These forces are blurring territorial boundaries and have a direct bearing on the economic, territorial and cultural resources that combine to give meaning to communal identity in Northern Ireland. It is argued that the structure of the state will continue to develop along supranational, national and subnational lines in the EU. Consequently, on-going European integration is assessed in the context of being the primary catalyst for a change in the structural alignment of northern Irish Nationalist and Ulster Unionist identities. Parallel changes in the approach of the United Kingdom government to the governance of Northern Ireland, particularly after 1985, are also indicative of the tentative adoption of a postmodernist approach in that specific context whereby communal interests are prioritized over the modern emphasis on territorial sovereignty. The potential impact of postmodern economic development on individual perceptions and communal identities in Northern Ireland is a major consideration. The implications of structural change for the dominant 'territorial' resource of northern Irish Nationalist and Ulster Unionist identities will, of course, be at the heart of the book's concerns.

Postmodernism is used as a means of discussing these substantive structural changes in conceptual terms. The modernist/ postmodernist debate is the conceptual framework that binds the book. Postmodernism in general offers a critique of the objective-rational epistemological approach established in modernity. Nietzsche set the conceptual scene for postmodernism with his replacement of objective rationality, the central tenet of modernity, with the 'will to power' (Dallmayr, 1993, p. 20). By challenging the rectitude of ideas such as universalist knowledge and objective truth that have been processed by modernity, postmodernism offers a route through which such a conceptual transition can be made. It is argued that a more schismatic culture-bound idea of knowledge is undergoing a renaissance in contemporary society and that postmodernism is fundamental to a strategy, based on interpretation, whereby the reactions of increasingly diverse agents to structural change may be grasped. The distinctions that exist between the modern and the postmodern are thus used to differentiate between the modernist approach to analysis, based on empiricism, and postmodernism's interpretative approach. The focus for the empirical approach has been the territorial context of Northern Ireland. In contrast, postmodernist interpretation emphasizes the import of the culture-bound ideas of knowledge held by communities in Northern Ireland and the implications that their particularist readings of territorial and transterritorial entities may have for a contemporary understanding of these identities. A 'postmodernism of resistance' enables a postmodernist approach subsequently to step beyond the bounds of critique and advocate forms of deconstruction and reconstruction that may contribute to an accommodation among diverse agents.

The dialogues in Part 2 aim to depart from the authoritative approach of modernity by providing the unadulterated responses of diverse agents in Northern Ireland to structural change. The intention of using this postmodernist approach is to contribute to a paradigm shift away from the modernist 'internal conflict' understanding of political interaction in Northern Ireland. The 'internal conflict' understanding prioritizes the conflict between Irish Nationalist and Ulster Unionist identities within the territorial confines of Northern Ireland as the essential political dynamic affecting the perceptions of these communal identities. This understanding either ignores or underestimates extraterritorial sites of influence. It also assumes the 'objective' viewpoint of authoritative intellectuals and has dominated the literature on Northern Ireland for the past 30 years (Whyte, 1990).

THE DIALOGUES

The dialogues attempt to present the subjective truths of representatives from the five main political parties in Northern Ireland. Such an exercise in communication signals the abandonment of the orthodox scientific quest for objectivity and the beginning of an intersubjective engagement.

In deciding on the participants I felt that it was important to choose those likely to represent the positions of communal identities in Northern Ireland best. It might be argued that this contravenes the principle of the dominant versions of postmodernism where the notion of representation is rejected in favour of a participatory form of democracy that directly empowers the individual. However, my choice of interviewing elected political representatives does not contravene the position adopted by a 'postmodernism of resistance' which does not reject the community in favour of the individual or the creation of communal alliances in favour of individual freedom. Elected politicians are entrusted with the task of acting as a conduit for the perceptions of the individuals that they represent. In Northern Ireland, they are also the accepted representatives of communal identities. Evidence of change in individual perceptions and communal identities is, therefore, related through interviews with elected political representatives.

The inclusion of representatives from the five main political parties furnishes the book with perspectives from the broad spectrum of identity perception in Northern Ireland that includes the conventional categories 'Ulster British', 'Ulster Loyalist', 'Irish Nationalist' and 'Irish Republican'. However, the book attempts to side-step the use of these conventional categories where possible because shifts in alignment within communal identity blocks, as well as the salience of subjective perspectives in contemporary political discourse, can undermine conventional categories allotted by authoritative intellectuals. For example, association with and/or support for paramilitary groups has traditionally distinguished 'Irish republicanism' as a corollary of 'Irish nationalism'. However, a more schismatic picture of the Irish Nationalist identity begins to emerge in this book, reflecting the contemporary development of nationalism in the EU. Moreover, the subjects themselves have used these terms interchangeably, for example, interviewee Denis Haughey (SDLP) has described the nominally 'constitutional nationalist' SDLP as 'a Republican party in the proper sense of that word' (Flackes and Elliott, 1994, p. 176). Conversely, the subjective perspective of Ulster Unionists perceived the congealing of a 'pan-nationalist front', incorporating the Irish government, the SDLP, Sinn Féin and the US administration, in the aftermath of the IRA cease-fire in 1994. As far as unionism itself is concerned, 'Ulster British' and 'Ulster

Loyalist' are the two variants of Ulster Unionism identified by Jennifer Todd (Todd, 1987). Similarly, Steve Bruce has focused on the 'Ulster Loyalist' political vision which includes the DUP, the Loyalist paramilitary groups and their political associates (Bruce, 1994). However, Colin Coulter has argued that the 'character of unionism' is much more diverse than Todd's conventional categories would allow (Coulter, 1994). The development of fissures within unionism and loyalism in the aftermath of the 1994 Republican and Loyalist cease-fires would appear to lend support to Coulter's thesis. Conventional categories, therefore, while useful, do have their shortcomings in attempting to pigeon-hole communal identities.

For the practical purposes of analysis, I have taken each of the five main political parties – the Ulster Unionist Party (UUP), the Social Democratic and Labour Party (SDLP), the Democratic Unionist Party (DUP), Sinn Féin, and the Alliance Party of Northern Ireland (APNI) – to represent differing political perspectives on communal identity in Northern Ireland.[2] These perspectives may not fit neatly into conventional categories but may be denoted by some or all of the following terms:

SDLP	Irish, non-British, European integrationist, constitutional, republican, traditional nationalist, liberal nationalist, postnationalist, consociational devolutionist, social democratic.
Sinn Féin	Irish, anti-British, anti-European integrationist, traditional nationalist, modern nationalist, republican, socialist, conservative, revolutionary, reactionary.
DUP	Ulster Protestant, Ulster Unionist, Ulster Loyalist, British, anti-Irish Nationalist, anti-European integrationist, reactionary, fundamentalist, devolutionist, constitutional.
UUP	Ulster Unionist, Ulster Protestant, British, anti-Irish Nationalist, anti-European integrationist, constitutional, conservative, UK integrationist, devolutionist.
APNI	Reconciliationist, Northern Irish, British, Irish, Liberal, European integrationist, devolutionist, constitutional.

Obviously this does not preclude points of convergence in the perspectives of two or more parties or points of divergence in the perspectives of those represented by a single political party. These five largest parties in Northern Ireland represent between 90 per cent and 96 per cent of the electorate in the 1990s.[3]

Participants are public representatives in Northern Ireland who are either actively involved in EU institutions or have a keen interest in EU processes. Liam O'Dowd has warned that employing such a methodology can lead to an excessively top-down approach (O'Dowd, 1991b, p. 102). As a result, I have tried where possible to contrast the representation of a senior party official with that of another representative from the same party working at local level. Participants include:- John Alderdice (APNI, Leader 1987–98); Nigel Dodds (DUP, Party Secretary); Mark Durkan (SDLP, Party Chairperson 1990–5); Reg Empey (UUP, EU Committee of the Regions, member); Denis Haughey (SDLP, EU Committee of the Regions, member); Mitchel McLaughlin (Sinn Féin, National Chairman); Francie Molloy (Sinn Féin, Councillor); Maurice Morrow (DUP, Councillor); and Jim Nicholson (UUP, MEP).

CHAPTER OUTLINE

Chapter 1 describes the conditions and concepts associated with modernity and postmodernity. It presents the argument that the condition of postmodernity is pervading politics and that the discourse of (resistance) postmodernism is a useful way in which to conceptualize the changes that are taking place. The postmodernist concern for the 'representation of difference' can already be found in the conceptual base of EU and Anglo-Irish processes. This change of direction undertaken by political decision-makers may be echoed in academic accounts of contemporary conditions. One way of producing such an account is for the subject to contribute through dialogue to an understanding of how new forms of relationships between individuals, collectivities and the state might be expected to develop in changing European and global-local contexts and how these might find political expression in Northern Ireland.

Chapter 2 aims to establish the key indicators of how nations as political-cultural forms have come to dominate in the modern world and consequently how they have affected communal identity, with particular emphasis on Irish Nationalist and Ulster Unionist identities in Northern Ireland. The role played by communication in this development is highlighted. Consideration is then given to the future development of the relationship between communities and the state in the 'communications age'. An emerging form of nationalism in the EU, described as liberal and postmodernist, rejects the notion of the modern nation-state as a structural *nirvana* for the nation. Its uptake offers possibilities for re-imagining northern Irish Nationalist and Ulster Unionist communal identities as Northern Ireland experiences the shift from modernity to postmodernity.

Chapter 3 provides an account of the formative experience of Ulster Unionist and northern Irish Nationalist identities in the modern sub-state of Northern Ireland, 1921–72 and in the UK state, from 1972 to date.[4] Intimations of postmodernity in the declarations and proposals of the UK government, particularly after 1985, are considered subsequently. It is argued that these intimations signify the beginning of a paradigm shift in the political context of Northern Ireland from an exclusive interest in territorial autonomy to one focused on the inclusive accommodation of diverse communal identities.

Chapter 4 deals with European integration. In particular, the chapter evaluates intimations of postmodernity in the development of the EU through a consideration of the contingencies of integration; subsidiarity; regionalism; the Committee of the Regions; and citizenship. It is argued that the EU's intention of becoming a community of nations instead of a homogeneous cultural community points to the development of a system of multilevel governance that promises to secure the 'right to roots' of communities, as well as the 'right to options' of individuals. The implications of the development of the EU for the economic, territorial and cultural resources of Ulster Unionist and Irish Nationalist identities in Northern Ireland are considered in **Chapter 5**. It is suggested that EU integration and structural initiatives have postmodernist contingencies that are beginning to redefine the structural space of Northern Ireland.

The dialogues in **Part II** aim to provide: (i) a reflection of the perceptions of structural change among the representatives of communal identities in Northern Ireland; (ii) an indication of the degree of conflict and consensus on future structural parameters for Northern Ireland among these representatives; and (iii) a sense of the degree of reinterpretation of the territorial, economic and cultural resources of communal identities induced by such on-going changes.

The combination of premodern ethno-religious identification and modern territorial aspirations has undoubtedly shaped the conflicting nature of northern Irish Nationalist and Ulster Unionist communal identities. However, understanding of 'the nation' and 'the state' – the key concepts on which communal identity is founded – has shown signs of fundamental change at the end of the 20th century, even in what is commonly perceived to be the glacial political context of Northern Ireland. The dawn of the third millennium is, therefore, a propitious time to re-evaluate the contemporary relationship between communities, politics and change in Northern Ireland. The viewpoint, themes and methods associated with (resistance) postmodernism provide a novel approach to the study of change and its real and potential impact on communal identities in Northern Ireland.

Part One:
Intimations of
Postmodernity

1 A Postmodernist Approach to Communal Identities in Northern Ireland?

The bulk of the ten thousand plus books on Northern Ireland politics published since 1969 have subscribed to a modernist 'internal conflict' paradigm. However, such a conceptual position, with its emphasis on objectivity and the establishment of a dominant socio-political truth by 'the majority', appears to be somewhat at odds with the increasing saliency of multiple culture-bound interpretations in the EU and in the Anglo-Irish political approach to Northern Ireland. Since 1985, the Anglo-Irish political process has striven to avoid an authoritative approach in favour of an interpretative one. In addition, this process seeks to arrive at a structural accommodation for northern Irish Nationalist and Ulster Unionist communities that represents a move beyond the structural model offered by modernity – the nation-state. The emphasis of the internal conflict paradigm on the territorial boundary as the parameter of critical analysis, therefore, begins to sit uneasily alongside the contemporary political realities facing communal identities in Northern Ireland. The representation of communal difference and the development of extraterritorial alliances is the pursuit of Anglo-Irish and EU political decision-makers, suggesting intimations of postmodernity for the political process. This chapter sets out to describe the nature of the shift in the political process from modernity to postmodernity in terms of conditions, concepts and methods.

CONCEPTUALIZING 'THE MODERN' AND 'THE POSTMODERN'

There is a surprising lack of specificity on terms relating to conceptions of 'the modern' and 'the postmodern'. Barry Smart has identified the terms 'modern', 'modernism', and 'modernity' being used as synonyms in the work of Habermas and Berman. Similarly, 'postmodern', 'postmodernism' and 'postmodernity' have been used in an interchangeable way. There is also a problem in distinguishing definitively between modern and postmodern 'conceptual constellations' (Smart, 1990, pp. 15–17). Indeed, Smart suggests that there has been a strong tendency in aesthetic and sociological discourse to discuss postmodernism within the context of 'the modern' (Smart, 1990, p. 20). This is confirmed in the work of Soja who maintains that:

> Modernity and postmodernity are not singular and homogeneous concepts to be categorized neatly by their opposing essences. Rather than being mutually exclusive, they are 'in' one another in ways that make their intertwining as important as their differentiation (Soja, 1993, p. 113).

Consequently, distinguishing continuity and change between 'the modern' and 'the postmodern' is reminiscent of a similar difficulty in separating 'the premodern' from 'the modern'.

Postmodernism gives rise to a recognition of the impossibility of the 'project of modernity'. This is not to say that the modern era and its political manifestations, such as the modern nation-state and nationalism, as defined by modernity, no longer exist. Rather, it is our own vantage point on such phenomena that has changed from one of subjugation to the process of modernity, to one of critical detachment with a view to change (Bauman, 1991, pp. 271–2). To proceed with caution entails accepting as a starting point David Harvey's assertion that there have been important changes taking place in contemporary society (Harvey, 1989). However, while Harvey continues to contextualize postmodern developments within the continuum of the 'project of modernity', a more overtly postmodernist position subscribes to Zygmunt Bauman's argument that postmodern conditions prevailing in society give rise to questions challenging the existing doctrines of modernity.

In terms of politics and society, modernity is synonymous with the emergence of new conditions, concepts and methods in seventeenth-century Europe (Giddens, 1990, p. 1). Preceding traditional societies had centred on small homogenous ethnic groups and their ancient codes based on custom, superstition and religion. Modernity describes the new order that emerged with the industrial revolution, the dawn of capitalism, and the twentieth century process of modernization. According to Hollinger, modernity may be understood as ' . . . the rise of industry, cities, market capitalism, the bourgeois family, growing secularization, democratization and social legislation' (Hollinger, 1994, p. 25). The concept of progress through scientific method underpinned modernity and represented a direct challenge to the influence of religion and superstition:

> The Enlightenment aimed at human emancipation from myth, superstition and enthralled enchantment to mysterious powers and forces of nature through the progressive operations of critical reason (Docherty, 1993, p. 5).

The certainties advocated by the Enlightenment metanarrative include the idea of progress towards an ideal state of society through the problem-solving power of scientific endeavour, and a correspondence theory of truth in which universalist knowledge is assumed to be representative of reality. The aim of the 'project of modernity' was to introduce rational order to everyday social life (Bauman, 1987, p. 110). At the outset, it was the belief of the Enlightenment philosophers that rational organization would not only enable man to control natural forces but would also yield an understanding of the self and morality (Habermas, 1985, p. 9). In this way, the modern emphasis on progress through rational order replaced the premodern marker of faithfully maintaining the status quo.

The nation-state became the structural manifestation of the triumph of modernity. In essence, therefore, modernity describes a world-view formed by a combination of two developments: the substantive development of this new model of state power that was effective in imposing preconceived notions of order; and the establishment of a relatively autonomous discourse that generated this model of order, replete with the practices that its implementation required (Bauman, 1987, p. 2). However, substantive changes associated with postmodernity give rise to concern for the central tenets on which an understanding of politics and society is to be based. While the nation-state continues to represent the dominant form of polity in the contemporary world, its modernist contingencies of objectivity, coherency and the domination of the nation-state centre fail to account adequately for the contemporary complexity of economic, political and social interaction with which it has to contend (Lyotard, 1984, p. 14; Harvey, 1989, pp. 284–307). It raises questions about political strategy based on the autonomy of the nation-state, as well as the efficacy of attempts to apply the notion of objective rationality to the functioning of society.

Such conditions suggest that a re-assessment should be made of the validity of the doctrines of modernity when considering the implications of structural development for communal identities in Northern Ireland.

A postmodernist approach facilitates a critical detachment from modernist concepts, such as the universality of knowledge, when considering concerns expressed for the representation of difference in the EU and in the territorial space of Northern Ireland. Furthermore, it encourages the formation of an intellectual alternative to the authoritative knowledge of the intellectual-as-legislator or the knowledge of a dominant socio-political group, as represented in the North by the Unionist hegemony between 1921 and 1972, and in the South by the Catholic and Gaelic hegemony of modern times.

TOWARDS A POSTMODERNISM OF RESISTANCE

The condition of postmodernity is underpinned by a revolution in technology and communications. In the economic sphere, communications developments have given rise to the internationalization of capital. The result has been the globalization of manufacturing industry; the dislocation of the structure of finance and disillusionment with the principles of macro-economic management (Harvey, 1989; Camilleri and Falk, 1992; O'Donnell, 1993). With the decline in the profitability of mass production, business has had to become more flexible as it pursues smaller, more diverse and specialized markets (Harvey, 1989, pp. 141–72).

David Harvey's neo-Marxist perspective inevitably concentrates on the economic dynamic of a structural change from modernity to postmodernity. For him, postmodernity is characterized by post-Fordism or 'flexible accumulation' in business. Emphasis on the pursuit of profit in business has necessitated the rapid development of new products and the recycling of old ones. The relentless pursuit of profit and the decline of mass production as a profitable enterprise has encouraged entrepreneurs to exploit ever smaller markets in order to satisfy more specialist tastes. This has required a flexibility in the labour market and in technology in order to meet the more complex and rapidly changing demands of the postmodern consumer society. Increased flexibility has been achieved by the exploitation of the cheaper Third World labour market; cheaper and more efficient transportation; and the instantaneous international communications which have facilitated time-space compression between production and consumption (Harvey, 1989, pp. 121–200). These changes in communications, production and consumption have reinvigorated local contexts which offer greater flexibility. They have also proved to be an expedient for the maturation of the supranational political structure of the EU through their ability to subvert the cornerstone of modernity – the nation-state centre. Adjustment in the structure of the state to meet the postmodern condition, described by globalization and localization, is a result of a re-appraisal of the role and competence of the nation-state centre in society.

Rapidly developing national and transnational communication networks have extended the dynamic of globalization/localization in the political sphere to the empowerment of marginalized voices in society. This has shifted the focus for politics from the emphasis of modernity on establishing a dominant truth as the basis of socio-political order to a postmodernist concern for the accommodation of communal difference. In the 1960s, television graphically depicted the African-American struggle for civil rights in Mississippi and in the United States generally. These scenes inspired the formation of a civil rights movement in Northern Ireland. In turn, the Northern Ireland Civil Rights Association (NICRA) made successful use of new national and transnational television networks to highlight the anomaly of the denial of democratic rights to a minority in a region of the United Kingdom. This political development empowered the voice of the marginalized northern Irish Nationalist community and marked the beginning of the end for the Ulster Unionist hegemony in Northern Ireland. In the 1990s, it might be argued that political parties associated with paramilitary groups – Sinn Féin, the Progressive Unionist Party (PUP) and the Ulster Democratic Party (UDP) – successfully used the media spotlight to articulate the culture-bound truth claims of the respective communal identities that these parties purport to represent, as well as enhancing their own respective positions as a medium of representation.

Changing conditions have implications for the concepts that describe the structure of society. Harvey asserts that concepts associated with postmodernity which describe contemporary structural change, such as decentralization, deconstruction, anarchy and flexibility, are not exclusive to the postmodern period. He suggests that these concepts have struggled with their counterparts – centralization, authority, hierarchy and permanence – throughout history.

However, Harvey perceives that contemporary society, afflicted as it is by late capitalism, bears witness to a sea-change towards the condition of postmodernity described by decentralization, deconstruction, anarchy and flexibility (Harvey, 1989, pp. 338–42). Nevertheless, the use of postmodernism to give a conceptual perspective is not unproblematic. The hallmark of postmodernism has been the ambiguity associated with the discourse, an ambiguity that can be attributed to the fact that the condition of postmodernity has yet to run its course.

Two waves of postmodernism have emerged (Foster, 1985, pp. xi–xii; Graham, Doherty and Malek, 1992, pp. 6–11). These postmodernisms differ radically in their relationship with modernism and can shed some light on our understanding of the conditions prevailing in contemporary society. The first wave, as conceived by Derrida and Foucault in postmodernism's early period, represents postmodernism as another phase in the development of modernism. In this postmodernism, the emphasis is on continuity with postmodern developments already linked to existing concepts and conditions. In substantive terms, this means that postmodern economic developments represent an extension of the encroachment of capitalism on space; in conceptual terms, postmodernism's recognition of all voices in society extends from the Enlightenment idea of autonomy and equality; and the postmodern methodological emphasis on dialogical anthropology and intersubjectivity also originates from Enlightenment ideas (Jones, Natter and Schatzki, 1993, p. 1).

While Foucault and Derrida endorse the tenor of the Enlightenment, that is, its capacity for honesty and criticism, both have strong reservations about the faith it places in the doctrines of scientific progress, positivism and value-neutrality. According to Foucault:

> The thread that may connect us with the Enlightenment is not faithfulness to doctrinal elements, but rather the permanent reactivation of an attitude – that is, of a philosophical ethos that could be described as a permanent critique of our historical era (in Rabinow, 1984, p. 42).

The more radical wave of postmodernism, encapsulated in the second wave of writing, as represented by Lyotard, is divorced from the conditions, concepts and methods of modernity, and challenges the rectitude of the Enlightenment metanarrative which is assumed by the process of modernization (Lyotard, 1984, pp. xxiii–xxiv). In its attempt to escape that modernist paradigm and avoid the modern predilection for structure and coherence, the more radical wave of postmodernism simply wishes to steer clear of the contemplation of the ethos and doctrines of the Enlightenment and the ambivalence of modernity (Hollinger, 1994, pp. 35–6). For Lyotard, the progressive promises of modernity are not feasible and the totalizing discourse of modern social theory and philosophy cannot, after all, be applied to social conditions and human nature. As a consequence, modernity has lost its credibility (Lyotard, 1984). Instead, 'the reality of hyperreality' has prompted an apolitical postmodernism that recognizes only fragmentation, change, conversation, usefulness, efficiency, experimentation, irony, and myth (Smart, 1990, p. 24; Graham, Doherty and Malek, 1992, pp. 6–11; Soja, 1993, p. 123; Hollinger, 1994, p. 172).

Soja discerns three versions of postmodernism emanating from these successive waves. In contrast to the apolitical 'Humpty Dumpty' version of postmodernism, nominally represented by Lyotard; or the 'right leaning' version that succeeded 'in shifting contemporary political discourse to its own simulations and dissimulations' (illustrated by Ronald Reagan's earnest assertion that the stagflation and unemployment crisis of the early 1980s was merely a state of mind); a 'postmodernism of resistance', with which Soja affiliates himself, shares the progressive instinct of modernity-in-general (Soja, 1993, pp. 121–2). This latter version of postmodernism is identifiably postmodern in its rejection of totalizing visions and universalist knowledge. However, its progressive instinct necessitates an emphasis on creating alliances commensurate with changing conditions in the 'post-Modern' world. According to Soja,

> ... a primary political challenge to radical postmodernism is to gain strength (rather than despair) from the fragmentation of progressive political projects that the Modern Left has traditionally seen as one of its major sources of weakness (Soja, 1993, p. 122).

Such alliances, based on gender, class, ethnicity, the environment, peripherality, social deprivation, economic interests or conflict resolution, are increasingly finding structural support in criss-crossing networks created in the context of the EU (discussed in chapter 4).

From a 'postmodernism of resistance' perspective, it is important to consider the import of conflicting readings, representing different and even opposing communal truths, for an understanding of the conflict between northern Irish Nationalist and Ulster Unionist communities. As Bauman explains, the strategy of interpreting the multiple truths that emanate from multiple communities of meaning differs from modern strategies of legislation in that

> ... it does abandon overtly, or put aside as irrelevant to the task at hand, the assumption of the universality of truth, judgement or taste; it refuses to differentiate between communities which produce meanings; it accepts those communities' ownership rights, and the ownership rights as the only foundation the communally grounded meanings may need. What remains for the intellectuals to do is to interpret such meanings for the benefit of those who are not of the community which stands behind the meanings; to mediate the communication between 'finite provinces' or 'communities of meaning' (Bauman, 1987, p. 197).

The conflicting cultural and political aspirations of Ulster Unionists and Irish Nationalists in Northern Ireland raises questions about the efficacy of attempts to apply the notion of objective rationality – a central tenet of modernity and the nation-state – to the functioning of such a society. That these communities can present conflicting versions of fundamental concepts like history, justice and truth underpins this sceptical approach. The differences that exist in the culture-bound knowledge of northern Irish Nationalist and Ulster Unionist communities are illustrated by the commentator Fintan O'Toole:

> Nationalist demands that Britain apologise for Bloody Sunday, for the Great Famine, or whatever atrocity is brought to mind by a convenient anniversary, are usually ways of avoiding responsibility for 25 years of IRA violence. Selective Unionist memories of those same years are often no more than a mechanism for forgetting what caused the violence in the first place, and for avoiding the messy business of making peace (Fintan O'Toole in the *Guardian*, 26 August 1996).

Such differences of interpretation between imagined communities highlight the relevance of a sceptical, culture-bound idea of knowledge in society.

Modern texts on Northern Ireland politics set out to give an authoritative version of knowledge that contrasts with this culture-bound knowledge of imagined communities. However, the representation and interpretation of culture-bound knowledge has formed the basis of some texts on Northern Ireland. Dennis Kennedy's interpretation of Ulster Unionist/Ulster Protestant culture-bound knowledge as presented by the Unionist newspapers in *Northern*

Attitudes to the Independent Irish State 1919–1949 (1988), and Fionnuala O'Connor's award-winning *In Search of a State: Catholics in Northern Ireland* (1993), which interprets the discourse of 'Northern Catholics', are primary examples of such texts. In the preface to his book on Ulster Unionism, *Under Siege: Ulster Unionism and The Anglo-Irish Agreement*, Arthur Aughey explicitly states the subjective nature of his work by disavowing 'any pretence to be impartial' (Aughey, 1989a, p. vii). Similarly, Norman Porter admits to writing from an 'engaged perspective . . . that does not aspire to be objective' in *Rethinking Unionism: an Alternative Vision for Northern Ireland* (Porter, 1996, p. 3). These accounts enable the reader to arrive at some understanding of the different worlds, indeterminately far apart, of the two imagined communities in Northern Ireland. Indeed, from this culture-bound perspective, O'Connor draws attention to the pitfalls of an analogical approach in a popular reference book on the politics of Northern Ireland – *Northern Ireland: a Political Directory 1968–88* (1989):

> The book begins with a chronology of major events that makes no mention of the forced migrations of the early seventies and includes no loyalist murders of Catholics in the events of 1972 (O'Connor, 1993, p. 161).

Some contemporary journalists, such as David McKittrick (1989; 1994), attempt to report news items through the culture-bound perspectives of identities within the communal blocks of Ulster Unionism and Irish Nationalism. The aim is to convey some sense of the multiple-truths that exist via the imagined communities within Northern Ireland.

With resistance postmodernism, it is possible for differing and even opposing beliefs to be equally valid. As a consequence, the objective rationality of the Enlightenment is challenged. The paradigm shift initiated by changes occurring in society encourages academics to drop modern pretensions to understanding a universal truth and consider instead the complexity of multiple truths that exist in the human world, not least in Northern Ireland.

OBJECTIVITY VERSUS INTERSUBJECTIVITY

To opponents of postmodernism, its rejection of the universality of reason and, by implication, the rejection of objective truth itself, represents an endorsement of pure capitalism and the triumph of nihilism. Postmodernists are thus perceived as having become detached from the real world and are consequently characterized as free-floating intellectuals (Callinicos, 1989, pp. 170–1). Undoubtedly postmodernism's rejection of a utopian vision through the power of scientific progress and the universality of reason does leave it open to the charge of nihilism. For some, it can exist purely as a runaway critique without political direction or moral responsibility (Simons and Billing, 1994 p. 6). Indeed, the emphasis of postmodernism on deconstruction leads Bauman to consider this as leaning towards an 'all-eroding, all-dissolving *destructiveness*' (Bauman, 1992, p. viii). However, in the contemporary world, where the dominance of Western conceptions has given way to the multiple-truth claims of the multifarious 'critical others' (including ethnic groups, feminists, homosexuals and environmentalists) the quest for objective truth becomes a stultifying experience at best and an oppressive one at worst. Ulster Unionists perceive that there were systematic pogroms carried out against Protestants in the South before and after partition in the quest to establish an Irish nationalist truth (Aughey, 1996, p. 32). Conversely, the northern Irish Nationalist community perceived itself to be the victim of oppression in the Unionist sub-state between 1921–72 because that sub-state represented the established truth-claims of the Ulster Unionist community. Recognizing the power of television, the Northern Ireland civil rights movement of the 1960s sought to challenge the legitimacy of this socially constructed truth and legitimize the alternative expression of communal identity to the established order that existed in the territorial space of Northern Ireland.

The impossibility of objective discourse is most apparent in Northern Ireland. The highly subjective readings of key concepts like 'justice' require a discourse based, not on objectivity, but on intersubjectivity. The Unionist concept of justice is formed purely in terms of rights for individuals in civil society. However, most Nationalists interpret the concept in terms of community, that is, in the cultural terms of national self-determination,

> full expression of the Catholic community's Irish national identity is treated as a demand of justice. Equally that community's right to have an effective say in government is demanded (Todd, 1990, p. 39).

A postmodern discourse, based on intersubjectivity, attempts to accommodate the multiple understandings of social and political reality that exist in Northern Ireland. The dialogue actually requires a multiplicity of voices covering the whole spectrum of communal reality. The dialogue in the business sector in Northern Ireland is at an advanced stage of development (Bradley, 1995, p. 27) and is due, perhaps, to a refusal to be deflected from the pursuit of profit. The dynamic surrounding the IRA and Loyalist cease-fires of 1994 may also have signalled a change in the perceptions of Loyalists and Republicans in working-class areas which can eventually facilitate dialogue (Bew, 1995, p. 33; Márie Nic Suibhne in the *Guardian*, 24 June, 1995). With the breakdown of the IRA cease-fire in February 1996, Loyalist paramilitaries threatened to respond 'blow for blow'. However, they also maintained that 'Northern Irish society was changing and would continue to change. New ground is constantly being broken and old animosities gradually laid to rest' (the *Guardian*, 13 March 1996). By tempering the threat of a return to violence with an invitation to pursue change by peaceful means, Loyalist paramilitaries appear to be amenable to pursuing the opportunities for change through dialogue. However, the beginning of 'inclusive' multi-party talks on the political future of Northern Ireland in 1996 (from which Sinn Féin were excluded until 1997) was marked by inter-party wrangling on procedure before substantive negotiation. Indeed, frustration at the lack of progress led John Alderdice, APNI leader 1987–98, to question the viability of an intersubjective approach that includes parties on the political extremes (in the *Observer*, 9 September 1996).

The initial inertia caused by this inclusive political process mirrors, to some extent, similar problems encountered by inclusive Anglo-Irish and EU intergovernmental negotiations. The 'advisory role' on Northern Ireland affairs granted to the Government of the Republic of Ireland in the Anglo-Irish Agreement (1985) proved to be a landmark in the UK government's engagement of the principle of intersubjectivity for Northern Ireland at the intergovernmental level. Intergovernmental conferences proceeded after 1985 despite keen opposition from Ulster Unionists. They involve high-ranking ministers from both governments who discuss a wide range of matters pertaining to Northern Ireland. An eventual eradication of the use of politically motivated violence and movement towards the structural accommodation of Ulster Unionist and northern Irish Nationalist communities are the goals of 'dialogues' at these different levels. In the shorter-term, such developments may facilitate the self-reflexivity required for the redefinition of politics and political space of Northern Ireland and a reassessment of the region's place in a European Union that has already embarked upon the process of postmodern structural schism. However, the intersubjective approach adopted by the British and Irish governments on Northern Ireland has led to difficulties. Meetings of the Anglo-Irish Intergovernmental Conference (IGC) often proved inconclusive and major policy statements, such as the Downing Street Declaration (1993), or structural proposals, such as the Framework Documents (1995), were highly complex and ambiguous when they finally arrived after many drafts.[1]

Despite the difficulties encountered by these postmodern political practices involving EU policy-making networks, the Anglo-Irish political process and the Multi-Party Talks (1996–8) on the political future of Northern Ireland, they nevertheless highlight the incremental shift towards a postmodernist paradigm for communal identities in Northern Ireland. The totalizing visions of Ulster Unionism and Irish Nationalism are disbarred from forming structural arrangements to their singular specifications by these practices. Such an approach would appear to pave the way for communal intersubjectivity and the reconstitution of political practice in Northern Ireland. However, 'live' premodern ethno-religious tensions between Ulster Unionists and northern Irish Nationalists, reinvigorated by constitutional flux, do have the potential to undermine movement towards political accommodation within a postmodern structural framework. Instead, they may perpetuate a climate conducive only to communal exclusivism, disempowerment and violence.

DECONSTRUCTION AND RECONSTRUCTION

Political practice, in the context of modernity, has been characterized by the enactment of a dominant political metanarrative secured by policy, planning and strategy. In such a context, the degree to which dominant political actors subdue opponents is the barometer of political success. The appropriateness of such practice in a democratic society is questionable, but in a communally divided society like Northern Ireland where the constitution of the modern state is a matter of legitimate dispute (for Irish Nationalists), a denial of the validity of communal identities that constitute over 40 per cent of the electorate in that society is not conducive to successful democratic practice.

With regard to rectifying the democratic deficit of modernity, the problem for 'Humpty Dumpty' postmodernism is that while it advocates the elucidation of all values in society, it feels unable to provide the dynamism required to elevate marginalized voices onto the political stage. Some on the political left interpret this position as being politically disabling because a rejection of the doctrines of the Enlightenment means that postmodernism is unable to enter the political arena and make judgmental statements in the cut and thrust of political interaction (Callinicos, 1989; Harvey, 1989, p. 117). Thus, by rejecting a utopian vision, this so-called 'radical postmodernism' deprives itself of the ideals that would provide it with the dynamic for political action. Ironically, through its political impotence, radical postmodernism could be said to be compliant in the perpetuation of the dominant metanarrative and in the wilful neglect of its own tenets of 'fragmentation', 'change', 'conversation', 'usefulness', and 'efficiency'. Postmodernism's difficulty with reconstruction is that such a strategy lends itself to constituting a metanarrative which postmodernism itself resolutely opposes – Lyotard defines *postmodern* as 'incredulity toward metanarratives' (Lyotard, 1984, pp. xxiv). However, Soja argues that it is for resistance postmodernists to highlight to those postmodernists sitting on the fence the importance of the political consequences of their immobility. Similarly, resistance postmodernists must attempt to deconstruct further the modernity of critics like Harvey who, while upholding the universalist vocation of modernity, also paint a cogent picture of the condition of postmodernity (Soja, 1993, pp. 121–4).

A valuable exercise in the deconstruction of communal identity blocks in Northern Ireland began in 1992, when the Opsahl Commission invited a rethink on the social and political problems that afflict Northern Ireland. The Opsahl Commission emerged from a project called 'Initiative '92' which was launched by a group of journalists and academics in Belfast. The aim of the project was to invite submissions from interested parties, groups, organizations and individuals on the future of Northern Ireland. The Commission received approximately 3,000 submissions, a cross-section of which it reproduced (in abridged form) in its report entitled *A Citizens' Inquiry: the Opsahl Report on Northern Ireland* (1993). Submissions were from people representing many different aspects of communal identity in Northern Ireland.[2] Its aims were consistent with postmodernism in that:

Postmodernism invites us to rethink the notions of self, society, community, reasons, values and history that dominate modernity, and to do so without nostalgia or regret and without utopian aspirations for what we create under the conditions of postmodernity (Hollinger, 1994, p. 170).

For Tom Garvin, the report of the Opsahl Committee's findings provided evidence of a 'massive rethink' on all aspects of Northern Ireland political affairs, including communal identity. The induced self-reflexivity challenged existing mantras of communal identity and replaced them with uncertainty and a desire to understand (Garvin, 1994, p. 124).[3]

The extrapolation of multifarious identities from modern identity blocks in Northern Ireland, which emerged as a major theme in the Opsahl Report, are grounded in postmodernism. Postmodernism has, thus far, overwhelmingly failed to offer a political strategy aimed at the accommodation of these multifarious voices. However, a less constipated 'postmodernism of resistance' is tentatively emerging (through Bauman and Soja and via Harvey) to promote deconstructivism and consider modes of reconstruction through alliance formation.

The postmodernist emphasis on deconstruction and schism is useful in an exploration of the different forms and expressions of communal identity that exist within the Irish Nationalist and Ulster Unionist communities in Northern Ireland. It is especially relevant in the political context of the European Union for communities and individuals: in terms of supranational/national/sub-national structural alignment and EU citizenship should it develop beyond the point of rhetoric. According to Bauman, postmodern developments have eroded the modern domination of the West and confirmed the plurality of the human world. As a result, there has been a refocusing on the significance of physical and imagined communities for political interaction (Bauman, 1992, pp. 136–9). The process of European integration is an attempt to integrate difference, through the incorporation of the multiple truths of EU nations, regions and localities in response to the condition of postmodernity. A concept of EU multinational citizenship could reflect the postmodern themes of intersubjectivity and the integration of multiple truths in an inclusive EU citizenship. Furthermore, the EU's tentative development of a criss-crossing multi-level polity represents a formula for postmodern reconstruction because it underwrites the fragmentation of the nation-state and promises an accommodation of a multi-cultural community of nations (discussed in chapter 4).

For the purposes of this book it is important to establish that the condition of postmodernity presents a challenge to the modern nationalist view that the nation can only be sustained by creating a modern state of its own. Postmodernism already describes signs of movement to integrate effective subnational and supranational units into an EU multilevel system of governance, albeit at a snail's pace. It also embodies the supranationalist designs on dismantling the territorial boundaries of the nation-state in the EU and restructuring the context of European capital. The conceptualization of contemporary structural change in terms of postmodernism points to a rejection of a totalizing doctrine of nationalism, as defined by modernity. However, if postmodernism suggests 'we draw from the old and the new in a recreative and non-dogmatic way' then the nation may still have a valid role to play in postmodern society. According to Richard Kearney,

> ... rather than constructing history as a *continuity* (leading inexorably back to a lost paradise or forward to a guaranteed future), postmodernism views it as a *collage*. It thus resists that naïve belief in history as demonstrating inevitable progress or regress, and suggests that we draw from the old and the new in a recreative and non-dogmatic way. The 'post' in postmodern refers not just to what comes *after* modernity' (Kearney, 1993, p. 149).

Certainly, adherence to the 'resistance postmodernism' signposts of multiple truths, intersubjectivity and alliance formation indicates that postmodernism may eventually have to climb down from its critical high horse and accept the reality of anti-hegemonic nations as a cohesive expression of communal identity. Furthermore, the empowerment of such identities in an evolving postmodern political network is conducive with a 'postmodernism of resistance' interpretation of democracy.

CONCLUSION

The process of structural change and paradigm shift is establishing itself in the political contexts of Northern Ireland and the European Union on the threshold of the third millennium. This change in conditions and concepts can be described in terms of the beginning of an incremental shift from modernity to postmodernity. The implications of such a shift in the policy-making process is that the authoritative throne offered by modernity to the dominant socio-political group is no longer tenable. Instead, a recognition of the multiple-truths that exist is required in order to engage fully the postmodern policy networks of the EU and Anglo-Irish structural arrangements for communal identities in Northern Ireland. Before conducting an in-depth examination of the intimations of postmodernity evident in the Anglo-Irish process and the EU polity, it is necessary to chart the key points in the development of the nation, Irish nationalism and Ulster Unionism. Such an exercise will facilitate an assessment of relationship between these entities and the state in modern and postmodern times.

2 Interpreting the Development of the Nation, Irish Nationalism and Ulster Unionism

As a concept, the 'nation' is beyond the realms of singular and comprehensive definition. It may be understood as a community of people who share some sense of solidarity, a national consciousness and a common heritage through shared memories, distinguishing cultural features such as religion, customs, language, and an historic territory (Seton-Watson, 1977, p. 1). The nation could be described more simply as a politically self-aware ethnic community. The nation does not have to possess a 'state', that is a centralized politico-territorial unit (Connor, 1978, p. 379). However, in the modern context such a community will have achieved, or aspire to achieve, political centralization through a single government.

Benedict Anderson's characterization of the nation as ' . . . an imagined political community – and imagined as both inherently limited and sovereign' (Anderson, 1991, p. 6) provides the basis for a postmodernist interpretation. This interpretation stresses the centrality of culture-bound knowledge and narration in the development of the nation. In doing so, it attempts to provide an alternative to the dominant explanations of this development that have been conducted in terms of history as continuity or history as revolutionary transition. A postmodernist interpretation indicates that postmodernism does not merely describe what comes after modernity; it is also representative of an alternative conceptual perspective in which history is interpreted as a collage that is (re)produced through the cultural narrative of different communities of meaning.

The nation is a concept that has preoccupied political life in Ireland, North and South, for generations. The mass mobilization achieved by Charles Stuart Parnell and his home rule party during the 1880s finally consolidated the rise of modern Irish nationalism which began with the rebellion of the United Irishmen in 1798. Yet, in the broader sense, the precise origin, meaning, function and future of 'the nation', and modern nationalism (the ideology that has inspired ideas of autonomy, unity and identity for 'the nation') is open to interpretation. The case of Irish nationalism reflects the nuances in interpretation. The emancipatory form of nationalism that is generally taken to describe Parnell's movement contrasts with the Ulster Unionist portrayal of contemporary Irish Nationalists as irredentist and aggressive.[1] When considering the imagining and reimagining of communal identity on the island of Ireland it is necessary to examine the different approaches to the development of the nation.

THE ETHNIC ORIGINS OF NATIONS

As political norms, 'the nation' and 'the state' would appear to be entirely modern. In late-sixteenth- and seventeenth-century Europe (and certainly after the religious wars in Europe concluded in 1648 with the Treaty of Westphalia) the prevailing social and economic circumstances enjoined the concept of 'sovereignty' (supreme power) to the state, giving rise to a system of European states with each an authority unto itself. With the onslaught of industrialization in the nineteenth century, they began to be termed 'nation-states' as attention focused on the whole population of these states and their recently developed 'national' character, steeped in a common history, sentiment and culture. The problem for a modernist interpretation of the development of nations and nationalism is that many of these traits of nations and nationalism are also recognizable in the premodern world. This gives rise to the possibility of 'premodern' nations and challenges the 'state-to-nation' sequence of events described by Breuilly (1982). Anthony D. Smith questions the assumption that nations are an entirely modern phenomenon (Smith, 1986; 1991). His concern has been to attempt to detect a link between premodern ethnic identity and modern national identity.

The battle between religion and secularism for influence over ethnic identity signified the beginning of the modern era. Up until then the spiritual and social aspects of religion had been crucial to the survival of ethnic identity. Its doctrinal and ethical aspects satisfied the need for spiritual salvation and its strictly codified regime provided a reliable environment for social bonding (Smith, 1986, pp. 34–7). Although the religious influence on communal identity persists in the modern world it has been disrupted and subsequently rarefied by the onslaught of secularization. Consequently, Smith does concede that the structural changes which signalled the beginning of modernity, particularly the bureaucratic activities of taxation, conscription and administration, did play some role in the transformation of ethnic communities to nations (Smith, 1991, p. 60). By examining closely events surrounding the decline of religion and simultaneous rise in the influence of secularism on ethnic identity, Smith attempts to clarify the degree of continuity/ transition occurring during that period. The aim is to stipulate the precise genealogy of nationalism and the nation.[2]

Modern structural change commenced with the West European revolutions in the spheres of the division of labour, the control of administration and the military, and in culture and education. These revolutions made their initial impact in England, France, Spain, Holland and Sweden. The revolution in the division of labour from the seventeenth century was representative of the change from feudalism to capitalism. It required a greater degree of economic integration within states and between states. According to Smith, 'lateral' ethnic communities, that is communities which were socially stratified by class and had an aristocracy with links to counterparts in other territories, were equal to the challenge that this revolution brought (Smith, 1986, pp. 130–4; 1991, p. 60). In the successful world of 'lateral' ethnic groups, urban and regional élites within territories were bound together in common economic purpose with a standardized economic state structure usually in place by the nineteenth century. Revolution in the control of administration and the military from the fifteenth to the eighteenth centuries gave the territory and political domain the burden of centralized responsibility. Aristocratic rulers of successful socially stratified communities broadened their base to incorporate middle-class bureaucrats into the power structure. The state was also implicit in the establishment of a standardized education system by the end of the nineteenth century. Aided by developments in mass-publishing, and preceding the bureaucratic revolution, the new modern state was able to replace the deity in an educator role within such communities and offered practical fulfilment through nationhood instead of the spiritual salvation assured by religious belief.

In contrast to successful 'lateral' ethnic communities, 'vertical' ethnic communities had an ethnicity that was pervasive throughout the population; they were ruled by others; and the centrality of religion in communal life proved to be more difficult to supplant.

As a consequence, vertical ethnic groups were initially unable to rise to the challenge of modernization and reap the benefits of the modern revolutions (Smith, 1986, pp. 76–88; 1991, pp. 61–8). Such groups required a secular intelligentsia of neo-classicists and romantics to reinterpret and mobilize this ethnic identity, based on religion, into a political force against the state to which they were subjected (Smith, 1986, pp. 129–49).

Ireland was a largely agrarian, peripheral colony during Europe's period of modernization. Despite the richness of its character, a socially cohesive Catholic Irish ethnic group had formed from Gaelic Irish and English-speaking medieval Norman antecedents. Unlike the lowland Scots and English plantation settlers of the sixteenth and seventeenth centuries, this 'vertical' Catholic Irish ethnic group lacked the qualifications to engage positively with the challenge of changes in wider European society.[3] Smith argues that the transformation of 'vertical' ethnic groups to nations was curtailed by the pre-eminence of religion in such societies. However, the rebellion of the United Irishmen in 1798, the Young Irelander's revolution of 1848, the home rule movement under Parnell and the Easter Rising of 1916 were symptomatic outcomes of a 'vertical' ethnic group introduced to nationalism by a secular intelligentsia, who tended to romanticize a collective history of the ethnic group. The leadership of the 1916 Rising included teachers, dramatists and poets.

The emphasis placed on a romanticized Gaelic past by groups like the Gaelic League (between 1900 and 1906) could be interpreted as proving vital in providing the Irish nation with a sense of security, particularly in times of modern structural change (Garvin, 1981). Indeed, the upheavals of modernization demanded that the nation reflect and embellish its ethnic past to ensure cohesion (Smith, 1986, pp. 200–8). Smith concedes that much of this embellishment may have involved some invention of tradition as described by modernist interpretations. Mythic pasts may well have been invoked in order to create the conditions for nations to survive modernization and acquire power. However, he asserts that the intelligentsia could not stray too far from the established historical past of the community if any invention was to retain an authentic flavour. Ethnic identity, therefore, had a direct input in shaping the modern nation and is not merely invention masquerading as authentic ethnicity (Smith, 1986, pp. 174–200).

The successful Gaelic and Christian past in Ireland was revived and provided the important buffer for the transformation from ethnic group to Irish nation. Multifarious grievances combined to form a catalyst for this transformation. The legacy of the Great Famine of 1845–51 acted as the principal dynamic of the modern movement of Irish nationalism. Other grievances emanating from perceived British misrule in Ireland included the failure of Ireland's malformed 'cattle economy' in the 1870s which had depended on the demands of industrial Britain (Boyce, 1982, p. 337); the government's opposition to Catholic emancipation prior to 1829; its underpinning of the actions of the landlord and tithe proctor in the early nineteenth century; and its execution of revolutionary nationalists, or Fenians, like the Manchester Martyrs who were publicly hanged in 1867 (Boyce, 1982, pp. 383–4). The execution of the leaders of the Easter Rising 1916 by the British government resulted in a reaffirmation of a collective Irish identity and further defined identity in terms of 'us' (the Irish) and 'them' (the British). Reaffirmation was brought about by mobilizing the myth of sacrifice which is endemic in the Irish nationalist identity. Indeed, this sacrificial myth of martyrdom is common to subject 'aggrieved' nations. It was reprised during the Hunger Strike (1981) in Northern Ireland when 10 Republican prisoners starved themselves to death in protest at the phasing out of their 'special category' political status by the British government. The election to the House of Commons of Republicans Bobby Sands, Owen Carron and Gerry Adams confirmed a successful reactivation of the myth of martyrdom in the Irish nationalist tradition during this period (Kearney, 1984, pp. 10–12).

Republicans are expert in the articulation and replenishment of the myth of sacrificial martyrdom. Unionists have relatively few myths; however, this does have the advantage of focusing hearts and minds on their one historical requirement – resistance to the dissipation of a perceived Protestant hegemony (Brown, 1985, p. 6). The Unionist 'siege mentality' has its origins in the Siege of Derry 1689. It sustains the self-image of an embattled people who must eternally resist the attempted incursions of their Catholic neighbours on their own hegemonic rights – to compromise would be to surrender. The insistence of the Protestant Orange Order on marching along the Garvaghy Road in Portadown in 1996, despite the objections of the road's Catholic residents and a police order prohibiting the march, is underscored by an Ulster Unionist 'siege mentality' which equates compromise with surrender to a growing and increasingly assertive Irish Nationalist community in Northern Ireland. Irish

Nationalists, meanwhile, read that insistence and the accompany-ing Orange regalia as being representative of a supremacist and triumphalist tendency within Ulster Unionism that has no respect for their wishes as a community.

In the Irish literary narrative, the most active sponsor of Irish mythology was W.B. Yeats. Yeats sought to provide symbols for unity and self-possession to counteract the reality of division and dispossession. 'Mother Ireland' represented a reclamation of national identity which was mythologized at the religious level, through the symbols of Celtic paganism; at the literary level, through a national literature which was to cut across class, creed and language; and at a political level through the mythic right of the blood sacrifice (Kearney, 1984, pp. 13–15). Against this embellishment of modern nationalism with mythology stood James Joyce and Samuel Beckett. Joyce wanted to re-mythologize the Irish nation and give it a Eu-ropean and universal context. He attempted to do this by intro-ducing exogenous mythologies (most famously the Greek mythology of Ulysses into the wanderings of Bloom around Dublin) into the Irish consciousness.[4] In doing so, Joyce confers conceptual intima-tions of postmodernity onto the Irish nation in his writing because he recontextualizes that nation outside the territorial confines of the modern nation-state. Beckett, on the other hand, wanted to forget nation, nationalism and their collective myths and concen-trate instead on the individual's fundamental alienation and pro-found inability to communicate. The social anthropologist A. P. Cohen would support Beckett's belief that nationalism offers a dis-traction from the individual's self-consciousness:

> The manufacture of national identity might reasonably be ar-gued as an attempt to diminish people's consciousness of their individuality, and superimpose over this a consciousness of both their similarity to their co-nationals and their difference from others (Cohen, 1994, p. 156).

Beckett derided the symbols used by Gaelic Revivalists as an exer-cise in illusion.

When considering a movement away from the code of national-ism through the concept of supranationalism and the project of a single global community, Smith's attitude ranges from the scepti-cal to the dismissive. He counters any argument that the forces of information technology and transnational political, economic and strategic co-operation are superseding the nation by pointing to the upsurge in minority ethnic nationalism which requires nation-states to reassert their authority. Transnational corporations may well transgress national boundaries through their business operations but they often do so in partnership with the government (either directly or through industrial agencies), or they do so at the expense of antagonizing nationalist feeling. Similarly, information technology and telecommunications may well signal the arrival of postmodern global culture by allowing instant access to a mishmash of ethnic style pastiche and eclectic concern for human rights and values, but Smith holds that '.... to penetrate their ethno-national forms or to challenge their assumptions does not undermine their power or destroy the hold of national discourses' (Smith, 1991, p. 160). The importance of ethno-history for Smith's concept of the nation cannot be understated. Ethno-history is the constant fundamental in the story of the nation and one which continues to ensure its hold on the individual because it promises that prosperity, security and collective dignity can be realized, even if their spatial and temporal distribution may be uneven (Smith, 1991, p. 177).

THE MODERN NATION

Ernest Gellner's modernist thesis of the development of the nation and nationalism differs from that of A.D. Smith in that Gellner interprets the industrial revolution as the dynamic for a transitional stage in history from the premodern to the modern (Gellner, 1964, p. 1983). He contends that, in order to meet the demands of the industrial revolution, the state aimed to homogenize culture from local intimate units, such as villages or clans, into cultures appropriate for the successful socialization of workers in a large industrial society. Gellner characterizes premodern societies as small, localized and intimate units that are ethnically and linguistically unique. They are also highly structured societies with individual members performing set tasks within a rigid structure. In contrast, industrialized societies engendered a 'high culture' which enabled the individual to become more geographically and occupationally mobile and able to perform a variety of roles (Gellner, 1964, pp. 153–6).

The state was central to the revolutionary transition from the premodern to the modern, in Gellner's interpretation. A prerequisite for occupational mobility and specialist expertise in the population

was a standardized education system. Only the state had at its disposal the resources to establish such a system which could enable
'strangers' to communicate with each other. The local ethnic units
offered a highly structured society where relationships were well
known and culture was not a necessary pre-condition for effective
communication. Bureaucracy of the modern state may offer some
of the structure of the old social order by employing terminology,
symbols and strict relationships, however, modern society is bigger
than bureaucracy. Cultural adaptation is necessary for communication in the modern world because encounters between people may
be spontaneous and unique. Structure is no longer omnipresent
and has to be replaced by culture. Identity is, in effect, uprooted
with the passing of structuralized society and rendered mobile by
its alignment to culture. Thus the task of the state was to promote
well defined 'high cultures', through the medium of education. The
expectation was that entire populations would adopt that standardized
culture and allow the creation of a socially and occupationally mobile
society able to meet the division of labour requirement of the industrial era (Gellner, 1983, pp. 35–8). For Gellner, the project of
modernity created 'an anonymous society of interchangeable individuals' to service the needs of the ascendant industrial capitalist
economy (Hutchinson, 1994, p. 13).

In Gellner's interpretation, the uneven spread of industrialization throughout Europe and beyond explains the differentiation
between nation-states and the tensions that resulted from power
imbalances. A lack of cultural differentiation in such circumstances
resulted in conflict based on class. However, some nations did form
through grievance because they were excluded from participating
in the industrial revolution on the grounds of communal identity
defined by features such as race, language and religion. The new
mobility brought with it an ethos of egalitarianism that served to
enhance the sense of grievance of those who were disenfranchised
in this way. Accordingly, grievance constituted a darker political
catalyst for the formation of nations (Gellner, 1964, pp. 153–6).

A point of departure among modernist interpretations is the
modernizing process attributed to the development of the nation
and nationalism. For Breuilly, nationalism was conceived as a response to the 'modern problem of the relationship between the
state and society' (Breuilly, 1982, p. 350). It is, therefore, the development of the modern state itself, rather than industrialization
(Gellner), capitalism (Hobsbawm) or print capitalism (Anderson)

that is the causal factor in the development of nations and nationalism (Breuilly, 1982, p. 355). The modern state created the conditions for a small political community to wrest power from a ruling monarch and act in the interests of society (Breuilly, 1982, pp. 360–1). In Hobsbawm's Marxist interpretation, the needs of capitalism dictated that nations had to be invented in order to provide the bourgeoisie with a vehicle to supersede the monarchical order and the religious establishment as the essential power-brokers in the modern state (Hobsbawm, 1990, pp. 101–30). These bourgeois political élites invented tradition[5] in order to legitimize their power during the turbulent times of the modern revolutions. However, in citing that premodern social groups, such as the Prussian monarchy, were able to maintain an influence on national politics in the new post-1871 Germany, Hobsbawm qualifies the modernist revolutionary-transition interpretation of nation-building in Europe (Hobsbawm, 1990, p. 184).

Gellner holds the modernist line more steadfastly with his insistence that the rise of nationalism and the nation was due to the prevailing economic circumstance caused by the transition of society from the agrarian to the industrial. The rise of nationalism and the nation was not accurately representative of a change in the political expression of ethnic communities to survive the modern era (Gellner, 1983, pp. 39–52). For Gellner, the connection between ethnicity and nationhood across the travail of modernization has been so distorted by constructed history and myth as to render it almost inconsequential: 'The cultural shreds and patches used by nationalism are often arbitrary historical inventions. Any old shred and patch would have served as well' (Gellner, 1983, p. 56). In this interpretation, nations and nationalism are the necessary product of a dispassionate modern rationality that recognizes their utility in the provision of an effective system of communication required by a newly industrialized society. However, the ability of nationalism to recreate a passionate sense of exclusive identity that taps into a real and imagined ethnic past for vitality is not explained by Gellner's 'nationalism-as-a-function-of-modernization' interpretation.

Indeed, the new mobility of the industrialized era deprived individuals of the security offered by their set social positions within their premodern society. Consequently, those individuals turned to the cultural resource of their communal identity in order to provide some sense of identity in a displaced modern society. By using the cultural and historical bonds of people to capitalize on the prevailing economic conditions, nationalism problematically confers political legitimacy on a unit which may refuse to be delimited by the state boundary. The real mission of nationalism may well have been to attempt to impose a high culture on society – to dissipate minority low 'folk' cultures and create a culturally homogeneous society – but the intimate relationship between nationalism and ethnic culture dictated that it could not be strictly controlled and contained by the state and its boundaries.

The Irish context provides an example of the ethno-religious features of the nation exerting a dominant leverage over the economic concerns of pivotal Irish Nationalists. Many of the Irish peripheral élite in the nineteenth century did not become conditioned into the 'British nation' even if it was in their economic interest to do so. Instead, they embraced Irish nationalism on the ideological principle of freeing Ireland from the colonial bind (Boyce, 1982, pp. 378–9). In effect, they constituted the secular intelligentsia that encouraged nationalism in Ireland, often to the detriment of their own economic interest. However, Gellner's interpretation does provide grounds for highlighting the neglected impact of economic and social factors in the emergence of Ulster unionism and Irish nationalism as the pillars on which communal identity crystallized in late-nineteenth-century Ireland.

Through its impact on the economic resource of communal identity, the development of the break in history after the onslaught of industrialization certainly exacerbated the widening chasm that was developing between Irish nationalism and Irish unionism at the turn of the century. The agrarian south, which had experienced economic and population decline in the nineteenth century, contrasted sharply with the prosperous industrial north-east of the island. Ulster farmers, who were mainly of Ulster Protestant stock, also managed to side-step the discontentment caused elsewhere by the land reform issue, benefiting as they did from Ulster customs which extended certain rights to them (Walker, 1994, p. 10). Nevertheless, other factors, such as the distinction made between the lowland Scots and English 'settlers' of the plantation era and the so-called Irish 'natives', as well as the notion of the fair minded and progressive colonizing the barbarous and backward, gave a retrospective integrity to the modern totalizing ideologies of Irish nationalism and Ulster unionism (Ruane and Todd, 1996, pp. 29–30). The religious component of ethnicity continued to play a dominant role. Catholic grievances over the issue of education were not experienced by Protestants and served to define communities further as 'Catholic' and 'Protestant'. By the elections of 1885 and 1886 the denominational cleavage was given political expression in the victorious home rule and Conservative parties (Walker, 1989, p. 256).

THE IMAGINED COMMUNITY

For Benedict Anderson, nationalism offers more than mere practical fulfilment. As it supersedes religion, nationalism actually borrows the central characteristics of religion, those of faith and the fear of fatality, by emphasizing its properties of everlasting life which the individual can enjoy through the allegiance of the individual and the family to the nation (Anderson, 1991, pp. 17–40). Anderson believes that this crucial act elevated nationalism above the status of political ideology and made it into a cultural system with religious characteristics. In Northern Ireland, premodern ethno-religious characteristics have continued to vitalize Irish Nationalist and Ulster Unionist identities and colour perceptions of these identities. However, the tenets and experience of social and political modernity have been instrumental in shaping these premodern characteristics into a modern mould.

The arrival of wide-scale print-publishing for the dissemination of nationalist propaganda was the essential precondition for modern nationalism and the consolidation of an 'imagined community' (Anderson, 1991, pp. 66–79). The possibility of an 'imagined community' arose primarily with a loss of faith in the concept of a universal truth represented by one particular language and with a questioning of the divine right of monarchs to rule. While modern economic change, scientific discovery and the development of communications were the underlying factors that were instrumental in this challenge to fundamental cultural conceptions, print capitalism was the decisive dynamic influencing change. When the limited market for books published in Latin became saturated around 1700, print capitalism turned its attention to publishing cheap editions in vernaculars. Thus a focus on individual identity and its place within the wider community came under scrutiny throughout Europe in the intervening period. The sacred community of Christendom, represented by Latin, was decisively undermined by

multifarious print-languages which established the national consciousness (Anderson, 1991, pp. 36–46).

The Irish language was not an issue for Irish nationalist movements before the Gaelic League was founded in 1893. Even the
Gaelic League had no formal political aims in its attempt to create
a uniform Irish language out of the complex dialects that existed
(Garvin, 1987, p. 50; Hobsbawm, 1990, p. 106). What mattered was
that the new modern cultural tool of newspapers could carry a
nationalist message directly to the imagination of the reader and
project as well as reflect a sense of communal identity centred on
the nation. The modern nation was too large for members to encounter one another but newspapers allowed the nation to become
a product of the imagination. They did this by drawing attention
to cultural similarities among members and cultural differences
between members and non-members (Anderson, 1991, pp. 13–15).

Young Ireland, a radical modernist group of Catholic and Protestant journalists who became disillusioned with what they perceived
to be the sectarian and integrative nature of Daniel O'Connell's
traditional nationalism[6] successfully used the technological innovation of print capitalism to communicate the doctrine of nationalism through education. They launched their newspaper *Nation* to
this end in 1842 (Boyce, 1982, p. 159). With an estimated reader-
ship of over a quarter of a million by 1843, *Nation* promoted the
aim of an independent, rural, Gaelic Ireland, free from the colonial rule of an alien, industrial, English neighbour (Hutchinson,
1994, p. 59). Provincial newspapers, like the *Connaught Telegraph*
and the *Kerry Sentinel* brought an Irish nationalist message to their
readers in local communities (Boyce, 1982, p. 205). Such newspapers
provided the conduit through which the 'land war' of 1879–82 became a catalyst for political action by the home rule party under
Parnell. Newspapers thus proved to be intrinsic to modern Irish
nationalism becoming a reactive force to British government policy
in Ireland. Modern Irish Nationalists believed that the Union sty-
mied the life-chances of Irish people. Furthermore, they perceived
that they were being subjected to persecution by the state. According to Benedict Anderson, those suffering victimization and alienation, real or perceived, find solidarity with those in a similar
predicament and commit to the nation in a solidarity of the vic-
timized (Anderson, 1991, pp. 113–141). Resonances of this 'reactive nationalism' in the North were initiated in the late 1960s by
the ability of television to relay pictures of the state subjugation of

the civil rights' marches in Northern Ireland directly into homes and imaginations.

(RE)IMAGINING IRISH NATIONALIST AND ULSTER UNIONIST IDENTITIES

Religion had provided the main source of social organization and cohesion in premodern Ireland. However, religious regimentation, combined with the strong sense of Irish identity, actually made it difficult for such a peripheral ethnic community to adapt to the modern circumstances for which 'nation' status was required. The theoretical course of action for a nationalist intelligentsia faced with this set of circumstances would have been to mobilize the community politically; secure a territory and co-ordinate its economic activity; instil secular values in the community by re-education and turn ethnic members into legal citizens. However, arguably the most successful Irish Nationalist intelligentsia – the home rule movement of the late-nineteenth century under the leadership of Parnell – did not mount a direct challenge to the authority of the Catholic Church in Ireland. Instead, it led the groundwork for a nationalist approach by securing a vital alliance with that Church in 1884–5 (Lyons, 1977, pp. 252–7). The result was electoral success in the general election of 1885 and the perpetuation of a traditional form of nationalism in Ireland with a Gaelic and Catholic ethno-religious core. Consequently, Irish unionism became redefined in a provincial Ulster context during the home rule era as Irish nationalism emerged to represent that which was religiously and, to some extent, economically alien. Again mass political mobilization occurred in Ireland. This time it was to secure the position of the ethnic Ulster Protestant community in the light of proposed changes in the structure of state power. Although the Ulster Protestant community was becoming politicized, it failed to adopt nationhood because it did not have the essential desire of modern nationalism to secure a state of its own. Rather, its political focus was resolutely anti-Irish Nationalist and, therefore, unionist.

The Ulster Convention (1892), the Ulster Unionist Council (1905) and the provincial nature of the Ulster Covenant (1912) against the third Home Rule Bill all served to confirm the consolidation of an Ulster Unionist community that felt itself to be distinct from, and indeed contradictory to, the Irish nation. In deciding not to oppose the Government of Ireland Bill of March 1920, which drafted the idea of the partition of Ireland into two Home Rule parliaments, the Ulster Unionist Council opted for the institutional expression of their distinctiveness from Catholic, nationalist, Gaelic, Ireland (Kennedy, 1988, p. 36; Jackson, 1994, p. 35). This distinction was compounded further by the perceived threat posed by Irish nationalism for Ulster Unionists from 1920. The decline of the Protestant population in the South by one third between 1911 and 1926 to 20,800 and by a further 12 per cent between 1926 and 1936, was taken by Ulster Unionists to be ominous evidence of this threat (Kennedy, 1988, pp. 154–73). However, violence between 1919 and 1922, and especially in the five months prior to the beginning of the Civil War in the South at the end of June 1922, was the most obvious manifestation of the threat for the Ulster Unionist community.

A major problem for the modern state-building on the island that occurred between 1920 and 1921 was that the distinction between the ethnic Ulster Protestant community and the Irish nation did not have a clear territorial boundary. The problem was highlighted by local elections in January and June of 1920 that resulted in Nationalist-Sinn Féin control of ten urban councils – including Derry, Strabane, Enniskillen, Armagh and Omagh – in the six counties due to be granted a northern parliament in the Government of Ireland Act (Bardon, 1992, p. 468). Despite the commix of Irish Nationalists and Ulster Unionists in the northern designated area, the British government pressed ahead with the Government of Ireland Act which became law in December 1920 and gave Unionists control of their own Home Rule parliament. However, the Anglo-Irish Treaty of 1921 constituted an immediate political threat for Ulster Unionists because it included Northern Ireland in the Free State, albeit with the option of leaving. In addition, the Treaty's financial provisions were thought to be unfavourable to Northern Ireland. Worst of all, the Treaty's proposal of a Boundary Commission to reconsider the territorial boundary of Northern Ireland presented the possibility of Northern Ireland losing territory to the Irish Free State (Kennedy, 1988, p. 69). Institutionally, the Provisional Government of the Free State represented a threat by initially encouraging and financing a policy of non-co-operation by northern Nationalists with the Belfast administration (Kennedy, 1988, p. 73).

The northern Irish Nationalists who subsequently found themselves on the wrong side of partition experienced feelings of dispossession and resentment at being cast adrift structurally from the rest of the Irish nation (Ó'Tuathaigh, 1994, p. 73). The promise of the modern era, that of nation-state fulfilment (albeit in a transitory home rule form) had seemed imminent for northern Nationalists in 1912. However, violent and political events and territorial circumstance were to conspire to deprive them of what they believed would best represent their interests and their identity. Instead, they found themselves locked in a structural arrangement that they perceived to be hostile to their identity and wilfully negligent of their interests. This perception was reflected and reinforced by the newspapers read by the northern Irish Nationalist 'imagined' community, notably, the *Irish News*.

The anti-Irish Nationalist narrative of Unionist newspapers like the *Belfast News-Letter*, the *Belfast Telegraph* and the *Northern Whig* played a vital role in galvanizing the Ulster Unionist community. Dennis Kennedy (1988) has shown how newspapers reflected and reinforced the particularist culture-bound knowledge of the Unionist 'imagined' community by constantly highlighting the perceived threat posed by Irish nationalism. In particular, Sinn Féin and the IRA were portrayed as the root-cause of all politically motivated violence during this period and after (Kennedy, 1988, p. 73). Provincial newspapers in Northern Ireland continue to represent this cleavage in varying degrees. The *News-Letter* and, to a lesser extent, the *Belfast Telegraph* (euphemistically subtitled 'the national newspaper of Northern Ireland') continue to reflect and reinforce the particularist culture-bound knowledge of the Ulster Unionist community while the *Irish News* continues to do the same for northern Irish Nationalist concerns. To assert that the communal conflict in Northern Ireland is not fed by a communications gap between the 'two communities', as the late Ernest Gellner would have done (1983, p. 71), is to overlook the influence of these exclusivist narratives on the communal imaginations of Ulster Unionists and Irish Nationalists in Northern Ireland.

There is, however, some evidence to suggest that nationalist ideology is responding to postmodern developments and changing as a result. The 'liberal nationalist' SDLP narrative of the nation represents a substantive threat to the modernist contingencies of Ulster unionism and Irish nationalism.[7] This narrative is founded on David Harvey's assertion that the flexible accumulation of late capitalism has resulted in a 'reterritorialization' of social power (Harvey, 1989, pp. 302–3). The SDLP narrative attempts to reimagine the Irish community in this reterritorialized postmodern context. As such, it is broadly in line with the pro-European liberal nationalism that has been developing at the level of the state and political class in the Republic of Ireland (Ruane, 1994, p. 185). Extraterritorial sites of political influence are actively engaged and nurtured; their salience for political interaction constantly highlighted. As a consequence, the hegemonic content of modern nationalism is rejected in favour of co-operation and cross-territorial alliance formation.[8] Such a narrative points to the emergence of a liberal form of nationalism in the postmodern world to challenge the mantle of modern nationalism. For Yael Tamir:

> The era of homogeneous and viable nation-states is over (or rather, the era of the illusion that homogeneous and viable nation-states are possible is over, since such states never existed), and the national vision must be re-defined (Tamir, 1993, p. 3).

This structural change does not mean that a code of post-nationalism is about to be observed or that a single global community is an inevitability. Rather, the challenge is for liberal nationalism to realign the relationship between national identity and the state in light of postmodern structural change (Tamir, 1993, p. 166).

CONCLUSION

Modernity provided the conditions for the development of the Irish nation from its ethnic origins (modern economic development) – albeit by the negative power of grievance – and the means by which the national 'imagined community' could be developed and consolidated (print languages). The Irish nation was not the product of divine ordinance emanating from a specific 'origin', nor was it simply the (by)product of the European drive to modernization – it was essentially narrated by Irish newspapers and other print media of the day. These narratives did collage and embellish historical events as they pertained to 'the Irish', they were also reacting to the processes of modernization: but it is these narratives themselves that are directly responsible for creating and moulding a 'national consciousness' in its ambiguous and ambivalent form. As a consequence, it is these narratives that will continue to play a pivotal role in the development of nations as they encounter the structural changes associated with postmodernity.

Communal identities in Northern Ireland, with their ethnic roots, territorial entanglement, and mutually exclusive culture-bound interpretations nourished by the communications media, have the complexion of a perverse mutation that has resulted, at least in part, from the enterprise of nationalizing ethnic communities. However, the continuing political conflict in Northern Ireland cannot be explained purely in terms of Gellner's notion of the temporal and spatial duality of modern socio-economic development and impoverishment (although this was a significant factor in initiating the revival of nationalism in Northern Ireland from 1969), it also involves a post-material identification of cultural heritage with modern nationalism. Into this mix comes a liberal form of nationalism synonymous with postmodern structural change. It rejects the notion of the modern nation-state as a structural nirvana for the nation. Its uptake offers possibilities for re-imagining northern Irish Nationalist and Ulster Unionist communal identities as Northern Ireland experiences the shift from modernity to postmodernity in politics and society.

3 The Governance of Northern Ireland: From Modernity to Postmodernity?

The northern Irish Nationalist and Ulster Unionist imagined communities have witnessed profound change since 1920 when the Government of Ireland Act proposed two Irish parliaments, one for the six counties in the north and one for the 26 counties in the south. The beginning of the modern state context for Ireland, which entailed the territorial separation of Ulster Unionists and northern Irish Nationalists from the rest of the Irish nation, was confirmed in the Anglo-Irish Treaty of 1921. Although the Treaty granted governing status to the whole island of Ireland, an article in the Treaty permitted the Northern Ireland parliament to opt out of the jurisdiction of the Irish Free State constitution and retain its status under the 1920 Act, which it promptly did. From 1921 until 1969, Ulster Unionists maintained hegemonic control in Northern Ireland (O'Leary and McGarry, 1993, pp. 133-4). Through hegemonic control, this dominant group successfully established its truth-claims as the basis of socio-political order in Northern Ireland. The culture-bound knowledge of northern Irish Nationalists was perceived to be the extension of the Catholic and Gaelic socio-political group that dominated in the South. Consequently, northern Irish Nationalists represented a threat within the territorial niche that Ulster Unionism had managed to carve out for itself on the island of Ireland. As a result, successive Unionist governments attempted to control rather than accommodate this Irish Nationalist community that found itself in the particular modern structure of state that Northern Ireland represented between 1921 and 1972.

Unionist attempts at reforming Northern Ireland in the 1960s initiated the collapse of their hegemonic control in the region. The period 1969–72 brought a sequence of civil-rights protest, Unionist reaction, Nationalist revolt, and the collapse of the Unionist hegemony. Thereafter, political accommodation in Northern Ireland became the priority of the UK government. In 1973–4, the Sunningdale power-sharing experiment accommodated the nationalist SDLP in a new and short-lived structure of government for Northern Ireland. The Anglo-Irish Agreement of 1985 initiated more durable developments in the governance of Northern Ireland, developments that began to chime with postmodernist concepts. The modern emphasis on upholding the territorial boundary and maintaining a dominant socioeconomic truth began to be steadfastly challenged by a postmodernist concern for the representation of difference that is not delimited by territorial consideration. Since 1985, the governments of the United Kingdom and the Republic of Ireland have been evolving this postmodernist context for Northern Ireland politics.

THE NORTHERN IRELAND CONTEXT: 1921–72

A state is 'a legal and political organisation with the power to require obedience and loyalty from its citizens' (Seton-Watson, 1977, p. 1). Organizationally and functionally, the modern political unit of Northern Ireland between 1921 and 1972 was, in practice, a substate within the United Kingdom of Great Britain and Northern Ireland because it had many of the attributes normally associated with a federal state. A Westminster-style parliamentary system of government was imposed on Northern Ireland in 1921 which granted the Northern Ireland parliament legislative powers on matters relating to law and order; to the police; the courts, other than the Supreme Court; and other common areas of public interest except foreign affairs and matters concerning the Crown and secession, the making of peace and war, the armed forces, external trade, coinage and legal tender. The minimal degree of fiscal autonomy granted to the Northern Ireland administration ensured that ultimate sovereignty was reserved at Westminster. However, British subvention allowed the Northern Ireland government to implement their legislative powers effectively, often extravagantly and with little interference from Westminster (Arthur, 1984, pp. 19–22).

The monopoly of effective force and the maintenance of a territorial boundary are recognized to be the cornerstones of the modern state (Rose, 1983, pp. 5–9; Poggi, 1990, pp. 22–3; Tilly, 1990, p. 1). Dyson asserts that the resources of physical power, a clearly defined territory and the quality of the authority the state commands within that territory, that is its sovereign powers, are integral features of the modern state (Dyson, 1987, p. 591). In Northern Ireland, the monopoly of force came to be manifested in a new police force which effectively consisted of the Royal Ulster Constabulary (RUC) and the Ulster Special Reserve (the 'B' Specials). In time, this force had to deal with the threat of external invasion from the South and the threat and actuality of internal rebellion from elements of the northern Irish Nationalist community. The new monopoly of force in the North could draw on contemporary lessons of states where the monopoly of force had lapsed, destabilizing the state. It was, after all, the Nationalist rebellion in the South, from 1916 to 1921, which altered the state of the United Kingdom and Ireland that was established by the Act of Union 1801. The newly formed Irish Free State was then challenged by Éamon de Valera's anti-Treatyites during the Irish Civil War which began on 28 June 1922, leaving the legitimacy of the Irish Free State in doubt until 1932. The Irish state only found stability when the electoral success of De Valera's Fianna Fáil party was recognized by the first Taoiseach of the Irish Free State, W.T. Cosgrave (Rose, 1983, p. 6).

Although one third of all RUC places were initially set aside for Catholic recruits, the uptake of places by Catholics has never far exceeded 8 per cent. In August 1969, the strength of the 'B' Specials was 425 full-time and 8,481 part-time constables, none of whom were Catholics. Such figures fuelled the Catholic perception of the police force as a Protestant force that was little more than the coercive wing of the ruling Unionist Party (Farrell, 1976, p. 97). Protestant domination of the monopoly of force was perceived by Unionists to be vital for the maintenance of the Unionist hegemony and remained effective until the civil unrest of 1969. Prior to 1969, any inclination by the Nationalist community physically to challenge the monopoly of force was met with the introduction of internment. It proved to be an effective security measure when implemented in 1921–24, 1938–45, and again in 1956–62 when the IRA launched its futile 'Border Campaign' against Northern Ireland (Arthur, 1984, p. 112).

The issue of the territorial boundary between Northern Ireland and the Irish Free State was left unresolved until the Boundary Commission reported in 1925. It decided to maintain the boundary, as constituted in 1920, which was based on the configuration of maximal land mass to secure Unionist majority rather than any historic, geographic or economic criteria. Prior to the 1925

Boundary Commission Report, Irish Nationalists in large areas of South Down, South Armagh, Fermanagh and Tyrone expected those areas to be transferred to the Free State (Arthur, 1984, p. 22). When the expected didn't materialize Irish Nationalists in those areas were angered but the territorial boundary was not threatened. Although the legitimacy of the boundary has been challenged, *de jure*, by Bunreacht Na hÉireann/Constitution of Ireland (1937) which stated that: 'The national territory consists of the whole island of Ireland, its islands and territorial seas' (Article 2), the Government of the Republic of Ireland[1] has recognized the boundary in the Anglo-Irish Agreement (1985), the Downing Street Declaration (1993), the Framework Documents (1995) and the Multi-Party Agreement (1998).

The Unionist sub-state did not incorporate features of nationality, universal citizenship and democracy into its infrastructure.[2] Nationality was generally perceived by Unionists to refer to the Irish nation from which they felt distinct. Politically, Unionists interpreted their identity in terms of citizenship and the modern state. Such an interpretation determined that an extension of equal citizenship to northern Catholics was deemed to be inappropriate because the Catholic community was perceived to be Irish Nationalist and, therefore, 'disloyal' to Northern Ireland. Manifestation of this denial lay in direct and indirect discriminatory practices in both public- and private-sector employment and in the allocation of public-sector housing; in the gerrymandering of some local authority boundaries (notably in Dungannon, Armagh and Derry city) to favour the Unionist Party; and in the continued restriction of the local government franchise in Northern Ireland to ratepayers and their spouses (with large property owners allocated up to 6 votes depending on the rateable value of their property) despite the abolition of such restriction in Britain after 1948. This latter practice disproportionately impacted on the Catholic community because Catholics were disproportionately poorer than Protestants. Discriminatory practices in the allocation of public-sector housing exacerbated that community's disenfranchizement (Moxon-Browne, 1983, pp. 131–3; Bardon, 1992, pp. 638–9; O'Leary and McGarry, 1993, pp. 119–25). Although concessions to universal suffrage would not have dramatically altered the substantial Unionist majority on Unionist-controlled councils, it did provide civil rights activists with the potent clarion call 'one man, one vote' in 1969 (Arthur, 1984, p. 116).

The grievances experienced by northern Catholics determined that they considered themselves to be second-class citizens in Northern Ireland. However, Unionists believed that territorial, economic, electoral, legal and coercive controls were necessary for their own survival (O'Leary and McGarry, 1993, pp. 107–41). This necessary Unionist hegemony could not countenance any form of political accommodation with northern Nationalists and the modern sub-state of Northern Ireland continued to defy the existing norm of liberal democracy elsewhere in Western society after 1945.

THE END OF THE UNIONIST HEGEMONY: 1963–72

Two factors combined to end Unionist hegemonic control effectively in 1972, when the exercise of public power reverted to Westminster and the Stormont Parliament was prorogued. A policy of pervasive economic and social modernization for Northern Ireland was announced by Terence O'Neill shortly after he was appointed prime minister in 1963 (Arthur, 1984, pp. 84–98; Lee, 1989, pp. 414–5). The new economic climate, dominated by multinational companies, required a reorganization of public infrastructure in order to attract business. In his view, Northern Ireland would be best placed to make economic progress after community reconciliation had been forged. Almost immediately, Catholic expectations were raised as were Unionist fears. In the event, the raised expectations of Catholics, and in particular the Catholic middle-class, were not met by substantive measures to correct housing and employment discrimination, electoral boundary abuses, restricted local government franchise, and the sectarian 'B' Specials[3] (O'Leary and McGarry, 1993, pp. 162–7). Public policy decisions continued to offend the day-to-day sensibilities of middle-class Catholics who had believed that O'Neill's commitment was genuine. A regional plan, which included the development of a new city, to be called 'Craigavon' after Northern Ireland's first prime minister, James Craig, did not inspire Nationalist confidence in the Unionist regime under O'Neill. Similarly, the location of a second university in the Protestant-dominated town of Coleraine instead of the Catholic-dominated city of Derry (which had campaigned strongly for a university in the city) appeared to be sectarian in nature (Bardon, 1992, p. 626).

O'Neill did attempt to pave the way for economic links with the Republic of Ireland through meetings in 1965 with the similarly business-minded Taoiseach Seán Lemass.[4] However, Unionist Party obduracy and Protestant community opposition, led by the Reverend Ian Paisley, blocked the transformation of O'Neill's intentions into genuine reform (Rose, 1971, pp. 99–101; O'Neill, 1972, pp. 68–80). While it appeared that expectations were not going to be satisfied by the introduction of new reforms, the dynamic created by the heightening of Catholic expectations had not dissipated. Inevitably, that energy was channelled into political action. The form of that political action was the second factor that contributed to the demise of the Unionist hegemony. It emanated from the new political approach to its problems that had been developing in the Nationalist community. While the Nationalist Party continued to be defined by the stale traditional nationalist ethos which focused on national identity, the continued denial of equal citizenship and inadequate democratic representation in the context of the UK state provided an impetus for the young and emerging Nationalist élite (the products of the 1947 Education Act) to mobilize a civil rights campaign. The principal agent in this new movement was the Northern Ireland Civil Rights Association (NICRA). By directly addressing the Labour Party in Westminster and contextualizing its campaign in terms of equal citizenship in the United Kingdom, it demanded the redress of Catholic grievances (Rose, 1971, p. 152).

The NICRA's programme of political action had three effective features. Firstly, by directly addressing the sovereign government of the UK in its capacity as the effective representative of the Catholic minority in Northern Ireland, the NICRA concentrated on the citizenship rights of the individual in the UK context, thus implying an acceptance of the operation of the British Constitution in Northern Ireland. Consequently, the NICRA could not be as easily ignored as previous Nationalist representatives who had presented their communal grievances to the Government of the Republic of Ireland. Secondly, an effective media campaign, particularly through the new development of national and global television networks, highlighted the anomaly of the denial of democratic rights to a minority in a supposedly modern democratic society and acutely embarrassed the UK government. Thirdly, the peaceful demonstrations of the founding civil-rights marches, the violent reaction to them by Loyalist protesters, and the subsequent rise in prominence of socialist militants and Republicans within the NICRA persuaded the UK government to initiate reforms through O'Neill (McCann, 1993; O'Leary and McGarry, 1993, pp. 167–71). However, any action taken by the UK government was too little too late. Attitudes shifted towards the extremities of both sides. O'Neill was forced to resign on 28 April 1969 and by August 1969 the level of sectarian violence was so intense that British troops had to be deployed to act as peace-keepers in a developing violent conflict. Open defiance of bans imposed on civil-rights marches by the Ministry of Home Affairs represented a challenge to state law and was, therefore, construed as an initial act of rebellion by many Loyalists. For them, the belief that the NICRA was conspiring to dissolve Northern Ireland by force of violence was confirmed when street-rioting escalated after the summer of 1969 and the Provisional IRA emerged. From 1971, the level of politically motivated violence increased acutely. In an effort to quell that violence the tried and trusted mechanism of internment without trial was re-introduced on 9 August 1971. On this occasion, internment not only failed (because leading members of the Provisional IRA were not identified and captured) it actually intensified the conflict because of its one-sided nature (no Loyalist suspects were arrested), the alleged ill-treatment of internees and the on-going arrests (Arthur, 1984, pp. 112–13).

Despite the increase in security personnel, the level of violence continued to escalate with the result that, on 24 March 1972, the Northern Ireland Prime Minister Brian Faulkner and his ministers were summoned to Westminster by the British Prime Minister Edward Heath. They were informed of plans to transfer control of security to Westminster, to end internment and to appoint a Secretary of State for Northern Ireland. Almost immediately thereafter the Northern Ireland cabinet resigned, Stormont was prorogued and the Unionist hegemony brought to an end.

THE UK STATE CONTEXT: 1972–

Centralization is traditionally viewed as an important facet of a strong modern state because it enhances the sovereign power (Tilly, 1975, p. 70). Consequently, an objective interpretation of the transfer of power back to the sovereign authority of Westminster after fifty years of devolved government in Northern Ireland might conclude that such a move strengthened the modern state of the United Kingdom of Great Britain and Northern Ireland (Rose, 1983, p. 16). In the event, the fall of Stormont and the introduction of direct rule was interpreted, not as an act of strength, by the Irish Nationalist community in Northern Ireland, but as one of weakness. The reason for this interpretation was the fact that the incumbent Unionist hegemony had been dissolved. This sense of UK state weakness was compounded by the continued devolutionist policy of the UK government with regard to Northern Ireland (Rose, 1983, p. 20).

A fundamental cause of UK state weakness was undoubtedly the recrudescence of militant Irish republicanism after 1968. Poggi asserts that the state must be able to control the population occupying the state territory. To do this the state claims a monopoly of force or 'last resort control' which can be exercised by authorized individuals. The practice or threat of coercion must be wholly convincing to the population (Poggi, 1990, p. 22). Evidently, the practice of coercive force in Northern Ireland was not limited to that of the Northern Ireland authorities or, after the introduction of British troops in 1969, the UK state. State force could not contain a section of the northern Nationalist community that was itself engaged in the use of force against the *status quo*.

The year 1972 proved to be the most violent in over a quarter century of troubles since 1969, highlighting the degree of UK state weakness. A total of 467 deaths were caused by politically motivated violence in that year (Arthur and Jeffery, 1988, p. 98). The monopoly of force, augmented by 22,000 British soldiers by 30 July 1972, was undergoing an extreme assault by the Provisional IRA. The Provo's perceived that their campaign of violence (especially their systematic bombing campaign which began in October 1972) had irreparably weakened the position of Northern Ireland in the United Kingdom. They were convinced that it was only a matter of time before the UK government would be forced to negotiate with them on a state realignment of Northern Ireland (Smith, 1995, p. 95). Faced with this assault, the Secretary of State for Northern Ireland, William Whitelaw, set out to undermine the will of Republicans through the implementation of a security strategy that sought to redress Nationalist community grievances, such as the continued detention of internees and the question of 'political category status' for detained prisoners. In addition, the dismantling of 'no-go' areas by the British army on 31 July 1972 undermined the capacity of Republican paramilitaries to store and disseminate guns and explosives (Bardon, 1992, pp. 698–9). Consequently, some legitimacy was restored to the state boundary even though the border with the Republic remained porous in military terms because Republican paramilitaries could easily find safe haven south of the border after carrying out an attack in the North.

Whitelaw combined his security strategy with a new political approach that aimed to create a political structure of government for Northern Ireland which could accommodate, rather than exclude, the minority Irish Nationalist community. Such a political structure would have implications for the integrity of the modern political boundary between the territory of Northern Ireland and that of the Republic of Ireland. The Westminster directive that an unspecified 'Irish Dimension' was to be included in any constitutional settlement confirmed the new approach of the UK government. This approach angered the vast bulk of Unionists because they remained adamantly opposed to any reassessment of the political frontier with the Republic of Ireland.

In 1973, the opportunity arose for the Nationalist community to progress from demands for civil rights to political empowerment through the principle of consociationalism. From a modernist perspective, the official proposal for power-sharing, contained in a White Paper called *Northern Ireland Constitutional Proposals* (20 March 1973), placed northern Irish Nationalists on the horns of a dilemma. Irish Nationalist élites had to make a straight choice between the modern pursuit of nation-state fulfilment in an All-Ireland state or empowerment, through consociationalism, in a modern state not reflective of the Irish nation. From this perspective, the obvious paradox of entering into such an arrangement for the 'constitutional nationalist' SDLP was that the party's emphasis on social democracy enabled it to enter into a constitutional arrangement with a modern state to which its nationalist credentials were opposed. In this structure of state, northern Nationalists would remain the permanent minority in Northern Ireland without the modernist fulfilment of their identity through political incorporation into the Irish nation-state.

A power-sharing structure for government in Northern Ireland was authorized in the Northern Ireland Constitution Act 1973. This arrangement included the election of an Assembly by proportional representation and the instillation of an Executive when the Secretary of State was satisfied that it had broad-based cross-community support. In their pursuit of an 'Irish Dimension' in the power-sharing agreement at Sunningdale in 1973, the SDLP attempted to transcend the orthodox arrangement of the modern state defined by the territorial boundary. The party argued for a substantial structural link between northern Nationalists and the Irish nation, embodied as an 'Irish dimension'. At the same time, the party engaged in an attempt at forging a solution based on social democracy within the territorial boundary of Northern Ireland, and thus, within the UK state (Arthur, 1984, pp. 116–18; Bardon, 1992, pp. 703–7).

The subsequent incorporation of an Irish dimension into the constitutional plans for Northern Ireland can be interpreted as an initial intimation of postmodernity in a structural arrangement for Northern Ireland. Under such an arrangement, the modern state as a framework for government is transcended because the focus for constitution-making shifts from an exclusive interest in territorial autonomy to the diverging interests and allegiances of communities in Northern Ireland. The concept of the Irish dimension was to reflect the interests of the Nationalist community in Northern Ireland and provide a counterbalance to the British dimension that was taken to represent the Ulster Unionist community.

The Sunningdale Agreement (December 1993) proposed the creation of a 'Council of Ireland' to represent the Irish dimension in substantive terms. O'Leary and McGarry describe the form and function that was envisaged for the Council of Ireland:

> The Council of Ireland was to comprise a cross-border body – drawn from seven members of the Northern Ireland executive and seven members of the Irish government, a secretariat, and a consultative assembly with thirty members of the Northern Ireland assembly and thirty members of Dáil Éireann. Unanimity was to be the basis of the Council's resolutions, and thus mutual vetoes were to operate. The Council was to be experimental, vested with minor consultative and research functions, but was to have a 'harmonizing' role, and the door was left open for it to expand into institutions capable of forging a united Ireland (O'Leary and McGarry, 1993, pp. 198–9).

In the event, attempts to set the Council of Ireland in motion provoked demonstrations and protest riots by Loyalists (Bardon, 1992, p. 706). Faulkner's unsuccessful attempt at selling the Council of Ireland to Unionists in terms of its security benefits was not helped by the escalation in the violent campaigns of Republican and Loyalist paramilitaries (O'Leary and McGarry, 1993, p. 199). Anti-consociational Unionists – the DUP, Vanguard and the OUP (now more commonly known as the UUP) – united behind the effective publicity slogan 'Dublin is just a Sunningdale away' in the

United Ulster Unionist Council (UUUC). The UUUC received 51 per cent of the vote in the Westminster General election on 28 February 1974, securing 11 of the 12 seats at Westminster. It had thus successfully cast power-sharing as part of a Republican plot to deliver the disintegration of the UK state. Thereafter, the position of Faulkner and his colleagues became untenable (O'Leary and McGarry, 1993, p. 200; Bew, Gibbon, and Patterson, 1995, p. 197). Anti-consociational Unionist opposition to the power-sharing executive gradually galvanized. A province-wide strike in May 1974, enforced by the Ulster Workers' Council (which had links with Loyalist paramilitary organizations) and indecisively handled by the newly appointed Secretary of State, Merlyn Rees, eventually brought an end to the Sunningdale experiment in consociationalism.

The intention of the 'Council of Ireland' proposal was to provide a structural link for northern Irish Nationalists to the rest of the Irish nation that was represented by its own modern state – the Republic of Ireland. However, that identity was also being represented by the violence of the Provisional IRA which continued to seek the absolute alignment of the Irish nation with the Irish state. Some Unionist leaders, such as the Reverend Ian Paisley and Bill Craig, perceived these constitutional and violent approaches to be a twin-pronged attack by northern Nationalists on the territorial integrity of Northern Ireland. In their interpretation, the aim of constitutional Nationalists was to complement the violent assault on Northern Ireland that was being waged by Republicans with a political approach aimed at gradually eroding the territorial boundary with the Republic of Ireland through the introduction of a Trojan horse to Northern Ireland, namely, the 'Council of Ireland'.

From 1974, the Government of the United Kingdom has remained committed to the principle of consociationalism for a devolved system of government in Northern Ireland, despite UUP and DUP antipathy. Defending the majority-rule principle which they favour, many Unionists have contended that the principle of consociationalism is 'un-British' because it is has no tradition in the Westminster parliamentary system, and that it represents a breach of democracy in Northern Ireland. It has been reported that Unionist leaders proved to be 'flexible' in the 1992 Mayhew Talks and that they even acquiesced to proposals for consociationalism (Bew, Gibbon and Patterson, 1995, p. 221; *Fortnight*, October, 1995, p. 18). However, the linkage of consociationalism with an 'Irish Dimension' has allowed anti-consociational Unionists to label consociationalism as a mechanism to aid the process of 'Irish unification'. Meanwhile, the increased confidence of the SDLP (derived from the role of the extraterritorial dimension embodied in the Anglo-Irish process, the EU polity and US diplomatic involvement), as well as the party's desire to maintain its majority share of the northern Nationalist vote, indicates that acceptance by the party of consociationalism without an empowered 'Irish Dimension' is not a realistic proposition. Moreover, the EU has become an important feature of SDLP policy. In the 1992 Mayhew Talks, John Hume refused to revise the radical SDLP proposal which included a direct role for the European Commission in the governance of Northern Ireland. In the Multi-Party Talks (1996–8), the SDLP proposed new North-South structures based on an EU Council of Ministers model. Here, members of a North-South executive body, drawn from the Irish government and a new Northern Ireland Assembly, would have joint decision-making powers but with separate powers of implementation (*Irish Times*, 25 November 1997). A similar model for the North-South dimension was proposed in the 1992 Talks.

The power-sharing Executive of 1974 did function successfully for five months with a satisfactory degree of agreement on matters of practical decision-making including social services, employment, housing. However, there remained the fundamental problem of the incongruity of establishing a system of government on the one hand, and the failure to reach consensus on the constitution of the state on the other. The proposed 'Council of Ireland' was to consist of Dublin ministers and members of the power-sharing executive with the possibility that it would acquire executive powers. Unionists could not accept such proposals and this political stand-off remains despite the optimism engendered by the Multi-Party Agreement (1998).

From May 1974, the 'temporary' measure of direct rule from Westminster has continued in the absence of an agreed structure of state for Northern Ireland. Persistent attempts to introduce consociational government after 1974, through the Constitutional Convention of 1975, cross-party talks 1978–9, the Prior experiment in 'Rolling Devolution' 1982, and the Brooke/Mayhew Talks 1991–2, have all failed. The Government of the United Kingdom remains committed to the principle of consociationalism for Northern Ireland.[5] However, the critical factors for successful consociationalism *in a modern state context* include the ability of a political élite to take decisions independently of their segmental followers and, with regard to Nationalist identity, that the emphasis be placed on cultural rather than political identity (McGarry and O'Leary, 1990, p. 283). These factors would appear to be wholly absent in Northern Ireland.

AFTER THE ANGLO-IRISH AGREEMENT (1985): POST-MODERN POLITY?

The Anglo-Irish Agreement (AIA) of 1985 has been described as 'arguably the most far-reaching political development since 1920 and the creation of Northern Ireland' (Flackes and Elliott, 1994, p. 84). The most notable feature of the AIA, contained in Article 2, involved an institutionalized Irish dimension for the governance of Northern Ireland in the form of an Anglo-Irish Intergovernmental Conference (IGC). The IGC was to be headed by the Secretary of State for Northern Ireland and the Tánaiste of the Republic of Ireland, and supported by a permanent secretariat at Maryfield that included Irish officials. The remit of the IGC was to promote cross-border co-operation and consult on political, security, legal and other issues. Particular attention was to be given to issues of discrimination, electoral arrangements, the status of the Irish language and the use of flags and emblems (Bardon, 1992, p. 756). Accordingly, Dr Garret FitzGerald[6] described the role of the IGC as 'more than consultative, but less than executive' (O'Leary and McGarry, 1993, p. 226). This description reflects the shortfall in the Irish government's aim to secure an executive role in the governance of Northern Ireland through the full participation of an Irish minister. However, it also indicates the influential role that the IGC has had in the formulation of policy, a role similar to the agenda-setting capability of the European Commission in the decision-making processes of the EU. In FitzGerald's opinion, this implied that the Irish government had responsibility without power (Bew, Gibbon and Patterson, 1995, p. 214).

The IGC revived the spectre of the Trojan horse for Unionists and confirmed that the demise of the power-sharing executive in 1974 was a pyrrhic victory for Ulster Unionism (Bew, Gibbon and Patterson, 1995, p. 198). In contrast to the Sunningdale Agreement, there was little that Unionists could do to bring down the Irish dimension, incorporated in the AIA, because it was institutionalized at the extraterritorial intergovernmental level and did not require Unionist participation to make it workable. Thus, the AIA signalled the end of the Unionist veto on structure and policy-making in Northern Ireland (O'Leary and McGarry, 1993, p. 227; Hume, 1996, p. 45). Unionists were offered the possibility of limiting the agenda-setting scope of the IGC, but only if they entered into a consociational arrangement for Northern Ireland that was essentially Sunningdale Mark II. Although the AIA did not constitute a system of joint authority in the context of the modern state, it did provide a framework for a form of joint authority in the event of political parties in Northern Ireland failing to reach agreement on a consociational form of government with an institutionalized Irish Dimension (O'Leary and McGarry, 1993, p. 239).

The seeds of Anglo-Irish co-operation were germinated by the civil rights' campaign, the collapse of the Unionist hegemony and the restructuring of Nationalist politics into distinctive and considerable constitutional and paramilitary forces (Bew, Gibbon, and Patterson, 1995, p. 214). Essentially, this co-operation was subsequently fostered through regular contact between UK and Irish governments in the supranational context of the European Community after 1 January 1973, when both states joined the EC. In terms of the operation and achievements of the AIA, the most obvious development has been the institutionalization of co-operation between UK and Irish governments on Northern Ireland. The nature of this co-operation has been described as 'direct rule with a green tinge' (Bew and Patterson, 1990, p. 217). However, substantive progress on the issues was hindered by the different priorities given to reforms and security by the Irish and UK governments respectively. Consequently, the Irish government's desire to pursue reforms that advance the interests of the Irish Nationalist community in Northern Ireland was offset by the emphasis placed by the UK government on improving cross-border security and curbing change in an effort to limit the antagonism of Unionists (O'Leary and McGarry, 1993, p. 245–6). Invariably, the latest violent atrocity dominated the agenda of IGCs during the first four years. As a result, the AIA became perceived as being little more than an instrument for crisis management. However, both governments have claimed that improvements were made in the area of cross-border security[7] (O'Leary and McGarry, 1993, pp. 272–3). It is also probable that the IGC acted as a catalyst for the upgraded Fair Employment Act (1989). Nevertheless, the pace of reform in the area of legal justice remained a source of disappointment for northern Nationalists and the Irish government (O'Leary and McGarry, 1993,

p. 265–7; Ed Maloney in the *Sunday Tribune*, 15 December 1996).
In substantive terms, the AIA is representative of postmodernity
in so far as its success in institutionalizing an Irish dimension that
was 'more than consultative, but less than executive' impinged upon
the integrity of the modern territorial boundary of Northern Ireland.
As a coercive device for the imposition of consociationalism
and maintenance of an Irish dimension in the government of Northern Ireland, the IGC can be interpreted as a prelude to a structure
of government for Northern Ireland that transcends the modern
state boundary of the United Kingdom of Great Britain and Northern
Ireland. Equally, it can be argued that, by entering into an arrangement with the UK government on the governance of Northern Ireland in 1985, the Government of the Republic of Ireland transcended
the modern irredentism of Articles 2 and 3 contained in *Bunreacht
Na hÉireann/Constitution of Ireland* at that time. In such a developing postmodern context, it is envisaged that economic interests
in areas such as agriculture and tourism could benefit from the
adoption of an island of Ireland perspective (Bradley, 1995; Attwood,
1995; Hume, 1996). The AIA also offers some demonstration of
the political benefits for northern Nationalists of receiving representation from the government of the Republic of Ireland in the
IGC. Conceptually, the enhanced priority given to the voice of the
northern Nationalist community in the governance of Northern
Ireland reflects the emphasis placed by postmodernism on the
empowerment of marginalized voices in society. However, the northern Nationalist voice still required translation in the policy consultation arena of the IGC by the government of its 'patron' nation-state
– the Republic of Ireland. While some progress on addressing minority concerns suggested intimations of postmodernity in the operation of the AIA, limiting direct contribution to the consultation
forum – the IGC – to the representatives of national governments
is suggestive of a modernist conceptual framework.

Unionists argued that the Irish government's consultation of the
SDLP during the negotiations that led to the AIA, and the corresponding failure of the UK government to consult Unionists, constituted an imbalance in the representation of communal identities
in Northern Ireland. However, a Machiavellian interpretation of
the AIA leads to the conclusion that it was the intention of the
architects of the AIA for Unionists to perceive that northern
Nationalists had benefited from the AIA (O'Leary and McGarry,
1993, pp. 234–5). In adopting this strategy, the AIA was manipulating

the psychology of the zero-sum game[8] in an attempt to procure an eventual inclusive settlement. The coercive consociationalist approach of the AIA suggested that the institutionalized Irish dimension could only be contained if Unionists became involved in a consociational arrangement. The AIA failed to produce consociational government in Northern Ireland, with Unionists remaining steadfast in their opposition to the Agreement. However, the AIA proved to be a durable (if slow-burning) dynamic for shifting the political context of Northern Ireland from an exclusive interest in territorial autonomy to one focused on the inclusive accommodation of diverse communal identities. This paradigm shift is reflected in the framework for formal discussions on the political future of Northern Ireland that have taken place in the aftermath of the AIA – The Brooke/Mayhew Talks (1991–2), and the Multi-Party Talks (1996–8). With its emphasis on the 'totality of relationships', this framework considers not only the 'internal' relationship between northern Nationalists and Ulster Unionists, but also the north-south relationship, and the British-Irish relationship. Such a framework begins to displace the emphasis of modernity on the territorial sovereignty of the nation-state in favour of creating trans-territorial arrangements that can accommodate diverse communal identities.

The Downing Street Declaration (1993) reinforced the paradigm shift for communal identities in Northern Ireland. Territorial majoritarianism was rejected in favour of communal consent. Paragraph 5 stated that:

> The Taoiseach, on behalf of the Irish Government, considers that the lessons of Irish history, and especially of Northern Ireland, show that stability and well-being will not be found under any political system which is refused allegiance or rejected on grounds of identity by a significant minority of those governed by it.

The postmodern context of the EU was recognized as providing a broader framework for this paradigm shift from modernity to postmodernity in a political strategy for Northern Ireland, agreed by both the Irish and UK governments:

> ... the development of Europe will, of itself, require new approaches to serve interests common to both parts of the island of Ireland, and to Ireland and the United Kingdom as partners in the European Union (Paragraph 3, *The Downing Street Declaration*, 1993).

Such an acceptance of the EU as an integral feature of a political settlement in Northern Ireland, by a representative of the Conservative government at Westminster, is in marked contrast to the anti-European integrationist thrust of the approach of that government at Maastricht and after. As such, that UK Conservative government could be said to have adopted a postmodernist agenda in relation to the search for a constitutional settlement for Northern Ireland – by shifting the emphasis from territorial sovereignty to the structural accommodation of northern Irish Nationalist and Ulster Unionist communal identities; and by advocating the relevance of supranational development in the structure of the state to that end. However, at the same time, that same government remained determinedly modernist in its attempts to frustrate European integration and uphold the territorial integrity of the UK as the unit of political administration.

Parallel changes in emphasis have been taking place in the Irish Republican discourse since 1988. Under the influence of John Hume (SDLP Leader), Gerry Adams (President of Sinn Féin) has moved significantly from outlining Republican aims in terms of territorial majority in the way he did in 1988:

> When a people are divided in political allegiance, the democratic principle is that majority rights should prevail ... (in the *Irish Times*, 13 September 1988).

The first Hume/Adams joint statement, issued on 24 April 1993, signalled a shift in emphasis by Adams on the concept of national self-determination:

> We accept that the Irish people as a whole have a right to national self-determination. This is a view shared by a majority of the people of this island though not by all its people.
>
> The exercise of self-determination is a matter for agreement between the people of Ireland (Sinn Féin, 1994, p. 29).

This qualification of the right to national self-determination[9] with a recognition that its diverse cultural and political content on the island of Ireland leads to problems with how it is exercised, represented some acceptance of the validity of the plurality of communal identity that exists. Gone was the 'ultimate pursuit of one set of values at the expense of the other' (Tamir, 1993, p. 6) that characterized Adams' stated position in 1988. Although Unionists were still perceived to be 'Irish people' their agreement was now required before any structural settlement could be made for the island of Ireland. By October 1993, Adams was framing his arguments in the context of communal consent and accommodation:

> Whatever agreement we come up with has to be an agreement that the Unionists, like the rest of us, can give their allegiance to. They have to be part of it and feel that it accommodates them (in the *Independent on Sunday*, 3 October 1993).

However, Adams' explicit recognition of the need to secure the agreement of Unionists appeared to apply only to the form All-Ireland structures take but not to whether they should be created in the first place.

The executive action proposed by the Framework Documents for 'sectors involving a natural or physical All-Ireland Framework; EC programmes and initiatives; marketing and promotion activities abroad; and, culture and heritage' (*Framework Documents*, 1995, p. 29) was the first attempt by the two governments at outlining the practical implications of their postmodernist conceptual approach, described in the Downing Street Declaration (1993), which prioritized communities over territory as the determining factor on which structural arrangements are based. Again, in proposing this framework, it was emphasized that 'the consent of the governed is an essential ingredient for stability in any political arrangement' (*Framework Documents*, 1995, p. 24). Problematically, however, Unionists did not give their consent to the proposed framework. In such circumstances, the principle of consent ceases to imply agreement and instead becomes a veto, that is the right to reject what is being proposed. Unionists point out that the principle of consent was not observed when the AIA was imposed as a coercive device, against their wishes (Guelke, 1996, pp. 14–15).

The Multi-Party Agreement (1998) both reflected and recommended the most conspicuous features of the postmodern condition, namely, institutionalized pluralism, variety, contingency and ambivalence. Indeed, it was some or all of these features that enabled parties from across the political spectrum – the UUP, the SDLP, Sinn Féin, the APNI, the PUP, the Women's Coalition, the UDP and Labour – to sign up to the Agreement. It provides for the establishment of important institutions that are aimed at reflecting the plurality of communal identity in Northern Ireland. The main seat of power will be a power-sharing executive with parties allocated seats in proportion to their strength in a Northern Ireland Assembly, itself elected by proportional representation. After the Assembly has been established it is required to work on the formation of a North-South Council. The survival of the Assembly is contingent on the establishment of the Council. However, the Agreement has been drafted in such a way as to allow a degree of ambivalence on the nature and function of the North-South Council and implementation bodies. Although the words 'dynamic' and 'executive' are avoided in order to spare the sensitivities of Unionist signatories, it is clear that 'areas for North-South co-operation and implementation' allow scope for the open-ended development of powerful structures beyond the boundary of the UK state.

CONCLUSION

A Unionist hegemony characterized Northern Ireland between 1921 and 1972. Thereafter, constitutional flux gave rise to intimations of postmodernity in the approach of the UK government to building a suitable structural arrangement for the accommodation of Ulster Unionist and northern Irish Nationalist identities. These postmodernist developments have included the doomed Northern Ireland Constitutional proposals (1973) with its 'Irish dimension' and the more durable Anglo-Irish Agreement (1985) with its supranational institution-building incorporating the Irish government in an 'advisory' capacity. Since the signing of the AIA, the UK and Irish governments have increasingly adopted the position of interpreter for their respective Unionist and Nationalist 'client' communities in Northern Ireland. Indeed, the AIA implicitly conferred responsibility on the Irish government to put forward representations on behalf of the northern Nationalist community at intergovernmental level. This approach may be perceived as a recognition by the Government of the United Kingdom that it failed in its self-appointed role as a unilateral arbiter in Northern Ireland after the collapse of the power-sharing executive in 1974. Furthermore, it is an implicit admission that the UK government is no longer willing to claim sovereign authority within the territorial context of the United Kingdom of Great Britain and Northern Ireland. The implications of the actions of the Conservative government are that it actively sought to advance an agenda with intimations of postmodernity for a constitutional settlement in Northern Ireland while it maintained a modernist anti-integrationist approach to the EU.

The Downing Street Declaration (1993) and its language of communal accommodation and consent continued to develop the postmodernist theme of UK government policy-making in Northern Ireland in the 1990s. As such, the Downing Street Declaration was a statement of intent by the UK government that it prioritized the structural accommodation of communal diversity in Northern Ireland over the territorial autonomy of the United Kingdom of Great Britain and Northern Ireland. By the same token, it was also an implicit refutation by the Irish government of modern irredentist claims that were contained in Bunreacht Na hÉireann/ Constitution of Ireland. The Framework Documents (1995) were a preliminary sketch of the envisaged manifestation of structural arrangements that might be required for communal accommodation. However, in an attempt to take account of UUP concerns this sketch was modified somewhat in the 'Propositions on Heads of Agreement' document presented by the two governments to the Multi-Party Talks on 12 January 1998. These modifications were evidently upheld to the satisfaction of the UUP signatories to the Multi-Party Agreement (1998).

The Multi-Party Agreement has been subject to multiple interpretation, not least by the signatories themselves. What is not in doubt is that its contents represent a paradigm shift from the emphasis placed by the modern state on territorial autonomy to a postmodernist consideration of communal identity that contradicts modern territorial demarcation. The backdrop of structural change in the European Union serves as an important macro-level dynamic for these Anglo-Irish developments.

4 Intimations of Postmodernity in the Development of the European Union

While 1972 was a year of sudden and tumultuous change in the modern state context of Northern Ireland, the following year introduced a development with potentially profound structural consequences for the region. On 1 January 1973, Northern Ireland, in its capacity as a region of the UK state, acceded to the European Community (EC). Although the Northern Ireland Common Market poll in June 1975 resulted in a majority in favour of remaining in the EC ('yes' – 52.1 per cent, 'no' – 47.9 per cent), European integration did not seriously challenge the political agenda of Northern Ireland until the integrationist dynamic, culminating in the Single European Act, gathered momentum in the late 1980s. In the 1990s, anti-European integrationists in Northern Ireland (including the UUP, DUP and Sinn Féin) breathed a collective sigh of relief at the slow-down of European integration, caused primarily by problems with monetary union. However, the loss of momentum cannot disguise the fact that the European Union (EU), as it is now known, is representative of a major structural change in the European state system.

The continued domination of member state governments in the political processes of the EU ensures the perpetuation of the modern order in the EU polity. Nevertheless, it can be argued that the vital aspects of European integration, including economic and monetary union, citizenship, subsidiarity and the Committee of the Regions, are displaying intimations of postmodernity.

INTEGRATION

The retention of decision-making power by member nation-state governments in EU institutions has, thus far, prevented the formation of a political federation and the emergence of a truly supranational political authority. However, it would be difficult to deny the originality of the EU. The reluctance of the nation-state centre to relinquish power to a postmodern multi-level state network that comprises supranational, national and subnational elements does not invalidate the thesis that postmodern forces are active in challenging the mantle of the nation-state. The project of European integration is testimony to the continued, if uneven, influence of these postmodern forces.

The European Council at Maastricht (December 1991) was symbolic of the consolidation of resolve among the overwhelming majority of member states to continue moving the EU towards economic and monetary union. The symbolism of Maastricht implied that renewed vitality had been given to Jean Monnet's aspiration of attendant political union because the European Council at Maastricht endorsed amendments ensuring the eventual creation of a European Central Bank, a single currency and a single community-wide monetary policy. Certainly, the endorsements did lead to the Delors Committee speaking explicitly of the transfer of power from member states to EU institutions (Cameron, 1992, p. 71). Consequently, tangible developments and accompanying rhetoric can give the impression of a supranational authority able to influence, if not determine, the economic policy of member states and poised to extend its remit to the political sphere.

Traditionally, interpretations of the development of the EU have been divided into two camps: neo-functionalists, who perceive that integrationist forces are indeed undermining modern nation-state autonomy through the on-going development of a supranational polity; and intergovernmentalists, who argue that supranational developments are consolidating the power of member-states. Neo-functionalists perceive European integration to have an inherent dynamic determined by functional and political spillover. A 'spillover effect' points to the consequences for related sectors when one sector is integrated (Pentland, 1973, p. 119). Functional spillover occurs when the economic inefficiency resulting from incomplete integration drives an ever greater strengthening of policy co-ordination within an integrated framework. Political spillover is underpinned by the institution-building of supranational organizations – notably the 'activist bureaucracy' that describes the European Commission. This political spillover is itself a result of functional spillover because an integrated European economy requires supranational supervision.

Neo-functionalism predicts that spillover will realize Monnet's ambition of a federal Europe (Pentland, 1973, pp. 117–19; Moravcsik, 1993, p. 475). Criticism of neo-functionalism by intergovernmentalists is based on the empirical flaws of the interpretation. Undoubtedly, the neo-functionalist predilection for prediction in terms of 'the trajectory and processes of EC evolution', and getting it wrong, justifies some of this criticism (Moravcsik, 1993, p. 476). However, the refusal of principal intergovernmental theorists like Moravcsik to recognize the toehold gained by supranational officials through autonomous influence in EU processes indicates an important weakness in the theoretical approach of intergovernmentalism. Moravcsik endorses perspectives which suggest that:

.... the EC is best seen as an international regime for policy co-ordination, the substantive and institutional development of which may be explained through sequential analysis of national preference formation and intergovernmental strategic interaction (Moravcsik, 1993, p. 480).

Moravcsik argues that EU institutions actually increase the control of national governments over their individual domestic political situations. They do this by 'increasing the efficiency of interstate bargaining' through the provision of negotiating forum, decision-making procedures and the monitoring of compliance to those decisions. EU institutions also provide national leaders with a high-profile arena in which they can gain the initiative over single-issue groups within the domestic polity (Moravcsik, 1993, p. 507). Such an assertion correctly emphasizes the dominance of national governments in the decision-making processes of the EU. However, it fails to account adequately for the policy-networks that are not confined to the national and supranational sphere but which traverse subnational, national and supranational levels thus enabling subnational entities to transcend the domestic scene and become involved in policy-making within an EU multi-level framework.

The present reality of the EU's political dynamic to some extent reflects the dichotomy in interpretation of the process of European integration because it appears to involve a struggle between the pioneers of supranationalism and the guardians of the modern order of nation-states. The outcome of this struggle, thus far, has been that the EU displays both intergovernmental and supranational characteristics. The principal intergovernmental institution in the

EU – the Council of Ministers – remains the dominant decision-making body. Although qualified majority voting can curtail the influence of individual member-states, the regard for consensus means that a compromise solution is usually sought. The overall direction of the EU is also decided by a powerful intergovernmental body – the European Council (Nugent, 1994, p. 432). However, despite the predominance of these intergovernmental institutions in the decision-making process, the Commission, the EU's principal supranational institution, has secured vital secondary and regulatory decision-making functions. The EU has been able to expand its regulatory function because member states, conditioned by the modern perception of the state as a spending and taxing power, failed to recognize that regulatory activity is not hindered by the traditional budgetary constraints imposed by member states. The result has been a movement towards re-regulation at EU level of the deregulation that occurred in the 1980s at national level (Majone, 1994, pp. 97–8). The EU's regulatory role now extends beyond the financial and industrial sectors into the areas of health, education, social welfare and environmental issues (Moran, 1994, pp. 158–60). As Müller and Wright explain:-

> To an extent which is not fully appreciated, the EU is slowly redefining existing political arrangements, altering traditional policy networks, triggering institutional change, reshaping the opportunity structures of member states and their major interests (Müller and Wright, 1994, p. 6).

The inclusion of co-decision in the Maastricht Treaty (1992) has also the potential to be effective in improving the co-operation and assent powers of the European Parliament. The European Court of Justice, as the final authority on the implementation of EU decisions constituted in EU law, is also a powerful supranational institution (Nugent, 1994, p. 433).

Although Monnet and Schuman had envisaged that the Commission would eventually form the central executive core of a European political federation, the extent of its executive power remains to be determined at Intergovernmental Conference level. Nevertheless, the Commission has an important agenda-setting ability, most notable in the area of the Structural Funds. Marks cites the blueprint for the 'reform of the reforms' of the Structural Funds, drawn up by the Commission in 1988 and approved with only minor revisions by the Council, as evidence of the Commission's agenda-setting ability (Marks, 1993, p. 401). In addition, the Commission has a representative role in international relations; it maintains its guardian role of EU treaties with the right of redress through the European Court of Justice; and it manages the Regional and Social Funds, CAP and the EU budget. In carrying out such functions, while at the same time seeking to extend further its supranational powers into executive policy-making, the Commission has succeeded in combining administrative and executive functions traditionally reserved for separate institutions. The blurring of the lines of demarcation between such functions has implications for accepted bureaucratic procedures – procedures that have formed a cornerstone of modernity – and underlines the unique political and dynamic nature of the Commission and EU itself (Holland, 1993, p. 97).

The decision-making process is evolving in the EU with supranational and subnational institutions providing valuable input. Such developments have prompted Gary Marks' 'multi-level governance' interpretation of European integration where policy networks are formed that transcend modern territorial boundaries and are not confined to the national and supranational levels (Marks, 1993, pp. 401–2). The multi-level-governance interpretation is postmodernist in the substantive sense because the modern national territorial boundary is no longer regarded as the demarcation line for policy-making processes in the EU. It is also postmodernist in the conceptual sense because it describes a set of circumstances where neither the nation-state centre or the EU centre are taken to be the sole arbiter in the policy-making process in the EU. As a result, the universalist knowledge-claims of the modern state centre are, to some extent, beginning to be challenged by particularist, culture-bound versions of knowledge emanating from the subnational level. The integrationist forces at the supranational level in the EU are aiding and encouraging subnational governments and non-government agencies and actors in their challenge to the universalist knowledge-claims of the nation-state. The Commission has, of course, been the pro-active postmodernist force in initiating the subnational level into EU processes. It is, therefore, through institutional innovation at the supranational level that multi-level governance in the EU will be determined.

Undoubtedly, the 1990s experience of economic recession, the Balkan conflict and the demoralizing experience of the Danish and French referenda on monetary union has slowed the integrationist bandwagon of the late 1980s. However, the Maastricht Treaty attempted to recapture the initiative and consolidate the gains made with the Single European Act, particularly the creation of a single market for capital and financial services. The primary aim of Maastricht was to attempt to ensure that the achievement of the efficient allocation of capital through the single market is complemented by a single currency – the formula adjudged to ensure future economic success. The alternative, a free movement of capital in an integrated financial market, ensures that perceived weakness in a currency leads to instability in exchange rates, threatening further EU integration (Pinder, 1994, p. 270). The Maastricht Treaty was an important milestone in the process of European integration although the precise implications of it for that process remains the subject of much debate. The general tone of the Treaty remained expansionist in terms of the appropriation of powers by the EU commensurate with federal union status (Duff, 1994, p. 20).

The main success of the Maastricht Treaty in the pursuit of its integrationist aims was a formal endorsement of the objective of economic and monetary union (EMU) and a timetable and schedule for its realization. Difficulties adhering to the schedule for EMU have subsequently been recognized by pro-integrationist member states. However, the treaty does represent a stage in the quest to create EMU. It also remains a widely held view that EMU would enable EU member-states to benefit economically from an improved environment for competition, scale and specialization and, as such, is a desirable and realizable goal (Pinder, 1994, p. 270). However, the UK Conservative government represented the major obstacle for progress on reforms such as EMU and co-decision at Maastricht and succeeded in making the treaty less transparent and consequently more difficult to implement than had been hoped for by EU federalists (Pinder, 1994, p. 271).

SUBSIDIARITY

Before being reinterpreted by the Maastricht Treaty, subsidiarity was generally understood to be the principle of leaving decision-making to the lowest 'feasible' level of government (Marks, 1993, p. 397). In a federal context, subsidiarity is interpreted as the principle whereby the level of government that is closest to the people is entrusted with the task of taking action in accordance with the needs of the people (Dehousse, 1994, p. 107). In the EU context, a distinct divergence in the interpretation of subsidiarity has emerged between pro-federalists and anti-integrationists. Pro-federalists consider it to be an important principle for the development of European federalism. Conversely, anti-integrationists interpret it as a mechanism to limit the competence of the EU. The pro-federalist movement envisages the EU undertaking those actions which can be 'better achieved or attained' at supranational level. This interpretation simply means 'more effectively' or 'more efficiently' (Adonis, 1991, p. 67). Anti-integrationists, on the other hand, maintain that only necessary or essential tasks should warrant EU attention. This means that the EU should only be empowered to carry out those tasks which prove to be impractical at nation-state level. Anti-integrationist elements in the EU believe subsidiarity to be the guarantor of exclusive control by member-states over their own internal political arrangements (Marks, 1993, p. 406).

The Maastricht Treaty attempted to satisfy both parties by simultaneously providing for an extension of EU power and optimal degrees of decentralization within existing fields of EU competencies:

> In areas which do not fall within its exclusive competence the Community shall take action, in accordance with the principle of subsidiarity, only if and in so far as the objectives of the proposed action cannot be sufficiently achieved by the member states and can therefore by reason of the scale or effects of the proposed action, be better achieved by the Community (Article 3(b) Maastricht Treaty).

There is potential for confusion in the application of subsidiarity caused by the inclusion of the two conditions, 'sufficiently achieved' and 'better achieved'. The lack of specificity is indicative of the fact that there is little agreement on the substantive issue at the political level (Spicker, 1994, pp. 6–13).

A postmodernist interpretation of the Maastricht definition of subsidiarity begins with the premise that it is an unsuitable concept to apply to complex contemporary conditions. Postmodern Europe is witness to a society that is becoming increasingly more complex in economic, social and cultural terms. As David Harvey points out, such postmodern complexity also requires a new flexibility brought about by decentralization and the deconstruction of the context of the modern state (Harvey, 1989, pp. 338–42). Consequently, issues that concern the EU, such as environmental protection or the economic development of peripheral regions, concern each of the levels of government in the EU simultaneously and require a new flexibility in the structure of the state. However, the assumption of the principle of subsidiarity (and of integrationists and intergovernmentalists) is that the different levels of government can act independently of each other depending on their particular competencies. Dehousse entertains the idea that the EU version of subsidiarity that emerges in Article 3(b) of the Maastricht Treaty attempts to side-step the difficulty of applying an ill-adapted concept to a contemporary situation where postmodern forces have determined that the centre and periphery can no longer have clearly defined and differentiated competencies. As a result, Maastricht has delivered a version of subsidiarity designed to regulate the use of Community competencies (Dehousse, 1994, pp. 123–4). Such an 'adjustment as required' approach leads to obvious difficulties for the European Court of Justice in interpreting subsidiarity.

While the postmodern complexity of the EU means that subsidiarity is difficult to apply, it must be remembered that the introduction of the principle of subsidiarity appears to have been an attempt to placate the anti-integrationist forces of the EU. It could be argued that the inclusion of integrationist and intergovernmental voices in Article 3(b) of Maastricht is conducive to the postmodern emphasis placed on 'dialogue' and the representation of all voices covering the EU spectrum of reality. However, this makes it difficult to assess the implications of subsidiarity because this 'dialogue' has rendered the principle vague and potentially meaningless.

For good reason, anti-integrationists assume that the Maastricht version of subsidiarity strengthens the position of nation-states in their balance of power with the EU. This position encourages further uncertainty in the interpretation of subsidiarity, namely, disagreement on what constitutes the lowest level of governance (Millan, 1991, p. 14). In its attempt to create consensus among integrationist and intergovernmentalists in the EU, the Maastricht Treaty has delivered a version of subsidiarity that deems the nation-state rather than the region to be the lowest competent level of government. However, this is not to say that the regional structures of power will not feature in future drafts of the EU's subsidiarity master plan – that will be dependent upon the struggle between intergovernmental and integrationist tendencies in the EU. Maastricht represents the beginning of the battle to determine, among other things, the lowest level of governance in a multi-level EU (Marks, 1993, p. 406).

Further schism in the allocation of authority across different levels of government for different policy areas, should it occur, will create the environment for an intersubjective approach to policy-making, rather than the rational standardization imposed by modern states. The postmodernist accommodation of 'all voices' that is implied by the concept of multi-level government signals potential problems for bureaucratic efficiency – a central tenet of the process of modernization. However, such inclusiveness also implies a strengthening of democratic accountability through movement away from the emphasis of modern democracy on the enactment of the dominant political metanarrative. The consensual principle of EU processes links the EU with a conceptual approach that is distinctively postmodernist.

REGIONALISM

While the Maastricht version of subsidiarity offers some encouragement to those who wish to see the formation of a federal Europe, it offers less comfort to those who entertain utopian visions of a 'Europe of the Regions'. The version of subsidiarity that emerged in the Maastricht Treaty has led to a myriad of interpretations – none of them favourable to the subnational level of government. Nevertheless, whatever long-term implications subsidiarity has for self-determination by regions and localities, reforms in EU structural policy are enabling regional actors to deal directly with EU decision-makers in the execution of regional development programmes. Such channels provide tangible evidence that the Commission is interested in mobilizing subnational entities and that the postmodern political values of deconstruction, decentralization and flexibility are taking hold in the EU.

The Commission has several regional offices already in operation. Subnational units in most EU countries now have offices in Brussels in order to establish contacts and form alliances; to lobby and present the regional case to appropriate EU decision-makers; and to monitor developments in EU legislation and gather relevant information (Marks, 1992, p. 212; Nugent, 1994, p. 421). The UK currently has at least 17 regions represented in this way and includes the 'Northern Ireland Centre in Europe'. However, to suggest that these measures enabling the development of centre/periphery relations (in an EU context) have made significant incursions on the autonomy of national governments would be inaccurate. National governments have made a determined effort to control communications between the EU and their own regional governments. In the process, member states have managed to maintain the equilibrium with national governments placed firmly at the constitutional centre of the EU (Keating and Jones, 1985, pp. 234–45). Indeed, it has been argued that the EU has inadvertently strengthened the link between national and sub-national governments with the introduction of structural reforms and national governments' response to them (Hickman, 1990, p. 21; Marks, 1992, p. 215).

The Government of the Republic of Ireland represents its regions at national level and treats Structural Funds awarded as a source of extra revenue for the national exchequer. This phenomenon is compounded by the fact that the EU treats the Republic of Ireland as one region because it was thought that internal regional disparities were insignificant compared to the disparity between the Republic of Ireland and the rest of the EU (Hickman, 1990, p. 21). The Republic of Ireland has, however, created subregions based on Irish counties to enhance further its application for Structural Funds. The UK government, meanwhile, has involved regional representatives in applications for Structural Funds with the primary aim of maximizing budgetary transfers from the EU. Whitehall is contemptuous of the Commission's efforts to stimulate regional planning, claiming that it is a wasteful bureaucratic measure designed to supersede national planning preferences (Marks, 1992, p. 215).

Despite the success of national governments in containing the autonomy of regional representation, the postmodern policy networks emerging between EU institutions, subnational governments and private interest groups do influence the EU political process. In representing their interests, regional actors are becoming increasingly integrated into a web of relationships that straddle regional, national, European and even international territorial boundaries. Regions and groups with mutual interests are establishing trans-European networks that deal with specific policy areas and issues such as sex equality, employment, culture, the environment and industrial regeneration (Meehan, 1993, p. 183). The primary aim of this horizontal flow of communication is to strengthen the case of each issue with exchange of information and the preparation of presentational packages for a vertical assault on EU resources. In conceptual terms, such alliances are evidence of reconstruction described by a 'postmodernism of resistance' because they are succeeding in transcending the rigidity of nation-state decision-making and can form, re-shape and disband according to the opportunities provided by the postmodern condition of the EU. The European Commission has encouraged the horizontal flow of communication at the subnational level and has become actively involved in establishing vertical lines of communication to the subnational level. 'Euro-speak' has coined the word 'partnership' to describe multi-level policy networks that have resulted. In the 'reform of the reforms' first suggested in 'A Protocol on Economic and Social Cohesion' which was annexed to the Maastricht Treaty, the Commission suggested, among other things, simplifying the planning process in the administration of the Structural Funds. This would involve emphasis being placed on the development of Community Support Frameworks (CSFs) – involving supranational, national and subnational levels – for establishing funding priorities and doing away with an initial stage that involved member-states establishing broad planning goals in a national development plan. The aim of such reforms is to develop partnerships whereby subnational, national and supranational actors work together in preparing, implementing and monitoring development programmes for EU Structural Funds (Marks, 1993, p. 396).

Multi-level partnership is clearly important for the preparation, implementation and monitoring of Structural Funds since the Commission has a relatively small staff.[1] CSFs encourage interaction between administrators at the supranational, national and subnational level with the biennial meetings of the monitoring committees for each CSF providing a formal focus for partnerships. The Commission is also endeavouring to include non-government organisations in a 'social partnership' for the administration of Structural Funds (Marks, 1993, p. 397). The EU Special Support Programme for Peace and Reconciliation in Northern Ireland and the Border Counties of the Republic of Ireland (1995–) is a postmodern laboratory for 'social partnership' because the Commission has engaged non-government organizations in the implementation and monitoring of the package. Postmodernity also describes the extension of the remit of the initiative beyond the boundary of the modern nation-state to include border counties of the Republic of Ireland (discussed in chapter 5).

Should a future definition of EU subsidiarity overcome the exclusive competence barrier of national and supranational levels, and also lend itself to a regional capacity for self-determination, then partnerships through postmodern networking with sympathetic counterparts will gain in significance. Nevertheless, it must be emphasized that the empowerment of the subnational level, through EU subsidiarity, is extremely unlikely for the foreseeable future. What can be argued is that, while the withering away of the nation-state apparatus should be confined to the realms of abstract theory, emerging policy networks will challenge modern national governments' position as sole arbiters in the policy-making and implementation process and a system of criss-crossing multi-level governance in some of the policy-making areas of the EU will continue to gain in stature.

THE COMMITTEE OF THE REGIONS

To explore the potential for regionalism within the EU, Maastricht established a Committee of the Regions. The Committee of the Regions joins a list of specialist organizations representing subnational interests, including the following: the Assembly of European Regions, the Conference of Peripheral Maritime Regions, and the Association of Border Regions (Marks, 1993, p. 404).

The Committee of the Regions' first session in Brussels in March 1994 was attended by interviewees Denis Haughey (SDLP) and Reg Empey (UUP), the regional representatives from Northern Ireland (Conlon, 1994). The idea is to provide decision-makers with a more effective means of taking the temperature on regional affairs (Nugent, 1994, p. 421). As a result, the Committee of the Regions is a purely advisory body although Maastricht did stipulate that it must be consulted on issues such as education; training and youth; economic and social cohesion – specific actions; the aims and rules of Structural Funds (but not their financing); the implementation of decisions of the ERDF; trans-European networks – guidelines and implementation; public health and cultural matters (Laffan and Moxon-Browne, 1992, p. 28; Nugent, 1994, p. 244). It is free to issue opinions on its own initiative and without restriction. Such provision makes the Committee of the Regions' status in the hierarchy of EU institutions no higher than the lowly Economic and Social Committee with whom it shares staff resources. (Nicoll, 1994, p. 201).

In creating a new EU institution, the Maastricht Treaty has expanded the potential for democratic practice. However, the longer established and infinitely more powerful institutions – the Council and Parliament – are likely to make concerted efforts to thwart the potential for growth in the role of the Committee of the Regions. Although the principle of subsidiarity theoretically provides the Committee with the opportunity to extend its role into decision-making, the EU version of subsidiarity that emerged in Article 3(b) of the Maastricht Treaty makes it clear that the lowest level of representation is interpreted as that of the nation-state. For nation-states anxious to retain control over their regions, Article 3(b) can be interpreted as something of a safeguard against Article A which advocates that decisions be taken as closely as possible to the people (Nicoll, 1994, pp. 201-2).

The Committee of the Regions faces tremendous obstacles in creating a meaningful role for itself. However, analysts believe that much will depend on the quality of regional representatives appointed to the Committee; the quality of their work for the Committee; and their ability to influence the domestic political scene to which they belong[2] (Laffan and Moxon-Browne, 1992, p. 29; Nicoll, 1994, p. 202). In the context of Northern Ireland, the Committee of the Regions is a fledgling version of the European Parliament platform in that Northern Ireland representatives can transcend the territorial battle lines drawn by the modern state and co-operate in common interest.

In its work, the Committee of the Regions can expect an ally in the Commission which continues to seek to strengthen the links between supranational and sub-national level (Nicoll, 1994, p. 202). As such, the Committee of the Regions platform for the elucidation of more culture-specific voices in the EU orbit is a signifier of postmodernity in the EU. However, having been conceived in a treaty indelibly marked by the conflict between federalist and intergovernmentalist elements in the EU, it was inevitable that the Committee of the Regions would have a difficult birth. Conflict between the modernist and postmodernist forces in the EU will continue to thwart the development of the Committee of the Regions as an effective practitioner among EU institutions for the foreseeable future.

CITIZENSHIP

Strong modern states emerged in Europe after the fall of the Roman Empire. These modern states were instrumental in aligning differentiating national identities with differentiating citizenship. The intention of Monnet was that the process of European integration produce a supranationalist consensus in Europe with a common citizenship. The modern convergence of citizenship with nationality is something that EU integrationist forces appear to intend challenging. The notion of EU citizenship rights first emerged in The Foreign Ministers Paper (June 1990) and became a legal identity in the Treaty of Maastricht (February 1992) which announced, somewhat dramatically, that 'Citizenship of the Union is hereby established' (Article 8(1)). However, Citizenship of the Union retained a modernist context through being defined as 'every person holding the nationality of a member state'. The rights identified were limited to those specific to the sphere of competence of the EU and included the right to freedom of movement; the freedom to choose one's place of residence; and the right of political participation in the place of residence. This small step represented a not insignificant supranational advance for the Union, establishing an important federal precedent. Such an integrationist step is consistent with Monnet's argument that attitudinal change will progress once the legal commonality of citizenship is firmly established. However, major limitations remain to the basic rights and freedoms of citizens in the EU context. These limitations include: the remaining restrictions on voting rights – by not applying them to general elections of member states and by allowing electoral provisions to be qualified by governments who deem any further restriction to be in the public interest (Meehan, 1993, p. 183); the lack of uniformity in social welfare provision between member states; and the absence of a system to equate the professional qualifications awarded by different member states (Gillespie and Rice, 1991, p. 25).

Meehan affirms the legitimacy of dual citizenship rights conferred upon the individual by membership of a member nation-state and subsequent membership of the EU (Meehan, 1993, p. 178). Although the individual member state remains largely responsible for establishing citizen rights through the specifics of traditional laws and practices, a legal status was conferred upon individual citizens by the EU in the European Court of Justice. Citizens have thus been granted rights against their own national government and other governments in the transnational sphere of the EU. The new provision of rights is necessary, not least because

interests arising from social identities are becoming pursued through alliances of European pressure groups working through common institutions, possibly against the preferences of national governments (Meehan, 1993, p. 185).

Moxon-Browne charts the development of citizenship from the modern to the postmodern in the EU. This begins with the national sphere derived from the citizenship of member-states, proceeding through the 'privileged aliens' status conferred upon nationals of member states in EU treaties, and evolving into citizens of the post–1992 European Union (Moxon-Browne, 1991, p. 64). Moxon-Browne suggests that EU citizenship may be developed further on a broad range of personal and social rights such as abortion, divorce and homosexuality, by recourse to the European Convention on Human Rights (ECHR).

An emerging postmodern EU citizenship has potential implications for communal identities in Northern Ireland because these identities have traditionally defined citizenship in the mutually exclusive terms of the Irish nation (northern Nationalists) or the UK state (Ulster Unionists). As European interests increasingly transcend the modern territorial boundary of the nation-state a citizenship that caters for the structured space of the EU, granting a 'right to options' for citizens, would appear to be a logical requirement and adds a new and potentially inclusive context to the definition of citizenship in Northern Ireland. Certainly, a postmodern EU citizenship would transcend national boundaries and provide individual identities and abilities with appropriate 'rights to options' for the successful expression of those identities and abilities in the supranational sphere. However, with EU citizenship centred on the right to freedom of movement within the Union, as expressed in Article 8 (a) of the Maastricht Treaty: 'the right to move and reside freely within the territory of member states' – this 'right to options' is linked more clearly with the economic freedom of the single European market than with the political rights associated with citizenship, as defined by the modern nation-state (d'Oliveira, 1994, p. 132).

With EU citizenship coming to represent a 'loosening of the metaphysical ties between persons and a State' (d'Oliveira, 1994, p. 147) postmodernists of the anti-government school might conclude that an economic focus for citizenship is to be supported since the individual is being freed from the limiting context of the nation-state and is instead contextualized by the market-place. Such a conceptual building-block for citizenship does have something to offer a wider postmodernist concern for the inclusion of difference. However, such a free-floating citizenship, which is not underpinned by effective political rights, risks being effectively powerless (and meaningless in the context of political realignment in Northern Ireland). In any case, the practical reality of Maastricht in this respect was merely to hail the arrival of EU citizenship without giving it substantive effect. The future development of the concept, in real terms, rests on a promise (d'Oliveira, 1994, p. 141).

Apart from the 'right to options' component of citizenship, a state that subscribes to the principles of pluralism and democracy also confers the 'right to roots' on its citizens. Urwin and Rokkan distinguish between these two kinds of citizens' rights in a system of democratic pluralism:

(1) the Right to Roots, that is, 'the right to respect for community of origin, whatever its language or ethnic composition'; (2) the Right to Options, that is, 'the right to opportunities for the full use of individual abilities within the wider territorial network' (Urwin and Rokkan, 1983, p. 115).

It is conceivable that, in the context of multi-level governance, the EU would eventually have at its disposal the capacity to defend the communal 'right to roots', through influence at the subnational level, while at the same time expanding the 'right to options' of the individual through EU citizenship. Certainly, the EU has demonstrated a concern for threatened aspects of communal identity at the roots through its creation of a bureau for lesser used languages in the EU. Tamir points out important implications of this concern for the community of origin:

Contrary to the usual justification adduced for regional [supranational] co-operation, namely, that it allows individuals to transcend their national attachments, the merits of co-operation can now be couched in terms of its value to the free pursuit of national life (Tamir, 1993, p. 152).

Interconnection between the institutions of the EU and national and subnational levels of government in a system of multi-level government could mean supranational influence in securing the 'right to roots' of a community. The paradox of such an input is that it would be a derogation of the principle of subsidiarity which confers exclusive authority on different competencies, as pointed out by Dehousse.

There is, of course, a potential clash of interest in the duality of citizens' rights – the 'right to roots' and the 'right to options'. Postmodern society, with its increasing complexity and increasing expectations, adds to the potential for a clash of interest between these rights. With this potential dichotomy of interest, a plea for tolerance would be the obvious recourse for modernists. Tolerance has been a much mooted goal throughout the so-called Nationalist-Unionist conflict in Ireland. Indeed, the Irish Association was founded in 1938 to remove 'passion and prejudice' in Ireland and replace it with tolerance and understanding (Bew, Darwin, and Gillespie, 1993, p. iv). A lesser goal of tolerance through a form of benign apartheid could be suggested as an appropriate goal for Northern Ireland in the third millennium. However, tolerance, in whatever form, often results in indifference and increases estrangement and non-co-operation (Bauman, 1991, p. 276). From a 'postmodernism of resistance' perspective, only an increase in political engagement and an increase in the political effectiveness of the individual and communities can make a practical success out of postmodern political values.

In practical terms, the development of EU citizenship after Maastricht is an interesting proposition. However, there is reason not to expect rapid change in this area. EU citizenship depends on measures taken in the intergovernmental pillar and, as such, will be tightly controlled by national governments. It must be emphasized that the substance of EU citizenship is very flimsy when compared to the array of social and political rights that could have been bestowed on citizens in relation to European institutions and member states (Anderson, den Boer and Millar, 1994, p. 122). The narrow range of rights conferred only apply to the 'right to options' component of a citizen's rights, with EU influence over 'right to roots' dependent on the development of an EU multi-level system of governance. Should the EU appropriate the power to protect the 'right to roots' of communities and the 'right to options' of individuals then the political context of a single European home will have been established. However, it must be stressed that EU citizenship, along with other aspects of European integration such as EMU, subsidiarity and the Committee of the Regions, remain as intimations of postmodernity in the EU polity at the close of the twentieth century. The practical fulfilment of these aspects of European integration will continue to be frustrated by the endemic conflict between modernist and postmodernist forces in the EU well into the third millennium.

CONCLUSION

The EU polity displays substantive intimations of postmodernity in its infrastructure because the developments in technology, and subsequently in financial and industrial markets, have necessitated a re-definition of the political and administrative function formerly delimited by the nation-state in Europe. A (resistance) postmodernist outcome, described by deconstruction, reconstruction and flexibility, is that policy networks are beginning to extend involvement in the policy-making process beyond national governments to subnational and supranational levels, and even non-government agencies.

In attempting to meet the challenge of the condition of postmodernity, the EU is adopting a postmodern view in the Bauman sense of representing a critical perspective on the contingents of modernity, in particular, the nation-state as the pervasive political and administrative unit. Having said this, it must also be recognized that the ideological enterprise of European integration does not necessarily represent a rejection of modernity's idea of progress through control in an ordered society. The founders of the European Community believed a federal European superstructure to be integral to alleviating Europe's modern problems of economic depression and war. As a result, the EU recognizes the requirement of the state to adapt to postmodern forces but it still holds progress as its ideal. Nevertheless, concepts associated with a 'postmodernism of resistance' are extending to the conceptual thrust of the EU and are evident in its policy processes.

Postmodern intersubjectivity is apparent in the formulation of EU treaties with their emphasis on consensus and inclusiveness. In addition, the accent of resistance postmodernism on fragmentation, heterogeneity, particularity and alliance-formation provides a conceptual backdrop for the shoots of multi-level governance that are beginning to appear in the EU policy-making process. To this end, there would appear to be a desire among integrationists to deconstruct the modern centred arrangement of state power and reconstruct that power in a way that incorporates different levels of government, as well as non-government agencies into the structures and processes of the EU. Communal 'right to roots' and individual 'right to options' are also beginning to have a postmodern context mapped out in the developing processes of the EU. The import of these intimations of postmodernity for politics and identities in the specific context of Northern Ireland are now considered in chapter 5.

5 The European Union and the Resources of Communal Identities in Northern Ireland

Communal identities have territorial, cultural and economic resources which can be mobilized to produce political action. These resources are the essential building-blocks of communal identity. However, for resources to become politicized, that is, to produce political action, a catalyst is required. According to Urwin and Rokkan:

> Resources are necessary, but not sufficient, conditions for mobilization. The latter occurs when catalysts operate upon the resources to transform cultural distinctiveness into political action (Urwin and Rokkan, 1983, p. 124).

Informed by theories of the development of the nation, Urwin and Rokkan cite industrialization and the nineteenth century democratic revolution as important catalysts of the modern era (Urwin and Rokkan, 1983, p. 135). In nineteenth-century Ireland, famine, Irish revolutionary martyrdom, the Government's attempts to block Catholic emancipation, the question of land tenure and general economic decline combined to vitalize the impulse of modern Irish nationalism (Boyce, 1982, pp. 383–4). Similarly, the Northern Ireland civil-rights movement of the 1960s provided the conduit through which the hitherto marginalized voice of the northern Irish Nationalist imagined community was projected onto the political stage. This movement sought initially to engage the economic resource of Irish Nationalist identities and other 'dispossessed' identities in Northern Ireland. The catalysts that moved it to political action were primarily the failure of Prime Minister Terence O'Neill's plans for inclusive economic and social modernization and the persistence of perceived discrimination in employment and housing. The mass demonstrations of the civil rights movement provided the incentive for the resources of Ulster Unionist identities to initiate a political reaction. Thereafter, the territorial resource of northern

Irish Nationalist identities was emphasized, with militant Republicans resorting to violence in an effort to terminate the Unionist hegemony and, after 1972, the United Kingdom (UK) state of Great Britain and Northern Ireland. The modern nation-state configuration on the island of Ireland has had a defining impact on northern Irish Nationalist and Ulster Unionist identities. However, it is at least feasible to contend that the condition of postmodernity may eventually effect further change in the constitution and structural alignment of northern Irish Nationalist and Ulster Unionist identities. Changing social, economic and political conditions are creating a climate of interdependency, signified by the development of the EU. Shoots of cross-border alliance formation are also beginning to emerge within this political arena, emphasizing changing conditions. Northern Ireland communal representatives are beginning to perceive change in the European state system. Consequently, the EU may well be a potential catalyst for the renewed mobilization of the territorial, economic and cultural resources of communal identities in Northern Ireland.

THE ECONOMIC RESOURCE

A central plank of the Ulster Unionist case for maintaining the union of Great Britain and Northern Ireland in a modern state mode has been the economic benefits for Northern Ireland resulting from that union. Northern Ireland's peripheral relations continue to be dominated by the modern state context of the UK. Indeed, it is this centre-periphery relationship that has become increasingly pervasive since 1969. Despite the large degree of autonomy enjoyed by the Stormont regime between 1921 and 1972, a centralizing trend within the UK, that was firmly established in the 19th century, continued after 1945 with the setting up of the welfare state and the regional development strategy of the 1960s. It accelerated after the outbreak of civil disorder in 1969 with the increased deployment of British troops to Northern Ireland; the subsequent proroguing of Stormont; the removal of major powers from local government; and the imposition of direct rule via the newly created Northern Ireland Office. Economic, as well as political centralization occurred with the expansion of public-sector employment and expenditure (NIEC, 1993, p. 28). British subvention to make up for the net deficit of expenditure over income in

Northern Ireland exceeds £3,500m per annum (NIEC, 1993, p. 13). In aggregate, government spending per capita in Northern Ireland is 43 per cent above the UK national average (Gudgin, 1990, p. 29). Over 40 per cent of the work-force is employed in the public sector (Kennedy, Giblin, McHugh, 1988, p. 113). This extensive economic involvement by the UK central administration was due to the need for intervention after the dramatic contraction of the comparatively large manufacturing base during the 1970s and 1980s; the expansion of the public-sector housing programme; and the years of violent conflict after 1969 making exceptional demands on the law and order provision.

The most obvious manifestation of the EU centre/periphery relationship in the Northern Ireland context is EU subvention for Northern Ireland made through the Structural Funds and, to a lesser extent, by donations to the International Fund for Ireland and other initiatives such as the Special Support Programme for Peace and Reconciliation.[1] The contribution to Northern Ireland for the tranche of the EU Structural Funds that runs from 1994 to 1999 is £1,020m. This figure represents about half the total UK allocation and is almost double the figure awarded in 1989–93. Set against the figure of £7,740m for UK public expenditure in Northern Ireland in 1994–5 alone (NIEC, 1993, p. 13), EU expenditure in Northern Ireland remains comparatively small. However, the principle of allocating Structural Funds is significant from a postmodernist perspective because it suggests the development of a European centre/periphery relationship that impinges upon the pre-eminence of the UK-state centre and begins to give substantive meaning to the concept of EU multi-level governance.

When placed in perspective, the Structural Fund allocation for Northern Ireland for 1994–9 represents less than 3 per cent of total public expenditure forecast for that period. Even when one considers the complicating factors of additionality (NIEC, 1983), the under-representation of the region in the EU, contributions to the International Fund for Ireland, and other contributions unaccounted for in this calculation, direct EU economic input into Northern Ireland remains comparatively small. However, the persistence of the longer-term European integrationist dynamic and the viability of an 'island of Ireland' peripheral region in the EU[2] are economic factors that are being used to support the case for the expansion of the economic and political context of Northern Ireland beyond the modern state context of the UK.

It has been argued that European integration is proceeding 'like an erratic marriage where love, loathing and lethargy' are the hallmarks (Teague, 1994, p. 33). However, EU integration shows no signs of dissolving. For Unionists, the fear is that the EU's incremental integrationist dynamic (which they perceive to be a danger in itself) will be complemented by a North-South integration process aimed at gradually integrating the two parts of the island of Ireland. The Cadogan Group (a unionist think-tank) seized upon the proposal, made by the UK and Irish governments in the *Framework Documents* (1995), that new North-South institutions should be 'dynamic' in nature (Cadogan Group, 1996, p. 26). Teague suggests that an alternative 'consensual' model of integration, based on functional cross-border co-operation, would provide 'non-dynamic' cross-border arrangements for appropriate sectors including energy, environmental protection and tourism, while not making infringements upon the distinct political entities of the United Kingdom and the Republic of Ireland (Teague, 1994, pp. 33–4). Integration as a dynamic process would, therefore, be displaced by supranational institution-building that reinforces rather than changes the modern nation-state configuration. The 'Propositions on Heads of Agreement' document (1998), presented by the two governments to the Multi-Party Talks, leaned towards such a 'non-dynamic' intergovernmentalist framework. However, the Multi-Party Agreement (1998) is purposefully vague on the nature and scope of the powers to be invested in North-South institutions.

As far as the wider EU integration process is concerned, Gerry McAlinden, chief executive of the Northern Ireland Centre in Europe, confirms that cross-border development and co-operation is an integral part of the European plan for economic and social cohesion, that was itself established in the Single European Act of 1985 (McAlinden, 1995, p. 77). The EU's INTERREG II programme directed £167 million for 1995–9 to the Irish border region (Robb, 1995, p. 137). It is aimed at cross-border development through investing in regional development, human resources, infrastructure, agriculture, fisheries and forestry, and the environment. The programme places some emphasis on promoting co-operative activity by offering cross-border partnerships with a proven track record[3] single packages of funding (McAlinden, 1995, p. 82). As a result it has provided the impetus for the creation of 'live' micro-level sites in the border region that are testimony to the intimations of postmodernity in the development of structural arrangements for northern Irish Nationalist and Ulster Unionist communal identities. The postmodernity of INTERREG II involves working towards the decentralization of the decision-making process; a re-focusing on local micro-economies; and the active promotion of alliances that may have existed prior to the creation of two modern states on the island of Ireland but which were ruptured with the onset of structural modernity. The implications of the beginning of a paradigm shift in the state management of border region micro-economies will be a restructuring of financial management and accountability procedures with input from the supranational European institutions, the 'national' UK and Irish governments and political and civil society in the border regions themselves. McAlinden believes that the cross-border partnership of the Euregio (Netherlands-German) border region, as well as examples of partnership along the Spanish-Portuguese border, may offer some guidelines to policy-makers and managers of the cross-border partnerships on the island of Ireland (McAlinden, 1995, p. 83).

The EU Special Support Programme for Peace and Reconciliation, providing £234 million in 1995–7, with the UK and Irish governments adding £78 million in matching funds (Robb, 1995, p. 138), also has a strong cross-border element (as one of the five priority areas of action attracting at least 15 per cent of the total package). The inclusion of non-government agencies in the implementation and monitoring of this package (not only in cross-border partnerships but also in 'social partnerships' dealing with the other priority areas of employment, urban and rural regeneration, social inclusion, and productive investment and industrial development) extends the postmodernist nature of the alliances formed. Through these initiatives, communities are encouraged to take control of their particular circumstances and develop the economic potential of their peripheral location instead of labouring on the territorial resource of their identity that was moulded and prioritized by the development of the modern state in Ireland.

European integration is the macro-level dynamic behind the positive discrimination of EU funds that are enjoyed by local communities on the island of Ireland. Should the economic interests of the periphery become further aligned to the EU multi-level government axis that incorporates supranational, national and subnational levels then the economic resources of northern Irish Nationalist and Ulster Unionist identities are liable to become redefined in this developing context of postmodernity. It is also possible that the modern state context for the territorial resource of communal identity in Northern Ireland will subsequently come under increased scrutiny should economic and political union make advances. As such, the responses of interviewees (in the dialogues) to a changing economic context for Northern Ireland provide an early indication of the degree of changing priorities in the structural allegiances of northern Irish Nationalist and Ulster Unionist identities.

THE TERRITORIAL RESOURCE

> A neutral concept, territory becomes politically significant because of the interpretation placed on it by people: it becomes a concept generated by people organising space for their own ends (Urwin and Rokkan, 1983, p. 123).

With the onset of structural modernity in Ireland, Ulster Unionists were presented with the opportunity to organize space for their own ends through their ability to influence the formulation of the Government of Ireland Act of 1920[4] (Phoenix, 1994, p. 393). With the formation of two modern states in Ireland after 1921 the territorial resource of Unionist and Nationalist identities became paramount. The perceived threat from Irish Nationalists necessitated an overriding emphasis on the integrity of the territory of Northern Ireland by Ulster Unionists. According to the Cadogan Group it is this territorial resource that remains the determining factor in the political actions of Ulster Unionist and northern Irish Nationalist communal identities: 'In Northern Ireland two sets of people claim the same ground, each wanting it attached to a different state. That is the essential quarrel, though over the years it has been obscured' (Cadogan Group, 1996, p. 32). The pre-eminence of the territorial resource of Ulster Unionist identities has been maintained since 1921. The Unionist approach has concentrated on defending the territorial boundary of Northern Ireland, especially with the Republic of Ireland, and guarding against any slippage of Northern Ireland's UK statehood (Cadogan Group, 1996, p. 24). Consequently, it would appear that the condition of postmodernity has so far failed to breach the modernist parameter encapsulating the territorial resource of the Ulster Unionist identity. After all, the UUP has preferred to concentrate efforts on lobbying for Northern Ireland to be further integrated into the UK, especially after the signing of the Anglo-Irish Agreement in 1985 which gave Dublin an advisory role on Northern Ireland.[5] The UUP maintains that Northern Ireland's allegiance to the Crown offers Unionists a secure identity, as well as large-scale subvention from the UK centre.[6] The UUP has argued that this position of strength could be severely jeopardized if EU integration continues apace, UK sovereignty is further eroded, and an empowered EU sanctions ever greater involvement of the Republic of Ireland in Northern Ireland affairs (Jim Molyneaux in *Unionist Voice*, November 1990). For evidence of the initial stages in this process, some Unionists might point to the improved relations between British and Irish Ministers occurring at EC level before the signing of the Anglo-Irish Agreement. The EU threat to the all-important territorial resource of Unionist identities is secondary to the Irish Nationalist threat for Ulster Unionists. However, it has been aligned with Irish nationalism as an enemy of Ulster Unionism by the UUP because it is also threatens the modern boundary of Northern Ireland.

The continuing pride of place reserved for the territory of Northern Ireland and the cultural resource of Ulster Protestantism in the Ulster Unionist identity, as well as the fear of being labelled 'traitor' by some Unionist elements, makes political manoeuvring by Unionist leaders an extremely difficult notion to contemplate. Consequently, it would appear that the catalyst that moves the territorial resource of the Ulster Unionist identity to political action is any perceived to threaten the union between Northern Ireland and Great Britain. Unionist politicians of all shades were furious at the announcement of a 'shared understanding' between the UK and Irish governments contained in the Framework Documents. This understanding envisaged the establishment of North/South institutions that included a North/South body involving Heads of Department 'on both sides' with executive, harmonizing and consultative functions (*Framework Documents*, 1995, pp. 29–33). By definition, the territorial objective of Ulster Unionism is to maintain the condition of political modernity. However, the UUP dialogue indicates that the two UUP Euro-representatives are not only prepared to engage EU institutions but that they are also attempting to develop a political discourse for Ulster Unionists that adapts to EU substantive and conceptual developments.

The Ulster Unionist cultural resource of Ulster Protestantism is the paramount concern of the Reverend Ian Paisley's Democratic Unionist Party (DUP). It perceives Irish Nationalists as representing a direct threat to Ulster Unionist identities. The DUP leadership has generally supported greater devolution from the UK centre to Northern Ireland so that the prospects for the survival of Ulster Unionism and Ulster Protestantism may be enhanced. The DUP has opposed EU membership from the outset. Opposition to the loss of sovereignty by the UK in the interest of European integration is the mandatory territorial objection.[7] However, an ethnoreligious concern for 'Protestant Ulster' is central to the politics and religion of DUP members and further accounts for DUP hostility to Europe. The European Court of Human Rights' ruling that permitted male homosexual activity in Northern Ireland, despite the opposition of the 'Save Ulster From Sodomy' campaign, was presented by Dr Paisley as evidence of the undemocratic and threatening nature of European institutions generally. Dr Paisley's exegesis on the EU emphasizes concerns such as the overwhelming number of member states that have a large Roman Catholic majority; the treaty which established the European Economic Community being named the 'Treaty of Rome'; and the Catholicism of those who drafted the treaty – Adenauer, Schuman, and Monnet. The 'main architects of Maastricht' received similar scrutiny:

> Never forget the Community as at present constituted is 187 million (78.5%) RC and 51 million (21.5%) Protestant. Kohl, Mitter[r]and and Delors, the main architects of Maastricht, are all faithful RCs (DUP, *The Surrender of Maastricht – What it Means for Ulster*, 1992).

In the past, Dr Paisley has cast the EC in the role of the Antichrist in his eschatological sermons (Bruce, 1989, p. 229). The DUP dialogue reflects these concerns.

With the inclusion of the United Kingdom and the Republic of Ireland in the extraterritorial polity of the European Economic Community in 1973, and that polity's subsequent development in response to economic and other extraterritorial forces, the territorial resource of peripheral identity is left vulnerable to the possibility of reinterpretation. The validity of the modernist context for the territorial resource of northern Irish Nationalist identities – an All-Ireland nation-state – is beginning to be questioned as the EU takes effect on the economic and territorial resources of that identity (Todd, 1990, p. 41). SDLP interviewees argue that this reinterpretation is at an advanced stage in the northern Nationalist identities that they represent. Certainly, the SDLP has been more adept in its utilization of the European dimension, in practical and theoretical terms, than have other Northern Ireland parties (Ruane and Todd, 1989, p. 170; Hickman, 1990, p. 21; Hainsworth and Morrow, 1993, p. 132). The SDLP has used the EU to broaden the territorial context of the Northern Ireland conflict and claims that the conflict is irrelevant in that context (John Hume in the *Irish News*, 6 June 1994). The SDLP anticipates the emergence of a 'Europe of the Regions' that will eventually dislodge nation-states as the pre-eminent political actors in the EU (Hickman, 1990, p. 21). The enthusiasm of the SDLP for a 'Europe of the Regions' is largely predicated on the notion that integration will diminish nation-state loyalties and deliver a highly decentralized, regionally autonomous regime that will facilitate a reconciliation within the North, between North and South, and between Britain and Ireland (SDLP, *Westminster General Election Manifesto*, 1992).

Unionist interviewees doubt the ability of the process of European integration to diffuse what they perceive to be the hegemonic content of Irish nationalism. Furthermore, they believe that the SDLP enthusiasm for European integration exists primarily because it provides Irish Nationalists with an alternative means of achieving a condominium in the short-term and 'Irish unification' in the long-term. Unionist academics, such as those in the Cadogan Group, interpret SDLP strategy as one of continually shifting the search for a resolution of the Northern Ireland political conflict to a wider context in order to dilute the British dimension. The first step in this process was to internationalize it in an Anglo-Irish context; the next step, to 'Europeanize' it, thereby continually weakening the Unionist voice until it is muted outright (Cadogan Group, 1992, p. 16). The SDLP dialectic that the internal market will render partition obsolete, thereby facilitating an 'agreed Ireland' is generally interpreted by Unionists as evidence of irredentism. A Unionist analysis might conclude that just as in the 1960s, when the Nationalist game-plan changed from emphasizing national communal identity to an articulation of the violation of individual citizenship rights (in the UK state context) in an effort to change Northern Ireland's constitutional status, so in the 1990s Nationalists exploited the European dimension with the same modernist goal of aligning the Irish nation with the Irish state.

While Unionists are convinced that SDLP enthusiasm for structural change that opens up modern state boundaries is driven by Irish Nationalist irredentism, SDLP commitment to the consent principle, whereby Nationalist and Unionist consent to a future structure of state is required before it can be established, indicates that the party does not prioritize the modern nationalist goal of creating a state in the image of the nation (McAllister, 1977, p. 33). Furthermore, SDLP promotion of a 'Europe of the Regions' (Social Democratic and Labour Party, 1992), however fanciful, is indicative of a position that contravenes the modern nationalist principle of the investment of power in a central nation-state authority. Instead, the Europe of the Regions evoked by the SDLP represents a vertical schism of power in an EU polity. The SDLP's desire for an 'agreed Ireland', a term viewed with deep suspicion by Unionist politicians and intellectuals, appears to be far removed from the modern ideal of an autonomous nation-state when the party's commitment to the principles of consent and EU regionalism is considered.

The northern Irish Nationalist identity which the SDLP represents would seem to be at a cross-roads between 'liberal' nationalism (Tamir, 1993), which is pro-European because the emphasis on state restructuring and economic concerns means that European integration is potentially beneficial for the Irish imagined community; 'neo-traditional' nationalism, which still prioritizes Catholic and Gaelic values and a 'united Ireland', despite the opposition of a substantial Ulster Unionist 'minority'; and 'post'-nationalism, which envisages a 'Europe of the Regions' that enables the 'European community' to co-exist with the Irish imagined community (Kearney, 1997, p. 59). Such an identity recognizes that modernity and its political manifestations, the modern nation-state and modern nationalism, have not disappeared. However, the emergence of these different takes on nationalism indicates that the vantage point on such phenomena has changed to one where it is possible to reinterpret the concepts of modernity in light of postmodern developments. Consequently, Kearney's 'postnationalism' makes many of the discriminations made by the liberal nationalism described by Tamir: between nation and state; between forms of nationalism; and between forms of state. As such, the debate within the SDLP reflects the on-going debate in the Republic of Ireland, the UK and the EU on the contemporary nature of the nation, nationalism and the state in the EU polity and is likely to continue for as long as the EU remains in a state of flux between modernity and postmodernity (Ruane, 1994, p. 190–2).

The Irish Republican identity represented by Sinn Féin would appear to be in a period of transition and drift in terms of the form of nationalism to which it subscribes. Sinn Féin certainly finds it difficult to reconcile the irredentism that is central to its nationalist political philosophy with the postmodern challenge that European integration poses for nation/state alignment. The main dynamic for this irredentism is the perceived injustice inflicted on the northern Nationalist community through the exercise of power by the UK government in Northern Ireland (Todd, 1990, p. 41). While Sinn Féin has been forthright in its opposition to European integration in the past, the EU is now presented as a means to end the partition of the island:

> The political and economic transformation of Europe provides a golden opportunity for Ireland to finally resolve its British problem and embark on a process of economic and political reunification and transformation (Sinn Féin, 1992).

However, the party is simultaneously opposed to continued European integration endorsed by the Maastricht Treaty because the transfer of power to EU institutions weakens the role of national parliaments (Sinn Féin, 1991). The Sinn Féin dialogue addresses this contradiction in the enthusiasm shown for European integration making infringements on the boundary between Northern Ireland and the Republic of Ireland, and the criticism of any manifestation of European integration because it weakens the power of national parliaments.

The APNI is pro-European integrationist because it holds that the EU will provide the dynamic required for movement towards its goals of increased secularization and liberalization for the region. The party also maintains that European integration will enable a movement away from concerns about national sovereignty providing the emphasis remains on decentralization (*Alliance News*, Summer 1989). The APNI dialogue attempts to ascertain the party's position on the implications of European integration for its advocacy of the devolution option for Northern Ireland. The APNI's vision of a 'Europe of the Regions' is contrasted with its UK devolutionist policy: it is pro-union with Britain in the context of the modern state but has a 'wholehearted' commitment to the EU and the development of a postmodern 'Europe of the Regions' polity (APNI, *Westminster Election Manifesto*, 1992). This analysis is used to highlight the position of identities represented by the APNI and the implications of European integration for them.

It is sometimes assumed that Northern Ireland MEPs, Ian Paisley (DUP), John Hume (SDLP) and Jim Nicholson (UUP), merely use the European Parliament platform to extend their territorial quarrel over Northern Ireland in a context beyond the territory itself (Hainsworth, 1989, p. 51). However, attention has been drawn to the fact that Northern Ireland MEPs co-operate at EU level where they have the common goal of maximizing economic benefits for Northern Ireland (Bevant, 1993, p. 101; Meehan in Opsahl, 1993, p. 215). Such co-operation has intimations of postmodernity because it is taking place at a level that challenges the exclusivity of modern nation-state interaction. It is also indicative of the possibilities for new alliances between Nationalists and Unionists on economic and social issues in the postmodern extraterritorial context. The 'region' itself is no longer defined solely by the modern state boundary in this supranational context since border counties in the Republic of Ireland are included in INTERREG II and the EU Peace and Reconciliation programmes. Northern Ireland MEPs also act as a conduit between the EU centre and the Northern Ireland periphery, leading delegations from Northern Ireland to Brussels on fact-finding and lobbying missions, as well as hosting visits of European Commissioners to Northern Ireland (Hainsworth, 1989, p. 63). Such developments suggest a potential anomaly between extraterritorial involvement in integrationist supranational structures of state by Unionist political representatives and their defining emphasis on the modernist territorial dimensions of their identity. The extraterritorial actions and interpretations of Northern Ireland's EU representatives are explored in the dialogues and are offered as evidence of the EU as a potential catalyst that will effect change in communal identities in Northern Ireland.

THE CULTURAL RESOURCE

The emergence of the modern state in Ireland presented the Irish nation with a divergence in the political experience of its northern and southern components. Thirty years of political conflict in Northern Ireland and the subsequent prevalence of anti-northern Nationalist revisionism in the South (prior to the 1994 IRA cease-fire) had served to exacerbate further the divergence in the political outlook of Irish Nationalist identities, North and South. The outcome of this for many in the South was an unease with declaring allegiance to an Irish Nationalist identity for fear of being labelled a 'Provo' (Mary McAleese, cited in O'Connor, 1993, p. 263; Cochrane, 1994, p. 392). Perhaps as a consequence of Northern conflict, Southern revisionism, generation turn-over and the on-going process of secularization in Southern society, it has been suggested that there is a 'new' Irish cultural identity emerging in the South that is increasingly pluralist and heterogeneous. For Rory O'Donnell of the Dublin-based Economic and Social Research Institute, this new Irish identity has the Irish international soccer team and Irish international musicians as its principal symbolic figureheads (O'Donnell, 1993, p. 36). Furthermore, it is suggested that this new identity begins to distinguish Northern Ireland as a separate entity and, by implication, northern Irish Nationalists as having a separate identity (Holmes, 1994, pp. 93–4).

There can be little doubt that individual perceptions in southern Irish society have been affected by the condition of postmodernity and the development of the EU. The resulting enthusiasm for the EU; the increasing geographical mobility of commodities and individuals; as well as the spiralling development of mass communications, have made other cultures more immediately accessible and have led to greater assimilation of aspects of these 'foreign' cultures, not least British culture, into aspects of Irish culture. However, although there is evidence to support the claim of an increasing secularization and internationalization of southern Irish identities in the 1990s, an analysis which suggests that this has resulted in contemporary Southern Irish cultural identity being reducible to U2, Irish theme bars and Riverdance is flawed. Contemporary music and soccer undoubtedly are high-profile components in the cultural identity of the Irish nation. However, longer established 'ethnic' components have been collaged into this postmodern Irish Nationalist identity. Religion, the Irish language, traditional Irish music and dance, Gaelic games, custom, and myths and symbols – conveyed through the Irish media – continue to make vital contributions to the cultural resource of Irish Nationalist identities. The assertion that 'new' components of Irish Nationalist identities seek to, or have succeeded in excluding northern Irish Nationalists is also severely hindered by lack of substantive evidence. Such exclusion would appear to exist only in the theses of the so-called 'revisionist Nationalists' who, because of Republican violence in the North, have attempted to redefine Irish Nationalist identity in terms of the modern state, that is, the Republic of Ireland.

Despite the political dislocation that exists within the Irish national identity as a whole, an examination of the components of that identity reveal an Irish nation that continues to embody a culturally cohesive peripheral European identity in many respects. Nevertheless, northern Irish Nationalists are the political adjunct of the Irish nation having been deprived of the representation and security that the modern state has had to offer. The result has been a discernible northern Irish Nationalist identity that has incorporated concepts of 'community' and 'justice' as well as that of 'nation' into its identity (Todd, 1990, pp. 31–44). The communal aspect of the northern Nationalist identity has the structures of power established by the Catholic Church as an alternative focal point. The existence of such structures to represent the interests of Catholics, when set against the structure of the modern state in Northern Ireland that is still largely perceived to represent the interests of Ulster Protestants, has perhaps resulted in a politicization of this cultural component of northern Irish Nationalist identity. A revisionist interpretation of northern Irish Nationalist identities might hold that this politicization of northern Catholicism, when combined with the participation of northern Irish Nationalists in the hothouse of political and violent conflict in Northern Ireland, has resulted in an identity tarnished by premodern sectarianism, locked into modern nationalism and ill at ease with the concept of a postmodern multi-level polity that can accommodate Ulster Unionists. The dialogues examine the attitudes of northern Irish Nationalist identities to Ulster Unionists; the extent to which northern Irish Nationalist identities can claim to be 'liberal nationalist'; and their interpretations of structural accommodation in the contexts of modernity and postmodernity.

Ulster Unionists bear many of the hallmarks of a distinct ethnic group. Ulster Unionist identities have a shared sense of history, values, symbols, customs and beliefs that are defined by Ulster Protestantism – the cultural core of Ulster Unionism. Unionists, therefore, rely predominantly on their Ulster Protestantism for a distinguishing cultural feature. Indeed, the terms 'Ulster Unionist' and 'Ulster Protestant' are commonly used as synonyms. The liberal unionism of the O'Neillites in the 1960s and the socialism advocated by the paramilitary Ulster Defence Association (UDA) in the early 1980s threatened to undermine the position of the Ulster Protestant identity in Ulster Unionism. Denying Ulster Unionism its cultural core of Ulster Protestantism threatens the ability of

Ulster Unionism to embody the vital aspect of an ethnic identity and, therefore, remain coherent and survive in the territory of Northern Ireland[8]. This reliance on Ulster Protestantism as the overarching cultural resource gives Unionism an anti-Catholic bias according to Padraig O'Malley:

> In Ulster . . . the question of identity, particularly among Protestants, is extraordinarily complex. Because they do not have a strong sense of political identity, they fall back on their religion for symbols of identity. And because they take their cohesion in religious matters from an anti-Catholic bias that is common to all their denominations, anti-Catholicism becomes an expression of shared identity (O'Malley, 1983, p. 151).

Despite appeals from some Unionists for the development of inclusive and non-sectarian unionism in the 1990s, the definition of Ulster Unionism as an ethnic identity that incorporates Ulster Protestantism excludes northern Catholics who may be pro-union (in the UK context) for economic and even political reasons.

The modern state's emphasis on territory, combined with the anti-Catholic bias of Ulster Protestantism, has necessitated a public attitude of communal exclusivism among Ulster Unionists towards Irish Nationalist culture in Northern Ireland. The very existence of the Irish Nationalist identity in Northern Ireland was implicitly questioned by John Taylor, MP, (UUP, Deputy Leader subsequently) when he declared:

> Much as I enjoy the Irish and admire many of their cultural pursuits, I have to remind them that we in Northern Ireland are not Irish, we do not jig at the cross-roads, speak Gaelic, play GAA (Gaelic sports) etc. (in the *Irish Times*, 7 December 1993).

However, Taylor subsequently struck a more inclusive note before the 1995 All-Ireland Gaelic Football Final, which featured the Ulster Champions, Tyrone, when he said:

> While no one would consider me a GAA enthusiast, nor do I agree with the objectives of the GAA, nonetheless, I recognise the GAA as one of the great sporting organisations which provides great physical sporting outlets for thousands of our people (in the *Irish News*, 16 September 1995).[9]

David Trimble, MP, (UUP, Leader) appeared reluctant to accept that there is a cultural dimension to northern Nationalist identities when he said: 'I haven't been up the Falls Road, but I bet you they're watching the BBC and the kids support Manchester United' (in the *Financial Times*, 11 September 1995). Repudiation of Irish Nationalist culture remains essential to the political manifestation of some Unionist identities. Such repudiation is emphasized by the tone and content of a comment by the DUP's Sammy Wilson: 'It is not my job to promote fiddley-dee music, dancing at the crossroads and a leprechaun language' (*South Belfast Herald and Post*, 11 January 1996). Unionist intellectuals have failed to diminish the reliance of Ulster Unionism on this sectarian dimension and many have opted instead to migrate to the UK centre and pursue the British dimension to their identity which can accommodate liberal democratic principles (Bruce, 1989, p. 261; O'Dowd, 1991, pp. 163–5).

CONCLUSION

Working in parallel with the postmodernist intergovernmental initiative on Northern Ireland taken by the UK and Irish governments in the so-called Anglo-Irish process (chapter 3), intimations of postmodernity in the EU, through a developing system of multi-level governance and a meaningful supranational citizenship (chapter 4), have the potential to mobilize the resources of northern Irish Nationalist and Ulster Unionist identities and produce political action. The modernist characteristics of the conflict, with its emphasis on the territorial resource, dictates that the alignment of northern Irish Nationalist and Ulster Unionist communal identities to postmodern structures is likely to be a slow and difficult process. This process is complicated further by the vibrancy of premodern ethno-religious traits in the identity collage of contemporary Ulster Unionist and northern Irish Nationalist identities. However, a sustained absence of sectarian violence would allow individual perceptions to become susceptible to changing circumstances and provide communal identities with the opportunity to refocus and give full consideration to the implications of extraterritorial economic forces and structures of political power.

The EU's INTERREG II and Peace and Reconciliation programmes are micro-level catalysts aimed at refocusing on the economic resource of communal identities in a postmodern context. As such, they complement the macro-level advances made by European integration and their impact on restructuring the priorities given to the territorial, economic and cultural resources of communal identity in Northern Ireland. The direction of political action taken by communal identities as a result of postmodern catalysts will, of course, depend on the way in which the EU develops along supranational, national and subnational lines and the tangible effect of these developments on northern Irish Nationalist and Ulster Unionist communities and their representatives. The dialogues that follow seek to provide representative interpretations of the potential impact of this postmodernity on communal identities in Northern Ireland in terms of their economic, territorial and cultural resources.[10]

Part Two:
Dialogues

6 Dialogue with the Social Democratic and Labour Party (SDLP)

INTRODUCTION

The SDLP was formally launched on 21 August 1970 with a promise 'to provide a strong alternative to unionism' and 'to promote the cause of Irish unity by the consent of the majority of the people in Northern Ireland' (McAllister, 1977, p. 33). The party brought together six Stormont MPs that had constituted fractured strands in northern Nationalist political representation. They included the Independents who emerged from the civil rights movement – John Hume, Ivan Cooper and Paddy O'Hanlon; Austin Currie, a Nationalist MP; Paddy Devlin from the Northern Ireland Labour Party; and Gerry Fitt, Republican Labour (RL), who became the first party leader. They were joined by Stormont Senator, Paddy Wilson, RL.

In the first election contested by the SDLP as a party, the District Council elections of May 1973, the party received 13.4 per cent of the vote. The following month, the SDLP established itself as Northern Ireland's second largest party in the Northern Ireland Assembly election when it secured 22.1 per cent of the vote. Despite experiencing a slight fall in its electoral fortunes in the 1980s, the SDLP's percentage share of the vote has stabilized in the 1990s with 23.5 per cent of the votes cast in the 1992 Westminster General election and 22.0 per cent in the District Council election of 1993. In the 1994 election to the European Parliament, the SDLP received its largest ever share of the vote – 28.93 per cent – a result that was hailed as a personal triumph for party leader John Hume, MP, MEP (Flackes and Elliott, 1994; *Irish Political Studies*, 1995). In the 1996 Northern Ireland Forum election the SDLP maintained a 21.37 per cent share of the vote, rising to 24.1 per cent in the 1997 General Election despite strong performances by Sinn Féin in both elections (*Irish News*, 3 May 1997).

Since becoming an MEP and party leader in 1979, John Hume has recognized the potential import that European Community developments have presented for SDLP policy on the constitutional position of Northern Ireland. Consequently, the party has been proactive in seeking to develop a political philosophy that both reflects and elaborates upon such developments.

SDLP PERCEPTIONS OF STRUCTURAL CHANGE

> We have always recognised that the nation state is no longer a sufficient political entity to democratically confront the economic, technological, social and environmental issues which confront us in the modern world. We have argued for growing co-operation and co-ordination between the countries of Europe to protect the common good of all Europe's people in a new unity (SDLP, *Westminster General Election Manifesto*, 1992).

Mark Durkan, SDLP Chairperson 1990–5, contends that wider changes in society permeate nation-state boundaries and require a response from a state structure that is necessarily supranational in nature. Furthermore, postmodern contingencies require this supranational structure to focus on interdependency rather than on the rivalry associated with the nation-state system. Durkan argues that such a superstructure is the best way of strengthening democracy in a changing society. For these reasons he maintains that the idea of nation-state sovereignty is an out-dated concept that is becoming incompatible with the principle of democracy:

> I think it's right that we haven't allowed the nation-state to be the last word in polity creation and in international political development. What we have in the European sense is a pooling of sovereignty. Now, what some people will say is that by going into Europe and by according certain functions in the pooled business of either the European Parliament or the Council of Ministers or just the whole aggregate institutions of the EU that people have diluted sovereignty. We, in the SDLP, look on it as not diluting sovereignty but dilating democracy because the fact is that we live in an age now where the forces and factors that have a direct effect on peoples' lives and well-being are not forces and factors that can be controlled or regulated by nation-state instruments. So, if democracy is going to keep pace with those forces and powers and factors that affect the lives of people within

the democracy then we have to find instruments at a new level – the supranational level. We have to constantly start widening the scope and the base and the reach of democracy. We have to heighten democracy, which takes us beyond the sovereignty question by creating democratic institutions at a supranational level. We have to widen democracy by having democratic influences affecting more areas of social and economic life and we have to deepen democracy by taking things back from the nation-state and putting them into the regions and local communities (interview with the author).

Intergovernmental theorists such as Moravcsik (1993) and Caporaso and Keeler (1993) have argued that the EU is actually consolidating the power of the nation-state in the changing postmodern political environment (chapter 4). It does this primarily by providing a supranational structure of state, designed to exercise control over postmodern forces, in which the heads of member states sitting in the Council remain the principal decision-makers. Furthermore, decisions reached by the Council have had to receive unanimous support in the past, thus reinforcing member state control. Such interpretation is challenged by **Denis Haughey**, SDLP member of the Committee of the Regions, on a number of counts:

Firstly, the Council of Ministers is gradually developing. In the beginning there had to be uniformity – there had to be absolute consensus. Now the rules are developing so that you have, in certain circumstances, majority decision-making within certain formulations (there has to be so many people on one side of an argument in order for it to be carried against opposition from others). You don't have a requirement for absolute uniformity and as a consequence there is a narrowing of the range of areas where national governments can cite national interest as a reason for opposing or blocking anything. The Council of Ministers itself is developing into a collegiate body where there is collective decision-making that isn't based upon the requirement of absolute unanimity. Secondly, the European Parliament is developing quite rapidly now. It is the major power in financial matters. The European Commission still maintains a very powerful position. However, in the future I can see a situation where the European Parliament will exercise greater control in the selection of European Commissioners (interview with the author).

Haughey argues that power is gradually being wrested from the grip of the nation-state in the EU. Nations will then have to redefine their relationship with other nations and interest groups in order to successfully interact with European institutions:

> You have a set of dynamic institutions that are developing and growing and changing, therefore, I don't see the nation-state having that essential power any more to block or prevent things happening. All nations are now going to increasingly find themselves in a position where, in order to get things that they want done, they are going to have to construct alliances and friendships and axes and do horse-trading and do all of the things that normally go on in the national parliaments, in the European institutions.

In their assessment of European integration, the SDLP interviewees are convinced of the durability of the process and its potential for reconstituting Northern Ireland politics. Mark Durkan perceives the structural change associated with European integration to be the latest overhaul by the state in reaction to changing socio-economic conditions in contemporary society. He believes that such change has important implications for democracy. Denis Haughey also perceives that structural change entails an inexorable move away from the nation-state structure. He cites the development of majority decision-making in the Council of Ministers and the gradual acquisition of power by the Parliament as evidence of the gathering momentum of integrationist forces in the EU.

DETERMINING STRUCTURAL PARAMETERS FOR NORTHERN IRELAND

The Extraterritorial Context

The SDLP became overtly committed to developing an extraterritorial context for Northern Ireland, *vis-à-vis* the Republic of Ireland, after the experience of the 1974 power-sharing executive in which the party served. The executive was brought down by a general strike organized and enforced by the loyalist Ulster Workers' Council in May, 1974. Thereafter, John Hume began to articulate an extraterritorial context. In 'The Irish Question: a British Problem' (Hume, 1979, pp. 300–13) he called for a joint-approach by both London and Dublin in initiating a process that would lead to an agreement: 'The time has come for a positive and decisive initiative. It must be taken by both London and Dublin, *acting together*' (p. 309).

Agreement, when it eventually came in 1985, was not between the political representatives of communal identities in Northern Ireland but between the Government of the United Kingdom and the Government of the Republic of Ireland – the Anglo-Irish Agreement (AIA). Unionists protested that Hume had a hand in drafting the AIA owing to his close relationship with the Dublin political establishment, a relationship that had been rejuvenated by the New Ireland Forum which sat from 30 May 1983 until 2 May 1984 (O'Halloran, 1987, p. 194). Certainly, the AIA reflects the joint approach by the two governments that Hume called for in 1979. While focusing on SDLP perceptions and strategy it is important to recognize the Agreement as a milestone in a process advocated in the Hume article. The AIA was the definitive point at which the SDLP, under the Hume leadership, turned its back on the possibility of an exclusively internal structure of government for Northern Ireland. During the Brooke/Mayhew Talks of 1991–2, Hume explicitly reiterated this position in a radio broadcast citing Unionist lack of appetite for power-sharing as a reason for the need to broaden the territorial parameters of a constitutional arrangement (O'Connor, 1993, p. 91).

An extraterritorial context had already been established in 1973 with the accession of the United Kingdom and the Republic of Ireland to the European Economic Community. From the beginning of his membership of the European Parliament in 1979, Hume has been developing a political approach that has been influenced increasingly by the European dimension. He believed that Europe could act as a 'healing force' if Northern Ireland were more constructively and positively represented in the European Community (*Belfast Telegraph*, 16 May 1979).[1] When the SDLP submitted its proposals on a structure of government for Northern Ireland to the Brooke/Mayhew Talks (that also involved the UUP, the DUP and the APNI) it was clear that its 'European discourse' had been developed beyond theory and beyond even the 'moral, political and economic involvement' advocated by Jacques Delors (O'Leary *et al.*, 1993, p. 132). The SDLP proposed a structure of government whereby the European Commission would become directly involved in the structural mechanics of government. The party's proposal for a six-person Commission for Northern Ireland was based on the European Commission and included three commissioners elected within Northern Ireland, and one each to be nominated by the London and Dublin governments and the European Commission. A Northern Ireland Assembly modelled in the image of the European Parliament and a North-South Council of Ministers were also proposed to support the work of the Northern Ireland Commission. The proposal traversed the modern state parameter that informed other proposals and was lampooned by other parties at the talks.[2]

Denis Haughey appeared reticent about pursuing the Commission proposal in the Multi-Party Talks (1996–8) when he said: 'The SDLP has never been hung up on structures. We have always elaborated principles' (interview with the author).

It is the democratic representation of Irish Nationalist and Ulster Unionist identities expressed through the institutions of a state structure that is the key principle which the SDLP adheres to, according to Haughey. He believes that such democratic representation of both sets of communal identities cannot be achieved purely within the territorial context of Northern Ireland:

> All sections of this community have a right to access the decision-making process. That cannot be done with simple majority-rule. Secondly, there are divided identities and allegiances here. Some of us look to Britain for the focus of their allegiance and identity, others look to the nation that they perceive to exist on the island of Ireland as the focus of their identity. Where these identities are strongly held then expression has to be given to both and not just one. Therefore, you can't have a solution that says 'Ulster exclusively is British', neither can you have a settlement that says 'Ulster is exclusively Irish'. For practical purposes that means remaining within the UK for as long as the majority in Northern Ireland wish. However, it means identifying certain areas where we can co-operate closely with the South to give expression to that feeling which many people in the North have, that Ireland is one nation. Those areas include agriculture, fisheries, the environment, where the island can be administered by North and South as one unit. Giving expression to that feeling of Irish people in the North that they are Irish people living in Ireland, it is one country, and if there are levels that are identified where that can be the reality for some purpose then that gives expression to their identity.

An eventual down-grading of the territorial resource of northern Irish Nationalist and Ulster Unionist identities that have been determined by modernity is thought by Haughey to be paramount if such consent is to be a viable prospect:

> We have got to allow Ulster to be simply a piece of earth and for the people who inhabit it to be whatever they want, and to be able to find the expression of their allegiance within the framework of the state.

The 'Europe of The Regions' Concept

> We in the SDLP have always believed in the 'Europe of the Regions'. We must seek to ensure that in the New Europe, the regions have a powerful role to play and therefore we also welcome the Maastricht Agreement decision to set up a Committee of the Regions. We in Northern Ireland must seek to play the fullest part in the growing regional dimension of European affairs, and to forge the natural alliances with other deprived regions of Europe which will give us increased power and influence at the centre (SDLP, *Westminster Election Manifesto*, April 1992).

A 'Europe of the Regions' has long been offered by the SDLP as its vision of a fully integrated European Union. John Hume gives an account of this vision and its virtues in Kearney (1988b). However, critics, such as Edna Longley, detect signs of modern irredentism in Hume's account.[3] It has been difficult for the SDLP to refute irrevocably accusations of irredentism because 'the region' in the postmodern European context is undoubtedly a nebulous concept. In modernity, the concepts of 'region', 'nation' and 'state' have been defined by an emphasis on sovereign territory. The process of reinterpreting these concepts is difficult for individuals and communities whose political identities are the subject of 'live' premodern and modern conflicts within a disputed territory. In an EU context, Haughey's reinterpretation of 'the region' suggests that it is a concept that is multi-dimensional; with concurrent 'island of Ireland', 'Northern Ireland', and 'periphery of Europe' contexts depending on the policy area:

> For some purposes it can mean Northern Ireland, it can mean Northern Ireland as a region in tandem with the Republic and other regions of a similar type. It can, for many purposes, mean Ireland as one region.

In order to explore the nature of the SDLP vision and the grounds for its advancement it is useful to consider the SDLP assessment of the actual progress that 'the region' can make as a political unit in a fully integrated EU. Mark Durkan is realistic about the omnipresence of the nation-state centre in the EU and the obstacle that it presents to the process of regionalization: 'In many ways it is the nation-states who are going to be the biggest barriers on the way to that rather than what would happen at the identifiably European level (interview with the author).' He proposes that the limited primary functions of the nation-state demonstrate the need for a structure of state that can cope with the increasingly diverse and demanding requirements placed upon it by a society which is itself evolving beyond modernity:

> If you consider that the notion of the centralized nation-state with delegated parliamentary representation was something that was born in a time when the main purpose of the state was essentially defence and tax-raising, the state didn't have the range of economic expectations and requirements on it as it does now. Certainly, there would not have been the range of public services and agencies but also there would not have been the same mass education, the same media and information availability – in circumstances where we now have all those I don't see why we should maintain structures that well pre-date the particular context in which we are living. That is why we have to find ways of re-dispersing and re-allocating a lot of those powers and functions.

Durkan is cognisant of the continued importance of territory for identity and particularly the over-riding emphasis placed on 'Northern Ireland' as a political unit by Unionists when promoting the concept of a 'Europe of the Regions'. He argues that the SDLP has attempted to incorporate this reality into its thinking on the territorial parameters of Northern Ireland:

> There are different levels. In certain aspects in Europe you have Northern Ireland being treated as a region as well as being treated as being part of two member-states. You also have the question of inter-regional regions in terms of cross-border regions and areas, so, again, we see it as being a much more multi-tiered thing than Unionists would. However, we have not precluded that there should be arrangements in Northern Ireland and particular

to Northern Ireland and, in fact, we made proposals [in the Brooke/ Mayhew Talks 1991–2] that would have had Northern Ireland enjoying quite direct access to Brussels as a particular region and the UUP rejected it. They were insisting on the security of Northern Ireland simply as a region of the United Kingdom and only in that context taking its place in Europe. We went for quite a different approach that would have involved partnership in Northern Ireland, Northern Ireland enjoying some direct regional access to Europe, and Northern Ireland maximizing the benefits of that through its engagement in North-South structures which could only work on the basis of the approval of the two jurisdictions. These would not have been free standing institutions with the power to over-ride anybody. We proposed all of that and they rejected it.

Denis Haughey recognizes the barriers to the development of regionalism within the EU but argues that such realignment would be beneficial for the island of Ireland:

I am not saying that central governments in London, Berlin etc. are going to disappear overnight but I can see a situation where we have a set of very strong institutions in Brussels or wherever they come to be established and very powerful regional authorities across the European Union. In John Hume's report on regional policy in the Republic he recommended the division of the Republic into a number of strong regional authorities. If you had a situation where the North was divided into two or three regions and the South divided into seven or eight regions you have a more kaleidoscopic picture there with bits and pieces of the jigsaw fitting together in different shapes and patterns for different purposes and you might find something like the maritime regions of Ireland for certain purposes co-operating together. You are into a much more flexible world where all kinds of alliances and friendships and axes are possible.

Complementing the SDLP argument for an extraterritorial dimension to structural arrangements for Northern Ireland is the party's subscription to the concept of a 'Europe of the Regions'. The 'region', as elaborated upon by the two interviewees, is strongly postmodernist in its conceptualization – flexible, decentred, deconstructed, transient and amenable to the creation of new formations and alliances. It is a multidimensional concept that may be territorially defined but is interchangeable with a particular policy area (for example, the island of Ireland for agriculture or the European periphery for sea transport). While both interviewees recognize that centralized member states pose a considerable impediment to the realization of this vision, they remained convinced of its merits, particularly for the island of Ireland.

The Committee of the Regions

The Committee of the Regions was established at Maastricht by Article 198c (EC) and had its first meeting in March 1994 (chapter 4). The limited extent of its powers are probably not what the Germans had in mind when they originally thought that the Committee would act as a second chamber of the European Parliament (*Financial Times*, 17 December 1994). According to Denis Haughey there is a simple reason for this shortfall between expectations and reality:

> The Parliament is antagonistic towards the Committee of the Regions, seeing it as an alternative source of elected authority within Europe and is apprehensive about it gaining any influence or power or distracting in any way from the role of the Parliament which they see as being vital to develop in order to effect the proper democratic control of the Community's institutions. Our budget is very small and we have not, therefore, been able to develop very quickly.

This reality would appear to deflate further the SDLP 'Europe of the Regions' thesis. Nevertheless, Haughey maintains the position that politically enhanced regions in Europe can create opportunities:

> We have always been very strong on the notion of a Europe of the Regions, taking the view that we are living in a post-nationalist age. John Hume talks now very often about the decline of the nation-state and the emergence of the region. I think that we have a lot to gain from that in Ireland, both North and South, in that many of the European regions are very similar in structure to our own and nobody is better at networking than the Irish, we are masters at it. I think that we can, acting as a region within a more regionalized Europe, construct the kind of alliances that enable us to exercise muscle.

The faltering start of a committee which could potentially give institutional expression to the SDLP ideal of a 'Europe of the Regions' undoubtedly puts a damper on such aspirations. Indeed, the hostility of the Parliament to the Committee of the Regions is recognized by Haughey as a major obstacle to its development from consultation to decision-making and is one that will not be overcome easily. As a result, there is a potential dichotomy in the SDLP position on the implications of the EU for the parameters of a structure of state for Northern Ireland. The party recognizes that the vital institutions of the EU that have been defined by their allegiance to the nation-state are unlikely to relinquish their power to integrationist EU institutions in the short- or medium-term. However, the party presents a view of the EU which suggests that regions, be they based on territory, community or policy-area, will eventually become the dominant form of polity in the EU. Although such an outcome is possible in the long-run, the SDLP adoption of a wholesale 'Europe of the Regions' outlook would appear to be premature.

Regionalism and Devolution

There must be effective direct representation of Northern Ireland in Europe, and joint approaches with the Republic if we are to maximize the advantages of EU membership (SDLP, *European Election Manifesto: Towards a New Century,* 1994).

Some Ulster Unionists, like Jim Nicholson, MEP (in the UUP dialogue), have attempted to draw parallels between an internal power-sharing relationship with the SDLP and the regionalist principle of the EU. The SDLP experience of power-sharing in 1974 and subsequent advances made in imposing elements of their extra-territorial strategy on the respective government policies of Republic of Ireland and United Kingdom have determined a less than enthusiastic response to such suggestions. Like John Hume, Mark Durkan cites the antipathy of Unionists to power-sharing in the past. Consequently, he rejects proposals for a purely internal 'Northern Ireland' structure of government. He also implies that such an arrangement cannot be representative of northern Irish Nationalist identities when drawing a distinction between regionalism in a postmodern European sense and the devolution of power to Northern Ireland from Westminster under the auspices of the modern nation-state:

Firstly, we have never ruled out or opposed power-sharing. Jim Nicholson and his party have done more to oppose power-sharing, whether at a Northern Ireland level or at a local level, than the SDLP. We would certainly see such partnership as part of the healing process and the process of political development. But if people are saying that political development here has to be confined to a purely internal Northern Ireland solution then it isn't on and it isn't going to earn anybody's allegiance. If the SDLP went along with that we would be either subject to our own revision in a number of year's time or subject to rejection in favour of another party on the basis that we had sold the pass on the issue of the Irish identity or self-determination. So, we are making it very clear to Unionists – yes, we agree that there are relationships within Northern Ireland that need to be looked at, we were the first party to coin the notion of the three sets of relationships. We have never gone into talks and tabled 'a united Ireland tomorrow', never done that at any talks that the Unionist parties have been at.

The issue is how do we create circumstances in which people can engage in such partnership at the Northern Ireland level. We can only do it in circumstances where we are not entrapping anybody. Just as Unionists shouldn't find themselves entrapped in some purely all-Ireland arrangement, so too Nationalists shouldn't find themselves entrapped in some purely Northern Ireland arrangement because history has told us already that isn't going to work, that isn't going to sustain sufficient allegiance across the community.

The other thing about the regionalist approach is that the regionalist approach will not just say 'take Northern Ireland as a region'. In many ways we in the north-west see the north-west as a region; there are four council areas that work very closely in the north-west – Donegal, Derry, Strabane and Limavady – so we see regionalism at that level as well. Whether you want to call it a sub-region or not doesn't much matter but this idea of just Northern Ireland as just one single region I don't think would stand up.

Unionists suggest that the SDLP 'Europe of the Regions' analysis is indicative of the irredentism of the SDLP because it is merely a ploy to subvert the integrity of Northern Ireland as a viable political construct (Cadogan Group in Opsahl, 1993, p. 234). Denis

Haughey, in turn, regards such an interpretation as out-dated and not in tune with the wider political reality:

> I know that is what they would say. It is very depressing and tiring. They keep going over the same tired ground. We are not talking about irredentism. We are talking about a new world where there is political integration of Europe so that the regions of Europe become important in their own right and Northern Ireland becomes an important region with an important set of common interests with the Republic where we can co-operate together.

By adopting the multi-faceted regionalist approach, the SDLP explicitly rejects a modern structure of state for Northern Ireland based on the territorial integrity. However, the territorial integrity of Northern Ireland is of primary importance to Ulster Unionists. The SDLP attempted to accommodate the emphasis on Northern Ireland in the internal component of its 1992 proposal. Nevertheless, SDLP interviewees express the need for government to represent the needs of communities that transcend the boundaries of the modern state. The alienation of northern Nationalists, resulting from this modern demarcation, is emphasized.

STRUCTURAL CHANGE AND NATIONALIST IDENTITIES REPRESENTED BY THE SDLP

The Impact of 'Humespeak'

'Humespeak' is synonymous with 'Eurospeak' and has been conducted in the terms of 'post-nationalism', 'consent', 'community', 'interdependency' and an 'agreed Ireland' with increasing frequency throughout the 1980s and 1990s. Yet, the conceptual nature of this discourse allows Unionists make the claim that its articulation by the SDLP is merely a ploy aimed at realizing the modern nationalist goal of an All-Ireland nation-state (Cunningham, 1997). What is not in doubt, however, is that this narrative is testimony to the political innovation of John Hume.

For Ulster Unionists as a whole, John Hume is perceived to be the 'evil genius' responsible for masterminding the AIA through his political influence in Dublin (O'Leary and McGarry, 1993, p. 238). Hume's sphere of influence is also perceived to extend to the EU and US, and even to the New Labour government elected in 1997. Meanwhile, Unionists are generally portrayed as languishing within the confines of their disempowered 'internal' context of Northern Ireland, with few political allies save for a handful of right-wing Tory MPs, and clinging to the hope of exercising political influence in times of slim parliamentary majorities. Such a juxtaposition gives the impression of a basic asymmetry in the political effectiveness of Unionist and SDLP political élites (Dixon, 1995, pp. 498–501).

Mark Durkan claims that the aims of the SDLP are not those of modern nationalists but are rooted in a desire to adapt to changing circumstances by, first of all, attempting to initiate a self-reflexivity among Nationalists, as well as attempting to challenge the preconceptions of Unionists:

> We as a party are engaged in the business of leadership. We are not out simply to challenge Unionists, we have always made a point of challenging Nationalists as well and we have always challenged traditional nationalist assumptions. We were the first party to articulate the consent principle. It's interesting that for many years Unionists rejected the consent principle as code for coercion. Now they are talking about consent, in fact, they are trying to lecture us on the consent principle, asking us do we believe in it. I hope that the same thing happens with another term that has often been associated with the SDLP – the notion of an agreed Ireland – where we have emphasized the need for an agreement. It's interesting that Sinn Féin are now using that term. Again, for many years they completely discounted this, as far as they were concerned agreed Ireland was code for agreed partition rather than united Ireland, whereas, for Unionists, agreed Ireland was code for united Ireland. Its interesting that some Unionists, not least Reg Empey, have started to try and take up the agreed Ireland term and tease it out. So, yes we have been trying to educate Nationalists and we are also trying to engage Unionists in that sense because the reality is that there is no point in saying 'let's set the clock back, we want to deal with Ireland as one single entity' – you just can't simply do that. We have to start from where we are and that means we are working on the basis of deep divisions that are there.

John Hume has been widely accredited with influencing the thinking of the London and Dublin governments in the Anglo-Irish Agreement (1985), the Downing Street Declaration (1993), and the

Framework Documents (1995) (Dixon, 1995, pp. 499–500). Hume is also adjudged to have played a pivotal role, through the Hume-Adams accord, in persuading the Republican leadership to call a cessation to its campaign of violent conflict in 1994 (Coogan, 1995, pp. 363–5; Bew, 1995, p. 33). Consequently, he has been pronounced the architect of the peace and political processes in Northern Ireland (*The Independent*, 27 June 1998).

Modern Politicization of Identity

Mark Durkan stresses the natural complexity of identity and the perpetual state of flux intrinsic to it when drawing attention to the paradox of the homogenization that was necessary for political identity in the modern era:

> Identity is an onion with a lot of different skins on it. Unfortunately, people have tried to forge one badge, one trade-mark identity in and around the nation-state as though that is the only identity. Generally, when people have tried to do that they have also tried to write in certain political values into that notion of identity. Looking at Thatcher's Bruges speech from a few years ago it was interesting that while she was saying that Britain needed to be back a bit from Europe and have its own rights as a nation-state, and she was trying to preserve the traits of the British identity, in a sense what she was offering as the traits of the British identity was simply the Thatcherite agenda.

There is also a recognition of the homogenizing agenda of De Valera in his attempt to promote a Catholic and Gaelic version of Irishness in the 1937 constitution: 'You see that right through, whether it's in terms of even the Irish constitution of 1937 where again identity was being used as a badge for certain political values.' Durkan is comfortable with the natural complexity and difference that is intrinsic to identity and is disdainful of attempts to create a uniform identity: 'I have always been very distrustful of single theme national identities because I think identity is a much more complex thing.'

In many ways, Durkan's emphasis on the multi-layered nature of identity and its affiliation with nation, region and even Europe is no less politicized than the modern homogenous political identity of De Valera or Thatcher. However, the identity that he describes is consciously multi-layered, self-determining and fluid, reflecting the postmodern concerns of difference and complexity. He subscribes to the view that identity is what Fionnuala O'Connor has called 'a slippery idea' (O'Connor 1993, p. 3). For him, the only certainty is that the northern Nationalist identity is changing. The territorial resource no longer enjoys pre-eminence and a greater appreciation by northern Nationalists of their own identity and the identity of others has been cultivated:

> In many ways, the thing we have got to remember too is that identity is something that grows and changes anyway. People discover and take on new aspects of identity. People also grow out of previous expressions of their identity. I think that increasingly, Irish Nationalists are doing that throughout the island and particularly in the North. I don't think that people are interested purely in the territorial issue, people do have a more sophisticated interpretation of identity. They have a more sophisticated appreciation of other peoples' identity so long as it's not shoved down their throat, as long as it's not a question of one identity supposedly having primacy over another.

This interpretation is not incompatible with the insistence that the political context of Northern Ireland alone is an inappropriate one for the representation of northern Irish Nationalist identities:

> While more Catholics now do have a better appreciation of the Unionist and British identity and the validity of that, what people aren't prepared to do is say we'll accept Northern Ireland arrangements that are made in the image of the Unionist identity, but we can be nationalists-on-licence and express ourselves as nationalists somehow on licence. That would be no more acceptable to northern Nationalists than a thirty-two county dispensation, offering Unionists the same, would be to them.

The failure of the modern state to represent the interests of northern Irish Nationalist identities has alienated the SDLP from its design. Mark Durkan reasons that this is because the homogenization of identity required by the modern state ensured that the identity of the Northern Ireland state was Ulster Protestant and the identity of the Southern Irish state was Catholic and Gaelic. According to Durkan, the diversity of identity that has survived modern attempts at homogenization on the island of Ireland requires structures of state that are not so rigidly defined.

The Territorial Resource of Nationalist Identities Represented by the SDLP

John Hume believes that the modern context of the territorial resource of northern Irish Nationalist identities has been transcended:

> The nation-state is based on two problematic concepts, territory and the feelings of superiority of one people over another. In Ireland, the nationalist mindset was a territorial mindset. But we have changed. Our position now is that people have been divided, not a territory. We need change to heal that division (in *The Independent*, 28 April 1995).

However, territory has been central to the conflict since the creation of two modern states on the island of Ireland in 1921. Mark Durkan advances the case for the sublimation or relocation of the territorial resource of northern Nationalist identities:

> Economists tell you that with a private good there are scarce resources, therefore there is competition, there are prices for it. With private goods some people are satisfied and others are left unsatisfied and left without ownership. What distinguishes a public good from a private good, however, is non-rivalry and non-exclusiveness. One person's sense of enjoyment of, or access to a public good doesn't deny or diminish anybody else's. So I think if we start to approach the question of identity and political allegiance from that basis and that it's not a matter of 'this place belongs to us and not to you', its a matter of 'we both belong to this place' regardless of what its called, that's one step. Also, within the Irish Nationalist tradition anyway people at certain levels look at things other than territory. Certainly, myself, as an Irish Nationalist, have never taken my politics from a map. It's not how I read a map that tells me I'm an Irish Nationalist nor would I ever express my politics in a flag. If you consider the rich sense of Irishness that people living in Ireland and people of Irish descent living away from Ireland attach to the whole Irish Diaspora across the world we have this sense of a nation that is not confined to the territory of the island. We can have that strong sense of nationhood extending beyond the territory. I don't see why we should pursue political aspirations here that are simply bound up in territory and nothing else.

Mark Durkan is blunt about the hopelessness of continuing to apply nationalism, set in a modern mode, to the contemporary political problem of Northern Ireland:

> Crude nationalism isn't going to solve those divisions, proprietorialism isn't going to solve it nor is majoritarianism – neither majoritarianism in a Northern Ireland setting or majoritarianism in an All-Ireland setting. This idea of 'majority condition equals ownership' we would completely reject.

> Just as we have criticized Unionists for taking that approach, 'majority equals ownership' as far as Northern Ireland is concerned, so too we would say to Nationalists in the All-Ireland context. We are dealing essentially with two minorities who have very much the same fear of being trapped and abandoned as the ultimate minority. In everything we are proposing for ourselves we have to try to put ourselves in the position of the others and think, 'well if this was in the context of their choosing would we accept what they are proposing or what they are offering'. That was put very well at the Forum for Peace and Reconciliation [in Dublin] by the Presbyterian Church when they took up something that I have used a few times – the basic issue of suggesting that people should read 'parity of esteem' as meaning 'do unto others as they would do unto you' and each think of themselves through unto the other minority's position. I hope we have been leading and re-shaping Nationalist opinion so that it's graduated from more than just a territorial mind-set of 'this is our land and you have no right to take part of it from us'.

He also spells out the role that the European Union has played thus far in terms of deflating territorialism by creating a neutral arena in which the relationship between the UK and the Republic of Ireland improved, engendering an atmosphere of co-operation where there had been antagonism:

> The first benefit in terms of the European process has been by actually co-housing both the British and Irish states, therefore, British and Irish identities are under a new umbrella. I think that has helped in some ways to ease the permanent tension between the two identities. I think that there is less rivalry between the two identities. That allows people to start expressing their identity simply according to its own integrity rather than as something that is counter to the other identity. If people are

allowed the privilege of their own identity in its own terms rather than in oppositionist terms to some other identity, that is certainly helpful.

Durkan applies the 'postmodernism of resistance' concepts of interdependence and alliance-formation in Europe to identity in Northern Ireland suggesting that there is a dynamic for conflict resolution through an emphasis on the convergence of interest and identity:

> The European process has also created a different psychological framework where we are looking to coincidence of interest as a basis for creating new arrangements and institutions to which, regardless of our diverse identity, we can all give allegiance. I think that developing a linkage between interest and identity, where they are actually intersecting, is important and is part of the learning curve that people from the two nationalisms in Northern Ireland can go through – that there are ways of defining and pursuing common interests without surrendering your distinctive identities. Europe has taught us that lesson at one level. It is always harder to translate those things from the more macro-level to the more micro-level but that is part of what we have to do.

Yet the frequent use of the phrase 'the right of the Irish people to self-determination' in the Hume-Adams communiqués of the 1990s is suggestive of the persistence of a Nationalist territorial mindset and the denial of the separateness of Ulster Unionist identities and their desire to be British. Denis Haughey suggests that this usage is understandable because it was an integral part in the first step of a practical attempt at achieving consensus. John Hume judged that if a political process was to stand any chance of success a cessation of violence was required. The objective of his protracted dialogue with Gerry Adams was to end IRA violence and bring Republicans into the political process:

> The work of politicians is solving problems, creating consensus, developing understandings which accommodate those who are wedded to particular views of the world. So what John Hume tried to do in his talks with Gerry Adams was to create a bridge between the old-fashioned notion of Irish national self-determination and modern notions of democratic consent. What John Hume was saying to Republicans was that 'you have always taken

the view that the future of Ireland can only be determined by the Irish nation, that is, the people who live on this island. However, the first problem we have got to face is that they are deeply divided about how they work out their future'. In circumstances where a society is deeply divided we have always held that simple majority-rule doesn't work. What you have got to do is create new agreements, new understandings that win everybody's allegiance. The first Hume-Adams statement is a masterpiece which said the people who live on this island have the indefeasible right to determine their own future. The problem is that they are divided about how to do that. If there is going to be effective national self-determination that means that we have to create a set of structures that have the allegiance of all traditions. What the Republicans were accepting when they signed up to that was that there cannot be Irish unity unless the Unionists agree. That was a quantum leap for Republicans but it was important for Hume to construct it in language that they could accommodate rather than saying to them, 'you can't have Irish unity without Unionist consent' which they could not swallow. It was important for Hume to say: 'Yes I agree with you, the people on this island have a right to national self-determination but the problem is that they are divided, we have to have effective national self-determination, we have to have an agreement that wins the allegiance and agreement and support of all sections of the Irish people' – and Adams signed. That was the break between the Provo past and the democratic politics of consent.

The evocation of the principle of consent by the SDLP, which dictates that the agreement of both Unionists and Nationalists is required before a democratic structure of state is established for the region, can be interpreted as representing a move whereby democracy is no longer defined by 'territory' but by 'community' – a shift from a code defined by modernity to one defined by a recognition of difference, which is symptomatic of postmodernity. Of course, the emphasis of Ulster Unionists on the territorial resource of their identities presents a major problem for the inclusive adoption of this shift in interpretation. However, SDLP interviewees believe that the EU platform provides a first step in establishing 'community' as the determining factor in deciding a future structure of government for Northern Ireland because it has engendered co-operation between the British and Irish governments. Mark

Durkan argues that European integration enhances this process further by its focus on the pursuit of overlapping interests in the EU.

The Economic Resource of Nationalist Identities Represented by the SDLP

That Northern Ireland has had to rely on substantial subvention from the British exchequer (accounting for approximately one third of Northern Ireland's Gross Domestic Product) and has consequently developed a dependency culture is not regarded as a factor detracting from the unionist case, but is cited by Ulster Unionists as the chief economic attraction of the constitutional status quo. However, as John Bradley of the Irish Economic and Social Research Institute, has pointed out:

> a problem with this kind of static analysis is that it fails utterly to take on board the fact that an island political settlement would be likely to release major economic forces that would work towards the regeneration of private sector activity in the north, and permit north-south synergies to emerge as businesses benefited from a larger truly single market of 5.5 million consumers (Bradley, 1995, p. 28).

Indeed, Anderson and Goodwin argue that the UK government would be likely to continue subvention because of their responsibility to Unionists; their moral obligation to facilitate post-conflict reconstruction; and their own self-interest dictating that a gradual reduction in subvention would be possible should reconstruction take hold (Anderson and Goodman, 1994, p. 16).

Unionists perceive such analysis to be nakedly irredentist. Mark Durkan focuses on the economic resource of northern Nationalist identities to argue that the Unionist perception of northern Irish Nationalist identities is simplistic:

> Obviously, for northern Nationalists, there are different layers to identity – even the term 'northern Nationalist' shows that there is something distinctive. In terms of their economic interest, the issue arises in terms of their circumstances in the North as opposed to what it would be if they were in a thirty-two county version of the South, but then, the corollary of that too is the picture of disadvantage and even discrimination that there is for

northern Nationalists in the North itself. There you get again certain economic sensitivities and interests either galvanising the notion of identity or qualifying certain expressions of identity or qualifying the immediacy of certain aspirations that might be pursued as a result of the sense of identity. So I certainly don't take any of these issues as being simple and straight-forward, I think there is a complex relationship between interest and identity.

Undoubtedly, northern Nationalists are more receptive than Ulster Unionists to the extraterritorial context. John Hume has declared that such pre-occupation with the union of Great Britain and Northern Ireland is becoming abstract from reality because European union is gaining in economic and political relevancy (O'Connor, 1993, p. 91). Similarly, Denis Haughey argues that in the present and future reality of the European Union, the defining of the economic unit in terms of the modern national state is becoming outmoded. For him, the process of redefining in terms of the regions of Europe is required for economic advancement:

> There are many European issues for which Ireland as an island is treated as one region, for instance, when the EFTA countries joined the European Union they had to contribute to a fund for greater cohesion and that fund was allocated to Ireland as a region.[4] Another low level example is that the sheep meat regime in Ireland is one regime. The whole area of agriculture is an area where, naturally, Ireland should be one region and where there should be a single regime applying North and South. It makes absolute common sense that that should be so. Now that gives rise to one or two problems as to how that region represents itself in the Council of Ministers but those are not problems that cannot be overcome with goodwill between the British and Irish governments.

It is difficult to distinguish the *bona fides* of a postmodern Europeanist perspective among Nationalist political elites when they cite the economic benefits of composing a 'Region of Ireland' for representation in the European Union.[5] Liberal Unionists conceded that a joint approach may indeed have extracted additional funding (Cadogan Group, 1992, p. 17) but the territorial resource of the Unionist identity, predicated as it is on the condition of modernity, begins to sound warning bells when it comes to the suggestion that a representation should be made under the banner 'the

Island of Ireland'. However, it is likely that representation by an 'Island of Ireland' delegation would result in the Northern region's economic interests being served in a more effective manner in the EU, particularly with the loss of Objective One status after 1999. Such a measure would then strengthen the position of the European Union as a catalyst for some realignment of the economic resource of northern Irish Nationalist identities and perhaps even, Ulster Unionist identities.

The economic resource of northern Nationalist identities has been an object of derision for many Ulster Unionist politicians who traditionally maintained that such a resource was overridden by the territorialism of modern Irish nationalism that demanded the formation of an all-Ireland state. A more complex picture emerges in the SDLP analysis. Mark Durkan acknowledges that while many northern Nationalists have suffered from discrimination and disadvantage because of their identity in Northern Ireland, many others have fared better than they might have done in a thirty-two county Irish Republic. He is aware of the complexity of the impact that has had on the economic resource of northern Nationalist identity and, consequently, the varying degrees of appetite for radical change in the structure of government for the region among those who share that identity. Meanwhile, looking to the future, Denis Haughey is keen to highlight the continuing incursions made by the EU on the economic life of Northern Ireland. He believes that an arrangement can be found that can maximize the economic benefits for all identities on the island.

SDLP Perceptions of the Implications of European Integration for Unionist Identities

It is an understatement to say that the process of European integration is problematic for Ulster Unionists. It is a process that erodes the political authority of the UK centre and has obvious implications for Ulster Unionist identities that define themselves in terms of their citizenship of the modern state of the United Kingdom of Great Britain and Northern Ireland. However, Ulster Unionists have a strong ethnic character that can be distinguished from the Irish nation. It is, therefore, important to establish whether or not the SDLP recognize that the ethnic Ulster identity of Ulster Unionists does actually require institutional expression that cannot be found in any All-Ireland nation-state formation. Mark Durkan says:

Firstly, it is up to people to define their own identity and we are quite happy with whatever identity people define themselves as. We have been accused in the past, for instance, of trying to tell Unionists that they are Irish and that is a mistake that many Irish nationalists have made[6] – this whole idea that Unionists are just some kind of political mutants who will revert to their true type once they are no longer exposed to some sort of harmful British rays, we don't accept that. People are whatever identity they choose and feel themselves to be. We fully respect that and just as we would say that the Irish Nationalist identity can't be accommodated simply within a purely internal Northern Ireland context, Nationalists have to face the issue as to whether or not the Unionist and British identity in Ireland can be accommodated in a purely internal All-Ireland context. What goes for one, goes for the other. Certainly, as I would see it, we have to tailor arrangements to harness the identity of both traditions.

John Hume and Gerry Adams, in one of their public joint statements, when they talked about any new peaceful and democratic accord here, they said it would be achievable and viable only if it could earn and enjoy the allegiance of all traditions. That means, if Nationalists agree with that then they have to look at what requirements follow from that. Allegiance is something you can't give to something you don't regard as legitimate according to your own particular ethos. So, Unionists, therefore, can't give their allegiance to something which hasn't been legitimized in terms of their own particular vernacular and that is that it has to be validated by the majority of the people in Northern Ireland. That is something we have to face. But equally, Nationalists can't give their allegiance to that which hasn't been legitimized in terms of their tradition either, that is, could have been validated by the majority of people on the island of Ireland as a whole. It is that issue, in terms of dual legitimacy, do we accept the legitimacy of both traditions? If we do, what follows from that? If we accept that parity of esteem has to extend to parity of allegiance then that brings us into the issue – are we prepared then to accept that parity of allegiance means that each sense and source of legitimacy has to be respected and indeed recruited to create and validate political structures?

Denis Haughey recognizes that the EU presents a special challenge for Ulster Unionist identities but suggests that there may be a difference in approach to integration between Unionist politicians and the identities that they represent:

Twenty years ago, when the issue of membership of the EU was alive, being discussed and we had a referendum on it, I think Unionists still conceded the notion that the British could be persuaded to get out of the Community. Now, I think the vast majority of Unionists believe that they cannot get out of the Community. Gradually and slowly I think they are accommodating themselves to that. I think the Unionist community generally are more relaxed about being part of Europe. I think there is evidence that the Unionist community is more prepared to contemplate change and accommodation than those active in Unionist politics would appear to be. I believe myself that there is some reason to think that there is an ethos within Unionist political structures that is notably different from the ethos within the Unionist community as a whole. Those who have been active in Unionist politics inherit an ethos from those who went before them, an ethos which is impatient at not having power. Over the last twenty-five years the Unionist community has become more attuned to the fact that they are never going to exercise exclusive power again and are more prepared to contemplate ways and means of getting power back under the condition that it is shared. But you still have people active in politics who grew up in political families and political circles where power was their natural inheritance and are impatient that they cannot have it.

The implication, of course, is that in terms of a political settlement, it might be advantageous for Unionists to witness a 'pooling of sovereignty' at the supranational level because then they may change from seeing things in absolute terms, Haughey agrees:

The Irish and British governments are co-operating within Europe and have now clearly decided that their own good relations are far more important than anything that goes on in Northern Ireland. The EU meetings also brought closer co-operation between the British and Irish governments on the Northern Ireland problem and that is set to continue. Unionists are beginning to absorb that into their thinking. Ten years ago, at the time of the Anglo-Irish Agreement, Unionists became perplexed at the notion that the Southern Irish government would make representations to the British government or that the British government might consult the Irish government about anything. That was institutionalized in the Anglo-Irish Agreement. Now Unionists talk quite commonly about the two governments need to do this, they need to do that etc. – they talk in terms of the two governments. So gradually people absorb things into their thinking and it becomes part of the way they see the world.

Such pragmatism is certainly not shared by the Unionist identities represented by the DUP. Their approach is defined by religious and political fundamentalism where compromise equals surrender. Haughey does not see them as a major obstacle on the road to political accommodation:

> You will find extremists in every society and the old notions of tribal loyalties with all of their add-ons of cultural manifestation will exist for a long time. However, what I'm talking about is trends and the way in which the majority of people come around to thinking over a long period of time. That doesn't mean that all of these things will disappear, what it means is that the great majority of people will come around, gradually, to a broad point of view of things. I imagine that in a hundred years' time there will still be Orange lodges, marches etc. but it will the last vestiges of old things that are dying out rather than a vital part of the political idiom of our society. There are also likely to be Ruairí Ó'Brádaighs[7] about saying that nothing is going to be right until we get the British out.

Mark Durkan emphasizes the concept of 'parity of esteem' when examining the SDLP's attitude to Ulster Unionists. He suggests that an insistence by northern Nationalists that an internal Northern Ireland arrangement is inappropriate for the accommodation of the diversity of identity in Northern Ireland should be weighed against the rejection of an all-Ireland state by the Ulster Unionists. For Durkan, those who preach parity of esteem must take account of the diversity of political allegiances when constructing a political model that seeks to accommodate all.

Denis Haughey perceives a divergence in the attitudes of the Unionist community and Unionist political leaders towards European integration. He believes that the Unionist community's perceived openness to change and accommodation will eventually be adopted by the Unionist leadership, particularly as they witness the continued transfer of power to the EU on major issues of government. In that environment, 'parity of esteem' and 'parity of allegiance' will be easier principles to establish.

European Integration and the Cultural Resource of Identity

Should European integrationist ideals be realized, Denis Haughey believes that national identity will continue in a more personalized and cultural form, free from the shackles of its territorial and economic resources:

> Identity, over a period of time, will become much more to do with the language that you speak, the cultural idiom that you are part of rather than the state to which you belong. In a multicultural Europe, therefore, culture becomes, I think, over the next hundred years, divorced from politics and identity becomes divorced from politics. You have the developing reality of a huge political block which will increasingly centralize certain aspects of its power in order to deal with the great economic issues, defence etc. and the whole question of cultural identity then becomes divorced from all of that because people are not European in the sense that there is no European language, there is no single European culture and therefore cultural identity, linguistic identity etc. becomes a much more informal thing related to the community in which we live.

Haughey sees any future political focus for identity as being necessarily European and, therefore, postnationalist:

> I see people conceiving of themselves, in a political sense, as European, and having a certain loyalty to that. But they will be no less Irish for that, or German or Basque etc. The political identity they will increasingly have is European and the identities which are now political will become much more cultural. Cultural manifestations of identity will become no less strong because the political allegiance which creates a separate dimension of identity is shifted from the nation-state to a European superstate.

There would appear to be some contradiction between this utopian vision of depoliticized communal identity and the increased empowerment of regional and local levels. Ironically, the divorce of identity from politics is resonant with the discourse of right-leaning postmodernists who anticipate the eventual extinction of the state in the lives of individuals. In such terms, it sits uneasily alongside the party's 'Europe of the Regions' thesis and commitment to the democratic representation of communities. It does, however, underline the radical nature of SDLP thinking in the conservative landscape of Northern Ireland politics.

7 Dialogue with Sinn Féin

INTRODUCTION

The current manifestation of Sinn Féin (formerly known as Provisional Sinn Féin) dates to a split in the Republican movement during the 1970 Sinn Féin Ard Fheis (annual conference) on the issue of dropping a policy of not recognizing the parliaments in Dublin and Belfast. Those in favour of recognition became Official Sinn Féin (forerunners to the Workers' Party and Democratic Left) and developed a Marxist approach to politics. Those who were against recognition formed Provisional Sinn Féin and concentrated on their opposition to British jurisdiction in 'the six counties' (Flackes and Elliott 1994, p. 284). It is this (Provisional) Sinn Féin that is commonly regarded to be the political associate of the current manifestation of the IRA.

Gerry Adams replaced Ruairí Ó'Brádaigh as President of (Provisional) Sinn Féin in 1983, the year in which he also became an MP. As Vice-President, Adams had already begun moving the party towards political participation. In the first election contested by Sinn Féin in Northern Ireland, the 1982 Northern Ireland Assembly election, the party gained 10.1 per cent of the votes cast. The figure fluctuated little thereafter, with the 1992 Westminster General election resulting in Sinn Féin securing 10.0 per cent of the vote and the 1993 District Council elections resulting in the party receiving 12.4 per cent of the votes cast. In the 1994 election to the European Parliament Sinn Féin received 9.9 per cent of the vote (Flackes and Elliott, 1994; *Irish Political Studies*, 1995). However, in the 1996 Northern Ireland Forum election and the 1997 General Election the vote for Sinn Féin increased to 15.47 per cent and 16.1 per cent respectively (*Irish News*, 3 May 1997).

Sinn Féin held the first in a series of talks with the SDLP in January 1988. Despite the setbacks resulting from initial disagreements and the strident criticism directed at the SDLP for entering into those talks, the line of communication was maintained. It eventually produced an agreed Hume-Adams 'peace process', announced on 25 September 1993. This led to Unionist accusations that a pan-Nationalist front had been formed by Adams and Hume, to be joined by the then Taoiseach Albert Reynolds and the Irish-American lobby in the wake of the 1994 IRA cease-fire. Whatever the nature of the relationship between Sinn Féin and the SDLP may be, the use of the term 'pan-Nationalist front' to denote that relationship deserves critical comment. On the face of it, the term suggests that the parties have similar nationalist aspirations. However, despite the revisionism of Gerry Adams after 1988, Sinn Féin still displays modern hegemonic nationalist tendencies and is strongly anti-European integrationist in outlook. In contrast, the SDLP has developed and maintained a strong anti-hegemonic, pro-European integrationist narrative that is indicative of a liberal-nationalist inclination in its political philosophy.

SINN FÉIN PERCEPTIONS OF STRUCTURAL CHANGE

> The implementation of the Single European Act and the Maastricht Treaty have had profound implications for economic, political and social life in Ireland. Although the consolidation of the European superstate has not proceeded entirely smoothly, the Single European Act and Maastricht have fundamentally altered Ireland's relationship with the other states in the EU (Sinn Féin, 1994b).

Mitchel McLaughlin, Sinn Féin National Chairman, acknowledges the development of the EU as an important political force in Ireland:

> I do think that the increasing dominance of the social, economic and political reality of the European Union is affecting Ireland, North and South, in a very dramatic way. Public opinion in Ireland, despite Sinn Féin's reservations regarding the capitalist ethos of the EU, is very strongly pro-European Union. So, I think politics will continue to develop in that context and I think that has an impact on this issue of conflict resolution and agreement on future political structures (interview with the author).

However, he remains unconvinced that the process of European integration will yield tangible results in terms of fundamentally restructuring the state system in Europe:

> I think that it is more in the way of a political aspiration – there are problems there already. The tensions, particularly between the Eastern European community (both as a market and as a

client and as a potential for economic development) and developed Western Europe is, in fact, the biggest threat to the whole subsidiarity theory. It is very doubtful, in my view, that it will survive intact. It was an idea that was good in its time but already late in its time because I think it was overtaken by the collapse of the Soviet Union.

Francie Molloy, a Sinn Féin Councillor, believes that the EU is beginning to make some impact at local level:

It hasn't had a big effect here in this Council [Dungannon District Council] although it is starting to develop. Up until this last while, with the Unionist position of not being prepared to consider cross-border initiatives, it has curtailed the involvement of Dungannon Council in the European structural funds and initiatives. It is starting to develop, the Council has a Development Officer who is now starting to bring about cross-border regionals. So, in that way, the EU is starting to have more influence (interview with the author).

DETERMINING STRUCTURAL PARAMETERS FOR NORTHERN IRELAND

The All-Ireland Nation-State Context

Apart from the problems caused by structural change for the political philosophy of Sinn Féin, the commitment of the party to pursuing the objective of establishing a modern state for the island of Ireland faces a more immediate and endemic problem – that of the complete opposition of Ulster Unionists to such a structure of state. As a result of the Hume-Adams dialogue that objective has been qualified to a recognition of the need to secure the consent of Ulster Unionists to the form such a structure of state would take. Francie Molloy argues that the failure of Northern Ireland as a political entity means that Unionists have to make the compromises necessary for a political settlement:

You can't impose a solution. We have had a situation where the six-county partitionist state has been imposed on the Nationalists of the six counties for the last seventy-odd years and that hasn't worked. We see also that there is no benefit in imposing an All-Ireland solution onto the Unionists either. So we have to work towards agreement. This is why, within the Hume-Adams document, it is clear that we want the consent of Unionists with regard to how we build a new Ireland and new all-Ireland structures.

He uses the old Republican antipathy towards some Southern political parties, categorizing them as 'pro-British', in an attempt to attract Ulster Unionists to the possibilities for alliances in an All-Ireland structure of government:

> We also think that we can persuade Unionists that within an All-Ireland context they wouldn't simply be as they see themselves – a minority – a Protestant community isolated in Ireland. We would point out that their Unionism or pro-Britishness, when aligned with the pro-British elements in the South at the moment – the Fine Gael's etc. that are already there – would mean they would be a very powerful voice within Ireland. They wouldn't be a minority – it would be in the region of a fifty/fifty basis. So the realignment of Irish politics is what I think we have to persuade Unionists of and that they can have a major part to play in new structures instead of being a small minority of thirteen or fourteen votes in Westminster.

Francie Molloy rejects a form of joint authority as the basis for a long-term settlement even though political analysts of the modern state and Northern Ireland endorse it as a viable option for settlement (Dent, 1988; O'Leary *et al.*, 1993). It is possible to interpret developments in British and Irish government policy on Northern Ireland, represented by the Downing Street Declaration (1993) and the Framework Documents (1995), as developments leading to some form of joint authority that includes local participation. Indeed, within a modern framework it is plausible to suggest that some form of joint authority would be a logical development to accommodate two sets of communal identities that have been defined by two modern states. Francie Molloy is not convinced by that argument:

> The idea of joint authority only prolongs the day for a solution. You already have had what Michael Collins talked about – the stepping stone. The next step was never taken. Joint authority would again just be prolonging the inevitable. What we say is you set in motion the British disconnection and then you start in

motion the Unionist participation within the whole of Ireland. Now, we accept that there will be a transition period needed, that you may have to have a Stormont assembly but that eventually people in the North will say 'well there is no purpose in having two parliaments', or you might have four assemblies on the federal basis and the people will say it's either good or bad. Our view is that until you actually get the British to say 'we're out of the equation' then Unionists won't start thinking along new lines.

The saying within older Republicans was that the Unionists would fight to the last British soldier and that they won't change until the last British soldier is away. I think that is still very relevant. A number of Unionist politicians will say 'well, we'll hold on for as long as possible' which is defeatist in one sense but it also prolongs the day of the inevitable and that is why I think we have to get away from the 'joint authority' idea towards building a new Ireland and new structures within Ireland with maximum support within the Unionist community which actually allows them to play a full part within Ireland.

The North-South structures proposed in the Framework Documents (1995) were interpreted as part of a transitory process leading to an All-Ireland state by Mitchel McLaughlin and, because of that, welcomed by him:

What we are saying is that if we have a process that is in itself organic and dynamic and we are identifying agreed objectives then we are perfectly prepared to work with transition processes that actually bring us from this position of a failed political system to one that may be a long way short of our own ultimate objectives but which actually represents a viable process of transition. The Government of South Africa is called the government of transition – the government of national agreement – there is nothing wrong with that and we certainly have publicly indicated that we believe that we are all faced with such a process and that it is a perfectly reasonable way out of the present political impasse.

Through their support for negotiation and a 'period of transition' Sinn Féin interviewees reflect a change in the political strategy of the party from one based on revolutionary struggle, informed by territorial majoritarianism, to a piecemeal approach that seeks to incorporate the concepts of accommodation and consent. There is some recognition of the need for Unionist consent to the form of new structures. However, Sinn Féin interviewees do not believe that consent can be translated into a Unionist veto on constitutional change. The 'Propositions on Heads of Agreement' document (1998) was rejected by Sinn Féin because it was perceived to support a Unionist veto on constitutional change (*Guardian*, 19 January 1998). However, the party eventually signed the Multi-Party Agreement (1998). A unitary state for the island of Ireland remains the primary objective of the party but the development of a purposefully vague 'period of transition' dialectic by Sinn Féin signals an attempt by the party at adopting a more flexible political strategy.

The Extraterritorial Context

The title of the Sinn Féin manifesto for the 1984 European Election, 'One Ireland, One People – The Only Alternative', indicates the negligible impact of the EU extraterritorial context on the Irish Nationalist identity represented by the party. A fundamental cornerstone for political conflict in Northern Ireland has been the existence of two modern states on the island of Ireland after 1921. Through the legacy of discrimination in Northern Ireland, northern Irish Nationalists have been conditioned into perceiving Northern Ireland structures as being hostile to their Nationalist identity. On the other hand, Ulster Unionists perceive the Irish state as being hostile to their ethnic identity and see their economic and cultural interests being best catered for in the context of the UK. It is conceivable that a system of EU multi-level governance and a European context for citizenship offers the potential to diffuse the political volatility of a future structure of government for Northern Ireland. However, Mitchel McLaughlin disagrees. He questions the self-professed Britishness of Ulster Unionists and believes that the anti-democratic nature of partition at the beginning of Ireland's modern political era needs to be addressed before considering the postmodern context:

> What is wrong with that theory is, first of all, it attempts to obscure or deny that the people who are born on this island are Irish people. But that is not the most serious problem, the most serious problem is actually built into the very partition of this

country, the sectarian head-count that set up the North. The fact is that the demographic trends are clearly pointing, at some stage in the indeterminate future, to a majority of those who are of the nationalist opinion. So, the decision that your formula would attempt to fudge would still have to be made. In my view the difficulty is that as we approach a levelling out of the population ratios – and we are approaching it – as you approach that you raise the fear and tensions unless in fact we approach such a point on the basis of pre-determined political structures and agreements. This is why we believe that this is the opportunity, this is the time to put down those structures that will evolve, that will be dynamic enough to accommodate the differences that are undoubtedly there, but we have to bridge them.

For Mitchel McLaughlin, movement towards an integrated EU merely perpetuates the modern problem of Northern Ireland:

Europe, by institutionalizing those divisions and by assuming this supranational perspective simply would be presiding over what I believe would be a heightening of tension as the day approaches. If you look at the constitutional guarantees that are so often referred to and depended upon by the Unionist community they are conditional precisely because there is a recognition that there will come a day[1] . . . the business of when it will happen is actually a distraction. Whether it is ten, twenty-five or even fifty years away, the fact of the matter of it coming is what gives the whole exercise the volatility that you referred to and everybody knows that.

Sinn Féin has attempted to use the fact of the developing supranational polity of the EU to argue for an end to partition. At the same time, however, the process of integration itself poses problems for the Sinn Féin objective of autonomous government for the island of Ireland. Mitchel McLaughlin denies that there is a contradiction between using the EU integrationist argument in the case against the partition of the island and maintaining the objective of an All-Ireland nation-state:

No, it is not a contradiction. In the first place the whole logic of socio-economic harmonization throughout Europe actually enhances the logic of All-Ireland socio-economic political structures. It does not mark out Sinn Féin's view on what we would like to see as an exercise of self-determination by the Irish people which is that they would either resist Euro-centralism or if they couldn't resist it that they would actually detach themselves from it.

Nevertheless, an ambivalent approach to the EU has been adopted by Sinn Féin representing a movement away from the openly hostile approach of the party on display in its 1984 European manifesto. The explanation for the shift lies in the dictates of an over-riding objective, according to the political commentator, Eamonn McCann:

> ... the European Community has been regularly portrayed in Republican statements and publications as, literally, the most dangerously evil institution on earth from the Irish nationalist point of view, intent on destroying the idea of nationhood in Europe forever, and a deadly, specific and imminent threat to Irish nationhood in particular. All this was dropped without so much as a by-your-leave from the membership, and replaced with a public proposal that the EC might intervene to help us out in our difficulties. And nobody has resigned in protest, or called on anybody else to resign. Remarkable.
>
> Or maybe not, if we consider that the general purpose of the Republican movement is to free nationalists from British rule, everything else being tactical' (McCann, 1993, p. 40).

For Mitchel McLaughlin, the concept of self-determination, exercised in the national context, forms the bedrock of his argument. However, he makes an important distinction between 'the Irish people' conducting self-determination through an autonomous national government and 'the Irish people' conducting self-determination through the negotiation of their relationships with other political entities:

> We recognize that Ireland, as a nation-state, has to have a negotiated relationship with other political entities, with other trading partners, with other nations. We are not talking about isolation and ignoring the rest of the world but we believe the Irish people should exercise self-determination in their own interest, in the negotiation of those relationships.

Exercising self-determination in the negotiation of extraterritorial relationships would appear to be distinct from acquiring nation-state autonomy. The implication is that the pooling of such authority in EU institutions may not be incompatible with the right of the Irish people to self-determination, so long as the people of the island act together in permitting that power to be transferred.

STRUCTURAL CHANGE AND NATIONALIST IDENTITIES REPRESENTED BY SINN FÉIN

Adapting to a Postmodern Context?

When it comes to the question of the relationship between northern Irish Nationalist identities and the evolving state-system within the European Union, Sinn Féin interviewees insist that this postmodern context should not be addressed until the modern problem of the partition of Ireland has been resolved. Mitchel McLaughlin dismisses the suggestion that it is incumbent upon Irish Nationalists to align their identity to developing structures of power in order to secure their identity and not wait around hoping that the problem of modern statehood in Ireland will be resolved:

> No, I would not concede it at all. The way it works at the moment, I would be very foolish to concede it. That is not to say that you couldn't develop relationships that are actually based on mutual respect for the rights of peoples to exist, to continue to exist, and to exercise self-determination. That would be a very democratic relationship and it might indeed be the future that would allow, within the umbrella of the European union of nations, if you like, different types of social and economic systems to co-exist.

He stresses the willingness of the party to participate in EU alliances aimed at influencing the direction of EU policy:

> I believe that the Irish people have always been European, have always been prepared to look outward, have always been conscious of the Diaspora, have always been conscious of the effect (even within their own society) of cultural and political colonialization. There are none of us pure Irish in any way and I don't think that Irish people are afraid of describing themselves as European or having been exposed to all of those external influences or of indeed profiting from them. So, the question is valid only if you are actually assuming that Sinn Féin is looking for an Ireland for the Irish and that we are going to be Euro-sceptical and that we are going to go into protectionism and

isolationism – that is not my view of the future. What I would see, for example, even in current circumstances where Sinn Féin is opposed to the capitalistic project that the EU represents is that there is a very broad band of opinion, even within the European Parliament, who would share our socialist analysis and who would also be opposed to the current direction of the EU. That forms a very broad and strong political alliance that we are a part of and proud to be part of.

Despite Unionist accusations of the formation of a pan-Nationalist front in the aftermath of the Hume-Adams Agreement, Francie Molloy emphasizes the differences that remain, particularly with John Hume's articulation of a European perspective for Irish Nationalists *vis-à-vis* the Sinn Féin perspective. For Francie Molloy, the EU represents a threat to Irish identity rather than the possibility of providing it with better representation in a changing society:

I think Hume would be quite happy with a United States of Europe. We wouldn't be as happy with that whole idea of a United States of Europe because Irish identity is lost within that. While there are many benefits that Ireland, as a small country, can actually gain from being part of a bigger economic unit, there are also the dangers of having to tie in with EU policy – neutrality, for instance, would go out the window. So Ireland wouldn't be able to serve some of the useful purposes that it serves at the minute being a neutral country against all of the multi-nationals and super-powers. There is a danger of Ireland losing its identity completely in the European context. John Hume has been totally pro-European. We want to see Ireland playing a role within Europe. We want to see the EU being re-negotiated with Ireland, as a body, having a say and playing a full part.

The Sinn Féin interviewees maintain that Irish Nationalist identities would be best represented by a modern unitary nation-state. Although extraterritorial structural relationships are not ruled out by Mitchel McLaughlin, a fully integrated EU is discounted by him. Francie Molloy believes that while such a development may be economically beneficial, it would also be to the detriment of other vital resources of the Irish identity.

The Territorial Resource of Nationalist Identities Represented by Sinn Féin

The concept of European union and open borders is at odds with a divided Ireland. Sinn Féin believe the EU can have a constructive role to play in facilitating a peace process in Ireland' (Sinn Féin, 1994b).

The territorial resource of the northern Nationalist identity represented by the SDLP would appear to be of lesser significance to that liberal nationalist identity than it is to the northern Nationalist/ Republican identity represented by Sinn Féin. Mitchel McLaughlin argues that the unification of the territory of the island of Ireland is vital for the well-being of 'all the Irish people' as he perceives them:

> We believe that you cannot have institutionalized division among the Irish people. If you are talking about defending the interests of all of the Irish people, particularly in the context of modern capitalist society, we believe in maximizing not just our resources but also our strengths. We believe that the territorial question is actually fundamental – both to eradicating division, whether it is cultural or political or economic, and that it will enhance Ireland's negotiating position in terms of the European mainland and the rest of the world.

Modern Irish Nationalists, broadly represented by Sinn Féin, appear to be fixed on the nation-state concept of a 'united Ireland'. However, the wholesale appropriation of the discourse of European integrationism by the SDLP poses new questions for the relationship between northern Irish Nationalists and the nation-state. Northern Nationalists represented by the SDLP are amenable to the party's complementary dialect of liberal nationalism/postnationalism and the redefinition of national identity along extraterritorial lines. In this context, a dichotomy in the northern Nationalist identity persists even if the Hume-Adams talks produced agreement on the need for the consent of Ulster Unionists in determining any future structure of state. This dichotomy has been wryly summed up by Fionnuala O'Connor:

> The day of the nation-state is dead and gone' says John Hume: 'But I haven't had mine yet' says Bernadette McAliskey (O'Connor, 1993, p. 371).[2]

There is, undoubtedly, a perception of structural change and the increased role of the EU in terms of the structure of state power among Sinn Féin interviewees. However, this perception merely serves to emphasize the isolation of northern Irish Nationalist identities from the modern structure of state power in Northern Ireland after 1921, according to Mitchel McLaughlin:

> Certainly for Nationalists there is the question of actually having sovereignty before you can give it away or you can agree to particular treaties or trade arrangements that would involve the sharing of sovereignty or an agreement to allow an agreed structure, such as the European Parliament, to interfere. That is an issue that will run through the situation here and is, in fact, clearly different from the type of decisions that have been taken on the European mainland and even in terms of the decisions taken in Westminster as it affects Wales and Scotland.

For Francie Molloy, the territorial resource has a strong historic and emotional, as well as pragmatic connotation for the Irish Republican identity:

> The whole history of republicanism, particularly in this country, has meant having control over your own destiny. Even the broad socialist movement was never really something that came into Ireland. Irish Republicans would always call themselves socialists and see themselves as people who would share with others but share with others within their own country as long as they had control over it. I think it goes back to the Land Wars in Ireland. There is a tradition that if you own the land you own the country. For republicanism that is probably a very strong motive – that you cannot make any decisions unless you actually have the power to control the country.

However, Francie Molloy's commitment to the right of self-determination within the modern state context is tempered by his perception that the extraterritorial structure of the EU is making incursions into the political autonomy that were once the preserve of national governments:

> We have to recognize that we are in a new situation – that no matter where you would have a republic, it is not totally independent. The European Union has a big say, a big control and so recognizing the political reality of the present time, you can

want to control your own destiny but you have to work within the broader structure otherwise you will simply be isolated as the Eastern European countries were.

It [the EU] is a contradiction, in some sense, with what we want. One of the sad things about it is that when we have basically got rid of one empire there is now being a new one created – the British Empire going out and the European Empire coming in. Irish history seems to show that Republican struggle has always come to a head at a time of broader change. The war was a factor in the 1916 era. At each stage there was always some big obstacle that made a bigger problem. I think our policies have to accept that there is a European Union but what we want to try and do is to create an alliance of the new nations that are getting their independence and are creating new national identities.

Territory remains central to Sinn Féin political analysis even though the party's interviewees recognize the encroachment made by extraterritorial forces on the configuration of state power. The feeling that the modern conflict over territory in Ireland needs to be resolved before the role of postmodern extraterritorial arrangements can be engaged is reinforced by Mitchel McLaughlin. Francie Molloy remains convinced of the viability of the modern Republican goal of creating an All-Ireland state structure. However, he recognizes that the EU is undermining such a goal by eroding the authority of national governments.

The Sinn Féin Perception of Ulster Unionists

By maintaining the traditional Republican position that Ulster Unionists are part of the Irish nation it would appear that Sinn Féin still fails to accept the self-professed, distinctive ethnicity of Ulster Unionist identities. According to Mitchel McLaughlin:

We argue very strongly and as reasonably as we can that we can construct a political structure on this island that respects the diversity of cultural and ethnic and religious affiliation. We believe that that in itself is the practical exercise of self-determination by all of the Irish people – not simple majoritarianism in any one part of the country, or even in terms of the island as a whole. We are not talking about suppressing or controlling or the domination of one section of the community or one section of social, economic and religious values by another. We have set out our

stall – we are looking for a more secure Ireland, we are looking
for accountable, functional and participatory democracy, we are
looking for a written Bill of Rights. All of those are the guarantees that will protect, even ourselves – we are going to be a political minority. We have a radical social and economic programme
that sets us apart from the other political parties. We recognize
that, at this point in time, realistically, we are a minority view in
the island as a whole. It would certainly be in our interests to
have the type of constitutional guarantees that would protect us,
as well as protecting the interest of those who belong to a different cultural tradition.

Defining Ulster Unionist identities solely in terms of culture is
erroneous. Ulster Unionist identities also have strong territorial
and economic resources that determine a distinctiveness from the
Irish nation. Ulster Unionist identities are, therefore, not merely
cultural but also political and the idea of being incorporated into
an All-Ireland state is anathema to them. Mitchel McLaughlin concedes that this analysis broadly reflects the Ulster Unionist position but is adamant that it can be changed through negotiation:

It is a major problem. The reality for all of us is that this problem has to be overcome or else we are going to be asked to live
with that division which is not just in contradiction to what I
believe to be the implicit tradition of nationalism and republicanism especially, but it also contradicts the ethos of the European Union and they will certainly bring their influence to bear.
Now, if we had, for example, in South Africa, acceptance that
the white South Africans could establish for themselves another
Orange Free State then we wouldn't have the peace process that
we have in South Africa. It was only when the white South African regime led from the front and the business class, in particular, negotiated with the ANC in advance of what appeared to be
a rush to democracy – in fact there was a lot of very careful
negotiation up to that point – it was when the white South African regime recognized that the apartheid era was over and decided that rather than wait for it to be finally defeated that they
would enter into inclusive dialogue from a position of relative
strength that the present opportunity was created. Now, Sinn
Féiners argue (we do this not in any way at all in an aggressive
or supremacist way) that is in fact the choice that is facing the
Unionist community and leadership at the present time, and this
is why we argue so strongly, for example, that the British govern-

ment should become persuaders for political agreement in Ireland and lead from the front and bring the Unionist community along with them. The future for all of us otherwise is one of division and continuing conflict.

Francie Molloy denies that Ulster Unionist political representatives are the main obstacles to the political change that Sinn Féin desires. In doing so he shows that the party is still conditioned by the traditional Republican analysis of the conflict whereby the UK government is perceived as the main problem and not the relationship between Nationalists and Unionists in its modern context:

I'm not so sure that it is Unionist intransigence that is causing it. I think it is the British using the Unionists and once again playing the Orange card. What we have been saying from the start is that the British have to become the persuaders – they have to persuade Unionists that they have to – not agree to anything – but they at least have to talk and that agreement would, hopefully, come out of that.

The Sinn Féin perception of Ulster Unionist identities is one that appears to accept their right to cultural tradition but which rejects their political *raison d'être*. Despite his own opposition to European integration, Mitchel McLaughlin indulges in the Sinn Féin tactic of pointing to the incompatibility of the broad movement towards European Union and the Ulster Unionist political requirement for the UK to retain authority over its own affairs of state.

The focal point of the Sinn Féin political philosophy is the ending of partition on the island of Ireland. As such, the territorial resource, conditioned by modernity and impervious to the influence of the condition of postmodernity, remains central to the Republican identity and to Sinn Féin's political analysis – 'Brits Out' remains the party's rallying cry. However, Francie Molloy presents a creeping realization that European integration is beginning to undermine his party's goal of an All-Ireland nation-state, a realization with implications for the territorial resource of the Republican manifestation of the northern Irish Nationalist identity. For the moment, the condition of postmodernity embodied by the EU is interpreted by Sinn Féin interviewees as another tactic to advance their modern objective of an All-Ireland nation-state. As such, the Sinn Féin interpretation of the EU as a possible means to a modernist end contrast sharply with the SDLP interpretation of a postmodern Europe as a utopian end.

8 Dialogue with the Democratic Unionist Party (DUP)

INTRODUCTION

The DUP emerged from its forerunner, the Protestant Unionist Party, in September 1971. The Reverend Dr Ian Paisley has led the party from its inception. The DUP professes itself to be 'right wing in the sense of being strong on the constitution, but to the left on social issues' (Flackes and Elliott, 1994, p. 134).

In its first electoral contest – the District Council Elections of 1973 – the DUP secured 4.3 per cent of the votes cast. The Democratic Loyalist Coalition, led by Paisley, received 10.8 per cent of the vote in the 1973 Northern Ireland Assembly election. In co-operation with other Unionist parties in the United Ulster Unionist Council (UUUC), the DUP received 8.2 per cent of the vote in the 1974 Westminster General election, a figure that was to increase to 14.8 per cent in the 1975 Convention election. Despite the demise of the UUUC and its skilful steering committee, the DUP proved to be a viable electoral force in its own right, securing 12.7 per cent of votes in the 1977 District Council elections. Indeed, the DUP momentarily eclipsed the UUP in the 1981 District Council elections with 26.6 per cent of the vote compared to the UUP's 26.5 per cent. Since the 1987 General Election, the DUP has polled less strongly with 11.7 per cent of the vote in that election and 13.1 per cent in the 1992 General Election. The party has faired better in the District Council elections during this period with 17.7 per cent of the vote in 1989 and 17.3 per cent of the vote in 1993. However, it is the elections to the European Parliament that give the DUP and its leader greatest electoral satisfaction. In 1979, the Reverend Ian Paisley was the only candidate returned on the first count, his 29.8 per cent share of the vote bringing him comfortably across the 25 per cent threshold. This led to the declaration by his supporters that he was 'Northern Ireland's most popular politician'. This success has been repeated in subsequent elections to the European Parliament, although with a narrowing percentage between himself and his nearest rival, John Hume, each time: from 11.5 per cent in 1984, to 4.4 per cent in 1989, to 2.2 per cent in 1994 (Flackes and Elliott, 1994; *Irish Political Studies*, 1995). In the 1996 Northern Ireland Forum election the DUP secured 18.8 per cent of the vote followed by 13.6 per cent in the 1997 General Election (*Irish News*, 3 May 1997).

The DUP is strongly anti-European integrationist, with its leader referring to the EU in disparaging biblical terms such as 'the whore of Babylon' and 'the Antichrist' (Bruce, 1989, p. 229). During the Common Market referendum campaign in 1975 the *Protestant Telegraph* recorded Dr Paisley's views on the implications of Common Market membership for the Ulster Protestant identity:

> There can be no future for Protestantism under the Common Market. The Common Market had a religious dimension, a constitutional dimension, an economic dimension, an Irish dimension and a legal dimension (*Protestant Telegraph*, 7 June 1975).

Dr Paisley took to referring to the Virgin Mary as 'the Madonna of the Common Market' at that time (Hainsworth, 1989, p. 56). When campaigning in elections to the European Parliament the DUP criticizes the encroaching nature of the EU; and what the party perceives to be the pervasiveness of Catholic influence and the corresponding threat for Ulster Protestantism. Perhaps Dr Paisley's most memorable contribution to the European Parliament is recorded by Flackes and Elliott:

> At the first session in Strasbourg in July 1979 he intervened twice. On the opening day he was the first MEP to speak, apart from the acting president, when he protested that the Union Flag was flying the wrong way up outside the Parliament Buildings. Later he interrupted Jack Lynch (president in office of the European Council), saying that he was protesting against the Republic's refusal to sign the European Convention on Terrorism (Flackes and Elliott, 1994, p. 261).

Dr Paisley reprised his protest tactic in October 1988 when he interrupted an address by Pope John Paul II. However, Dr Paisley does play an active role in promoting Northern Ireland's economic and social interests at EU level and works closely with fellow MEPs in this regard (Hainsworth, 1989, p. 64).

DUP PERCEPTIONS OF STRUCTURAL CHANGE

> We live in crisis days for our Province and Kingdom. What European countries could not do by force through the centuries – destroy the sovereignty of the United Kingdom – they are now accomplishing with the government's help (DUP, 1992).

The DUP perceives there to have been an erosion of nation-state sovereignty dating back to the beginning of the UK's membership of the EEC in 1973, and continuing after the Single European Act and the Maastricht Treaty. **Nigel Dodds**, DUP Party Secretary, maintains that the political implications of membership were played down when the UK joined the EEC:

> There certainly has been an erosion of sovereignty since we joined the EEC, as it then was. We were told that it was all just going to be about free trade and a common market and it was purely going to have economic impacts – things have moved a long way since then. If you actually look at what the Treaty of Rome talks about – 'an ever closer union' – this is bound to lead to a political union in the long-term and, politically, the UK's position would become less independent and more dependent on what the rest of Europe was doing. I think that is what has happened. The Single European Act and the Maastricht Treaty have, in our view, meant that a substantial amount of sovereignty has been transferred to Brussels from London and I think that is intended by the architects of Maastricht and they intend to continue that process (interview with the author).

He is, however, encouraged by the opposition to integration that he sees among the electorates of Britain, France and Denmark:

> Given the sort of reaction there was in France and in Denmark and on the ground in Britain I think the architects of a federal Europe are perhaps a bit more wary now that they shouldn't move so quickly. There was a tremendous backlash among ordinary people against this sort of move.

With regard to further moves toward European integration, DUP opposition is tempered by a realization that the process of integration is unlikely to unravel:

> I think the trend is to more and more powers for Brussels and that will increase no matter what – once you are in that process you are locked into it and, bit by bit, sovereignty is eroded.

Maurice Morrow, a DUP Councillor, is witnessing the beginning of European Union influence on politics at a local level: 'There has not been a marked impact, but I believe that as time goes on there will be. I can see it creeping in more and more as each year goes past' (interview with the author).

DETERMINING STRUCTURAL PARAMETERS FOR NORTHERN IRELAND

The Internal Context

Nigel Dodds believes that the interests of northern Irish Nationalists can be adequately represented by the SDLP in an exclusively internal structural arrangement for Northern Ireland:

This desire to have people from outside the UK involved in running Northern Ireland is the crux of the problem. I don't think there is much difficulty thinking we could find a system whereby the SDLP or people in the constitutional Nationalist tradition could work with Unionists to run Northern Ireland. The difficulty is the SDLP's insistence – and we saw it at the last talks [Brooke/Mayhew 1991–2] with their proposal for this 'Commission idea' – on the need for somebody from outside. Our view is that, really, it is the people of Northern Ireland who elect their representatives and it is those representatives who should run the show themselves without having to get somebody else in to run it for them. I think this is the difficulty – we cannot reach an accommodation with the SDLP in terms of the administration of Northern Ireland if that means Dublin having a role and of Europe having a role outside the normal European role for any region of the EU. John Hume seems to think that the only way the interests of Nationalists can be protected is by Dublin having a role in Northern Ireland's affairs. Our view is that if he has a role in the affairs of Northern Ireland then he is the protection for Nationalists' interests. He must represent the people who elect him and he must have the confidence to do that. If he wants Dublin involved in that then he is abdicating his own responsibility.

Maurice Morrow does not entertain the claim of northern Irish Nationalists that the internal context is insufficient to represent the resources of their identities. Majoritarianism, determined by the emphasis of the modern state on established territorial demarcation rather than on community, is the guiding principle:

> I think reality is going to have to finally come down upon everybody – that's Unionists, that's Nationalists, that's the British government, that's the Irish government. They have to accept, whether they like it or whether they don't, that Ireland is one island divided. People may not like that but then that's the way it is and unless and until there is a majority who say otherwise then I think it has got to stay that way.

He does accept that there are two sets of separate and opposing communal identities in Northern Ireland but rejects any process aimed at political accommodation that impinges upon the territorial boundary of Northern Ireland:

> There is a divided people within Northern Ireland but I believe that the people of Northern Ireland should find their own solution to their own problem. I do not believe that outside interference should come from anywhere – be it America, Europe, Dublin or anywhere else. The people of Northern Ireland should find their own solution.

He appears to suggest that Sinn Féin, the representative of a section of that 'people', may have a part to play in future inclusive political arrangements when he says:

> The first thing to do is to create a level playing field where everybody is equal. Sinn Féin want to retain their guns – that is not a level playing field. What they are actually saying is: 'if we don't get our way we will blow your heads off'. So, therefore, you can't talk with a gun at your head because you're not thinking rationally, you're not thinking straight and you're not allowed to think straight.

However, even if there is movement on the decommissioning of weapons by the IRA, Maurice Morrow reflects the DUP position that the party cannot contemplate positive participation in political structures that include Sinn Féin:

> I don't see in my lifetime, me sitting down with Sinn Féin. I don't see that happening in my lifetime because with Sinn Féin you have got to look at their history and their origins. Wasn't it Danny Morrison [ex-Sinn Féin Press Officer] who said there was

nothing wrong with the ballot paper in one hand and the armalite in the other. We have a cease-fire, we don't have peace. That is a cease-fire for expediency and when it is expedient not to have it, it will not be there. In other words, what it is saying is that 'we are not going to shoot you at the present time'.

The DUP's insistence that it will never negotiate with Sinn Féin on the future of Northern Ireland is echoed in the contributions of DUP representatives in this dialogue. The SDLP's desire for the representation of structures of power outside the UK and the DUP's antipathy towards any extraterritorial involvement in the political affairs of Northern Ireland would appear to rule out agreement on the constitutional future of Northern Ireland between the DUP and northern Irish Nationalist representatives.

The Extraterritorial Context

The prospect of the development of an extraterritorial context invokes hostility in the DUP interviewees. Nigel Dodds is dismissive of any suggestion that a developing system of multi-level governance in the EU provides an opportunity for the territorial, economic and cultural resources of identities that exist in Northern Ireland to be realigned. Again, the modern territorial boundary, especially the one between the UK and the Republic of Ireland, is sacrosanct in determining a structure of government for Northern Ireland:

I think an accommodation is possible in Northern Ireland but I don't think that it takes the European dimension to actually make that happen. Hopefully, that will happen and should happen. I think the best way of trying to do that is to hammer out an agreement on how Northern Ireland should be run – to have some sort of devolved administration in Belfast where the constitutional parties here who don't support violence and who don't have any role in violence are there working Northern Ireland PLC for the benefit of its people. That is across all the issues – education, housing, health and all those issues where there is a great deal in common between the parties. Getting them to work together on that basis, on those sort of issues in which people out there (Catholic, Protestant or no religion) can say 'I'm represented up there because my party is involved in that.' Not just there in the Assembly but actually running the thing, actually making the decisions. We have proposed ways in which that can be done and so have other parties. If you remember, at the last talks [Brooke/Mayhew 1991–2] there was a fair amount of agreement at Strand One. It was going back to John Hume's insistence that Dublin needed to be involved – that was the stumbling block of 1973 at Sunningdale, the real problem was the Council of Ireland.

Nigel Dodds cites the work of the three MEPs in securing the EU Initiative for Peace and Reconciliation as evidence that co-operation is possible: 'Obviously in Europe people see the three MEPs working together on these sort of issues and the Delors package is an obvious example where the three of them went together.' However, this co-operation has been conducted within the extraterritorial context of the EU. Indeed, the extraterritorial context was emphasized by John Hume when he shared a platform with Ian Paisley at a meeting of the Ulster Farmers Union on 29 March 1996. They were discussing the approach of Northern Ireland farmers to the EU ban on British beef in the aftermath of the BSE crisis:

> Let us remember, all major decisions on agriculture are not taken in London but in Brussels. So let us concentrate our minds on Brussels. We as a region have special regional status already. We are an Objective One region and our largest industry is now under threat. We have a very powerful case to put not just to the commissioner for agriculture, but to the commissioner for regional policy and to the President of the European Commission. (*Belfast Telegraph*, 30 March 1996).

Pointedly, Dr Paisley endorsed this approach adding that: 'Ulster is already a special case in Europe' (*Belfast Telegraph*, 30 March 1996).

Nigel Dodds denies that the EU provides the basis for a redefinition of political interaction and, consequently, a reinterpretation of identity:

> When the three MEPs go to represent a case to the Commission they go as representatives of Northern Ireland where there is no question of Northern Ireland's position as part of the UK being side-lined. It has to go through the European institutions, we are part of the United Kingdom with all that that entails. They may be arguing: 'Look, you gave the Irish Republic something or you gave Greece something – we should get the same because our situation is similar.' But they don't go there and argue – certainly Ian Paisley and Jim Nicholson, and when I'm there

John Hume doesn't argue it either – that this should be done because politically we are different.

Undoubtedly, when some Commissioner sees the three MEPs together, Europe likes to take the credit that they are the only ones who can get these three warring factions together and they think it is a marvellous thing. They see Hume and Paisley together and they think that they are doing this. They don't realize that on many issues the SDLP, the DUP and the UUP see eye-to-eye and would go on joint deputations to the Prime Minister or to Ministers here out of Belfast City Council. We are happy enough to play that game if it gets results. However, I think it would be wrong to say that is some sort of political thing where we are saying Northern Ireland isn't part of the UK – it doesn't come into it. The three MEPs see an issue like shipbuilding or farming and say, 'this is for the good of Northern Ireland – politics doesn't come into it – there is nothing to divide us on this issue, let's go together,' and they have worked that way. I think you could do the same in an Assembly. I think there is a lot of issues there where you would say, 'here are a whole range of issues which politicians here take a particular view on – we don't necessarily agree with the British government – let us do it our way'.

The successful working relationship of the three MEPs from Northern Ireland on European issues as they affect the region is interpreted by Nigel Dodds as a symbol of what can be achieved in an internal structure of government for Northern Ireland. He rejects the thesis that such co-operation is made possible by a changing political context which is not delimited by the nation-state boundary. However, an implicit recognition of the import of European integration for the economic resource of the Ulster Unionist ident-ity represented by the DUP is made through the participation of the DUP leader in the European Parliament and his willingness to deal directly with EU officials in an effort to have the 1996–8 EU ban on British beef applied only to Britain and not Northern Ireland.

The Role of 'Humespeak'

Maurice Morrow is unequivocal in his analysis of what John Hume is trying to achieve in his attempt to adopt a strong European perspective for the northern Irish Nationalist political discourse:

John Hume is an astute politician with one aim in mind and that is a united Ireland. John Hume would feel that the best way to achieve this would be through his influence and making us all, as he would call us, 'good Europeans'. But I'm not sure you can make a divided people – and I'm not talking now about Ireland divided, I'm talking about Europe – I'm not sure you can bring the French, the Belgians, the Germans, the British and the Irish together because we all have different cultures, we all have different backgrounds, aims and goals. I don't believe it is attainable. I think it is wishful thinking by John Hume. I feel that he has an agenda for it.

For Maurice Morrow, John Hume is still operating to an entirely modern agenda for the creation of an All-Ireland nation-state.

STRUCTURAL CHANGE AND UNIONIST IDENTITIES REPRESENTED BY THE DUP

The Territorial Resource

The territory of Northern Ireland clearly defines the Ulster Unionist identity represented by Nigel Dodds. This is demonstrated by his rejection of an identity describing itself as 'unionist' but with an Irish cultural resource. For him, those who see their economic interest best served by remaining within the Union but contend that they have an Irish cultural aspect to their identity cannot define themselves as 'unionist':

You have got to be either one or the other. I don't believe in this hybrid business: that you can be British and Irish at the same time. I don't think you can say: 'well it serves me economically to be part of Britain but I really want all of the advantages of being Irish as well'. I think that people, if they live within Northern Ireland, are British citizens – they are part of the United Kingdom. If they have an aspiration to be part of another state that is perfectly legitimate provided they pursue that by constitutional and democratic means, by argument and persuasion, not by violence. However, I don't accept this argument that you can have it both ways, at all.

Prior to partition, Unionists classified themselves as 'Irish' – they were, after all, 'Irish' within the political context of the United Kingdom of Great Britain and Ireland. The formation of the Irish nation-state in 1921 meant that a broad spectrum of Unionists identities, though not all, disavowed their Irish sense of identity and redefined it in terms of Northern Ireland. This redefinition has been intensified by the years of violent conflict after 1969 (Moxon-Browne, 1983). For Dodds, the formation of two modern states on the island of Ireland clearly dictated that identity should become defined in terms of 'Irish' or 'British', but not both. Thus, identity is defined by the territorial imperative of the modern state: 'I have no problem with people being Scottish and British or being Welsh and British or being Northern Irish and British – I have no problem with that.'

The Ulster Unionist identity, as represented by the DUP, is defined by the union of Great Britain and Northern Ireland, and is, therefore, committed to the retention of sovereignty within the boundary of the UK. Bearing this in mind, it seems anomalous for the DUP to have a participating member in the parliament of a supranational structure of state that is gradually diminishing the autonomy of the government of the UK upon which the Unionist identity depends. Nigel Dodds rejects this:

There is no contradiction whatsoever. In fact, it would be a dereliction of our duty and our responsibility towards our electorate if we were to opt out. The European Parliament is made up of a wide divergence of political views. At the last European elections there were quite a number of MEPs from various countries returned on an anti-Maastricht, anti-federalist, anti-European superstate ticket. There were twelve or thirteen from France, there has always been a strong element in Denmark of that view, so we are not unique by any means. There is now a strong voice in the European Parliament which is saying, 'Look, hold on a minute, people may be for free movement and economic freedom but they didn't vote for being rail-roaded into some European superstate.' We are part of that movement and we are there primarily to represent Northern Ireland's interests and make sure that Northern Ireland gets the best deal possible out of the European Union in economic and political terms.

Nigel Dodds does not envisage policy-making powers being transferred to the European Parliament so, therefore, he argues, there is no contradiction in Ian Paisley becoming involved in that parliament and the party's anti-integrationist stance:

> Lip-service will be paid to the role of the European Parliament by the national governments. The Parliament may shout and scream but they are not going to get the real power, that will stay with the national governments. The difference is that the Parliament is there as a democratic institution. Our role is to represent the people out there who share our views and to get the best deal for Ulster and we will continue to do that in the Parliament. There is no difficulty for us doing that and at the same time holding the views that we do on Northern Ireland.

The participation of the DUP leader in the extraterritorial institution of the European Parliament is justified on the grounds that he is representing the interests of Northern Ireland. Paradoxically, the relative powerlessness of the European Parliament is used further to justify participation.

The Cultural Resource

For Maurice Morrow, the perceived agenda of John Hume – 'the unification of Ireland' – represents a direct threat for the primary cultural resource of Ulster Unionist identities, namely, Ulster Protestantism:

> To Unionists, I believe it means the imposition of rule from Dublin where the Catholic church would have the dominant say, as it has in Southern Ireland. This has been proved conclusively when FitzGerald [former Taoiseach Garret FitzGerald] went for a referendum on divorce in the 1980s and Catholic church intervened and once they intervened that was the whole thing scuppered. It demonstrated quite clearly to the Unionist population who really does wield the power in Dublin.

A fear of 'Rome rule' probably does affect the political thinking of a sizeable contingent of Ulster Protestants. This perception holds that the decline in the Protestant population of the Republic of Ireland is evidence of the consequences for Ulster Protestants should they become directly exposed to a society in which the 'Church of Rome' is perceived to dominate. Such a perception is reflected by Maurice Morrow:

Southern Ireland is not a pluralist state – that has been proved conclusively. If you take, at the time of partition, the Protestant population in the South was ten per cent it is now three per cent. The Catholic population up here at that time was fifteen per cent, it is now thirty five per cent, some would say even higher.

The Catholic population has, in fact, not fallen below 34 per cent of the population of Northern Ireland since partition (O'Gráda and Walsh, 1994, p. 32). For Maurice Morrow this merely confirms his point that Southern society has been hostile to the liberty of Protestants while Catholics north of the border have suffered no such persecution:

> If it is higher it proves my point that in fact while the Catholic population has increased here, with all of the alleged discrimination, the Protestant population has decreased in the South.

The EU has also been perceived as a potential threat to Ulster Protestantism, particularly by the DUP. During the Common Market Referendum campaign in 1975, Dr Paisley's newspaper, the *Protestant Telegraph*, articulated this concern:

> The very mention of the EC charter the 'Treaty of Rome' would be sufficient to arouse most Ulstermen but, alas, not everyone has responded. It would be a gross miscalculation to assume that membership of the Common Market should be considered in purely economic terms. Ulster must record a 'no' vote to Europe. The Battle of the Boyne was Ireland's battle of the Reformation to keep popery at bay. The No Surrender of 1690 must still be our watchword when we record 'no' to Europe (*Protestant Telegraph*, 24 May 1975).

Maurice Morrow perceives European integrationism to be allied to Irish nationalism, with both representing a threat to the economic, territorial and cultural resources of Ulster Unionist identities. He looks to the religious make-up of EU member-states to distinguish the threat for Ulster Unionism's core cultural resource – Ulster Protestantism:

> I believe that Europe will be a super-Catholic state, so it will, because if you look at the make-up of European countries it is that way. That, of course, is something that I am fearful of and something I'm apprehensive about. I believe that it will not be

good for the Unionist or the Protestant community of Northern Ireland if such a thing continues.

Nigel Dodds argues against the sectarian notion that a unionist in Northern Ireland must also be Protestant. However, he does not deny the relationship between the political identity of Ulster Unionism and the cultural identity of Ulster Protestantism:

> There is obviously a very strong relationship but people can be a unionist without being a Protestant and many people are unionists without being Protestants. I don't think that anyone should make the mistake of thinking that only Protestants can be good unionists, that is not the case at all. As far as the DUP is concerned we have always argued that anyone who believes in the union, anyone who wants to see their future as part of the UK is a unionist. The question of religion, while it is important, is not important in the political sense.

However, Maurice Morrow holds the view that Ulster Unionism and Ulster Protestantism are more inextricably linked. He is sceptical of the suggestion that there is a sizeable Catholic unionist vote:

> I'm not one who would beat about the bush on this. I believe the two are interwoven. There are some who call themselves pluralists who don't like to admit that but it doesn't give me any problem saying that. By and large most Protestants are Unionist and most Unionists are Protestant – whichever way you want to put it. Yes, there is a section of the Catholic community that votes Unionist. I don't believe it is sizeable, but there is a section of it which does that. I have no doubt that there is a bigger section of the Catholic community who, because we have a PR system, will transfer from a pro-nationalist party to a pro-union party. The Official Unionists [the UUP] always feel that they can attract the Catholic community far better than the DUP can – I don't believe that. I haven't seen any figures that they have produced which sustains that.

There is a growing Catholic middle class, many of whom may conceivably see their economic interests being best served by Northern Ireland remaining as part of the UK. Maurice Morrow has problems with the idea of trying to accommodate such middle-class Catholic voters by recognizing their right to maintain their sense of Irish cultural identity. For him, the Irish cultural identity in Northern Ireland is synonymous with a modern Irish Nationalist identity that is anti-union and, therefore, 'treacherous and treasonous':

> There is the perception that the Irish Nationalist identity is treacherous and treasonous – no question about it whatsoever. It is the Dublin government to whom most Catholics look to vent their feelings of Irishness through. Right throughout the recent troubles the Irish government hasn't done anything to convince Unionists that they want Unionists to be allowed to live as Unionists choose provided that does not down the rights of the Nationalist community. I have no trouble whatsoever with saying, 'the rights that I have and I want – I want the same rights for people who call themselves Irish Nationalists or Roman Catholic'. I am not out to take from them their fundamental and their basic human rights. I believe they are just as entitled to them as my people are but what we have found is that if you take for instance the arrogant claim of jurisdiction – if the Irish government wanted to demonstrate that they are sincere in all of this, there was a nice gesture they could have made. That would have gone a long long way to try to smooth things out. You would have seen a lot of coming together. After 1969, some real grievances were used and cleverly used, then some of us in the Protestant community said this is another uprising of IRA sectarianism and we've been proved right.

Ulster Protestantism is recognized by both DUP interviewees as a cultural resource of the Ulster Unionist identity that they represent. Maurice Morrow perceives that the Republic of Ireland and the EU operate to a political agenda that is influenced by the Catholic Church. For him, both pose a direct threat to the Ulster Protestant cultural identity. Nigel Dodds, meanwhile, believes that it is possible for individuals who are Catholics or who belong to no religious denomination to be unionists. However, from his perspective, an Irish cultural resource of identity is incompatible with unionism. According to Dodds, this represents a 'hybrid identity' which he believes to be untenable. Maurice Morrow perceives that the phenomenon of a northern Catholic voting for either the UUP or the DUP is not significant. Furthermore, he maintains that the linkage of the resources of the Irish nationalist identity to the modern Irish state vindicates his assertion that such an identity is 'treacherous and treasonous'. The DUP, therefore, claims to defend the UK citizenship rights of all individuals in Northern Ireland, including individual Irish Nationalists, while the party opposes the right of the Irish Nationalist community in Northern Ireland to cultural self-determination.

The Economic Resource

Although increasing economic powers are being assumed by the EU, Maurice Morrow is sceptical that this will have any impact on the economic resource of identity in Northern Ireland because he believes any move to further integration will be countered by a growing anti-integrationist movement:

> I think what you want to consider is this – when the UK went into Europe, people, by and large, did not understand what the whole thing was about, it was a new concept. Yes, there was a referendum held and that referendum, by a small majority, said 'yes'. Now, if the tentacles of Europe spread and we have a common money, that will start to alert people right across the whole of the UK. They will say, 'we don't like this anymore' and I think that you are going to see a clamour on the mainland for changes. I believe that nothing stays the same forever, whether it is in our own country or elsewhere. As Europe begins to take a grip, and it is beginning to take a grip, then I feel that those who maybe were once for it will be no longer for it. Now, you might say 'but they can't get out', I don't know whether they can get out or not but I do know that it will cause an awful unrest right across the whole of the UK. Does the Dublin government want its authority completely immersed in Europe? Is it happy with that? I pose that question because I don't know the answer.

His opposition to the process of integration is tempered by the pragmatism of pursuing grants for Northern Ireland through participation in EU institutions:

> The DUP's stance on Europe is that we are opposed to European integration. We believe that every country should have its independence and Europe should not be allowed to interfere in its internal affairs. However, we also accept that it is a reality. In your own walk of life you might have things you don't like but they are real and that is it, you have to live with them – so it is

with Europe. I believe that the DUP got it right when we said: 'look, we are opposed to European integration, nevertheless, if there are grants or pluses for the people of Northern Ireland then we, as a party, will be in there fighting to get those things for the people'.

EU structural funding for Northern Ireland has done little to influence the economic resource of Unionist identities represented by Maurice Morrow:

> The accusation has always been thrown at the UK government that they have not poured into the regions, particularly Northern Ireland, the same money that they used to because they know there is money coming from Europe. My understanding was that any funding coming from Europe was additional to subvention from Westminster. However, it has been proved in the past that is not the case. Now we have this situation developing where there is a large package of money [the EU Special Support Programme for Peace and Reconciliation] thanks to the three MEPs and I think, in fairness to the three of them, they have done a good job. But it remains to be seen whether the UK government is going to sustain the same amount of funding on their part. I have my doubts about that but I could be wrong.

In the modern economic context, Maurice Morrow decries the lack of an economic argument for the establishment of an All-Ireland state:

> Sinn Féin and the SDLP must carry a big responsibility because have they put up one economic argument as to why there should be a united Ireland – it has always been a sectarian argument. Has ever there been an economic argument to try and convince me that my future lies in a united Ireland, in preference to the UK?

The predisposition of Maurice Morrow, and the DUP generally, to perceive the territorial, economic and cultural resources of identity in stark terms defined by the modern territorial context of Northern Ireland determines that any mention of a change in that modern territorial context is automatically interpreted as an overture to a 'united Ireland'. In order for him to countenance such constitutional change he says that

> The Dublin government has to convince me that: (i) I'd be better off in a united Ireland; (ii) that my Protestantism would not

be in any way interfered with and that my future and my children's future is in this new state. How are they going to convince me of that?

He believes that such a feat is impossible: 'They can't do it because history doesn't allow them. History has taught us quite clearly that the argument is not economic, it's a political argument all the time.'

The economic resource of the Ulster Unionist identity represented by the DUP is clearly invested in the UK state structure, according to the testimony of the DUP interviewees. Indeed, the possibility of European Monetary Union elicits little enthusiasm from Maurice Morrow. Instead, he perceives that such a development would be a signal warning of impending political union; a development that would overtly confront the present alignment of the territorial and economic resources of Ulster Unionist identities. However, pragmatism determines that the post-1994 economic yield from the EU is guardedly welcomed by him.

DUP Attitudes to Northern Nationalist Identities

Ultimately, many in the DUP believe that for Ulster Unionist identities to feel secure in Northern Ireland, Irish Nationalists north of the border have to be eliminated. Maurice Morrow issues a disclaimer on this stance by saying 'Some have said that to me, I don't personally agree with that,' before tentatively going on to predict future confrontation:

> Some have said that this is a situation where winner takes all. I must say that the more it unfolds it does seem to be that way. You could arrive into the scenario where people see no hope and it becomes a winner takes all situation. Now, I would hope that would never arise because I believe that the Protestant community has an awful lot to offer and the Catholic community has a lot to offer too. I think that if you were to go into that situation it would be regrettable, but, yes, realistically that scenario is unfolding and people are beginning to talk like that – it's a winner takes all situation.

I think that if the British government come out and say, 'Look, we are handing you over to a united Ireland – that's it', then that, of course, will bring out the worst in everybody.

Of course, the UK government has become too sophisticated to adopt such an approach. If the establishment of powerful 'Island of Ireland' structures are its ultimate intention the approach is likely to continue to be the piecemeal one announced in the Downing Street Declaration and given some substance in the Framework Documents, the 'Propositions on Heads of Agreement' document and the Multi-Party Agreement, where what is envisaged is, in large part, left open to interpretation. However, Maurice Morrow believes that he recognizes a drift:

> The old saying is 'By their fruit you shall know them'. If you plant a field of potatoes you don't expect to go out and reap turnips. If the British government are continually saying to us, 'Oh not at all, the Union is safe' (which we don't believe it is) and every move they make contradicts that, then I think that the British government is sending the Unionist people a signal that they want to see Northern Ireland cut adrift from the rest of the UK. Now, if that happens and if that is their thinking then what in fact they are saying is that democracy is not allowed to work and that puts people into desperate situations.

The implication is that such a course will bring about a doomsday situation with Unionists forced into violent reaction against political developments: 'You would know that if you put a man in a corner to fight for his life he will fight stronger than he has ever fought in his life.'

Maurice Morrow reflects the DUP perception that Irish Nationalists all come from the same traditional/modern mould and, therefore, pose a direct threat to the cultural and political identity of Ulster Unionists. He also echoes the party's deep suspicion of the motives of the Government of the United Kingdom with regard to the constitutional position of Northern Ireland in the United Kingdom. He implies that Unionists will react with all the means at their disposal should an attempt be made at constitutional change for Northern Ireland which provides for island of Ireland structural arrangements. Irish Nationalists, the UK government, the Irish government and the EU represent variable threats to the survival of the Ulster Unionist identity in the interpretations of DUP interviewees.

9 Dialogue with the Ulster Unionist Party (UUP)

INTRODUCTION

The UUP (sometimes known as the Official Unionist Party) represented the Unionist hegemony that existed in Northern Ireland between 1921 and 1972. The party had acted as a successful umbrella for those who prioritized the Union and the Northern Ireland Parliament over a normal left/right cleavage in politics. However, the O'Neill crisis signalled the beginning of the end for the Unionist hegemony in Northern Ireland and led, inevitably, to fractures developing in the Unionist Party. Eventually, the pro-O'Neill support in the party went to the APNI; Vanguard and the DUP captured the anti-O'Neill faction; while the post-Sunningdale supporters of Faulkner formed the Unionist Party of Northern Ireland (UPNI).

From 1921 to 1972, Unionists occupied as many as 40 of the 52 seats in the Northern Ireland House of Commons (Flackes and Elliott, 1994, p. 337). After the Sunningdale fracture, the rump of the party joined with Vanguard and the DUP in the United Ulster Unionist Council (UUUC) to fight the Westminster General Election of January, 1974. The UUP managed to secure 32.3 per cent of the vote, increasing to 36.5 per cent in the October General Election of the same year. The UUP maintained its percentage of the vote in the 1979 Westminster General Election (36.6 per cent) this time without the assistance of the defunct UUUC. In the 1992 Westminster General Election the UUP percentage of the vote was 34.5 per cent. At District Council level the party has fared less well – 29.5 per cent in 1977; 26.5 per cent in 1981; 29.5 per cent in 1985; 31.3 per cent in 1989; and 29.4 per cent in 1993. The dominant personalities of Dr Ian Paisley (DUP) and John Hume (SDLP) in Northern Ireland politics have ensured that successive UUP MEPs have finished third in what has come to be known as Northern Ireland's political 'beauty contest' – the election to the European Parliament. John Taylor received 22.1 per cent of the vote for the party in 1984 and Jim Nicholson received 22.2 per cent of the vote in 1989 and 23.83 per cent in 1994 (Flackes and Elliott, 1994; *Irish Political Studies*, 1995). The UUP secured 24.17 per cent of the vote in the 1996 Northern Ireland Forum election and 32.7 per cent in the 1997 General Election (*Irish News*, 3 May 1997).

In the 1979 election to the European Parliament, John Taylor called for an extensive re-negotiation of the European Community, in contrast to Dr Ian Paisley's outright opposition to the existence of the EU. In 1987, Taylor joined the ultra-right European Right Group when the European Democratic Group, to which he had belonged, gave its support to the Anglo-Irish Agreement (AIA). His successor, Jim Nicholson, joined the European Peoples' Party but announced a switch in allegiance to Sir James Goldsmith's 'Europe of Nations' grouping in December 1996 (*Scotsman*, 24 December 1996).

The UUP prioritizes the union between Northern Ireland and Great Britain in its political dogma and perceives EU processes as representing a threat to that union. Consequently, the UUP is anti-European integrationist:

> The Party upholds the sovereign role of the United Kingdom and refutes the plans for a transfer of defence, foreign policy and currency control to the Community (UUP, 1992).

European Monetary Union is singled out as the development that would shift the balance of power from the modern state to the extraterritorial polity of the EU. For the UUP, such a shift would be a derogation of democracy:

> Ulster Unionists . . . are opposed to the concept of European Monetary Union and a Single Currency since the inevitable consequence would be the transfer of this most fundamental power of Government from elected representatives of the people of the United Kingdom to an unelected body which cannot be dismissed from office by United Kingdom electors (UUP, 1992).

While UUP interviewees show signs of attempting to articulate a position for Ulster Unionism within the EU orbit, it should be noted that both interviewees are involved in EU structures in a representative capacity and may, therefore, not be as alienated from EU structures and processes as the rank and file UUP member.

UUP PERCEPTIONS OF STRUCTURAL CHANGE

Jim Nicholson, UUP, MEP, accepts that the sovereignty of the modern state in the European Union is being challenged but perceives weakness at the core of the movement for European integration:

> There certainly has been an erosion of sovereignty. Every country has had to pool their sovereignty to that extent and their overall control on their future destiny is less now than it was thirty years ago but it is the UK who feels it the most. To some extent that arises from what I call the 'island mentality'; because they are not land-linked to other countries they have always had an island point of view. That goes a long way to creating the concern in their minds *vis-à-vis* the whole future. How much it will erode in the future remains to be seen. A lot will depend, of course, on monetary union – if monetary union comes into being. You can't have a political union without monetary union.

The neo-functionalist concept of 'political spillover' predicts that once institutions establish themselves they often take on a dynamic of their own. EU integrationists argue this to be the case with European institutions. Jim Nicholson is stoical about the development of integrationist institutions and their implications for the autonomy exercised by the UK parliament:

> I think it will be very difficult for them to go back – there is no doubt about that. The present debate that is going on in the UK is proving that of course. What is sovereignty? It is not something you can touch and feel, it is something implied. It means different things to different people. Some people find it a powerful principle, others find it no problem at all. To an extent, the members are largely intertwined by trade. Everyone is trying to gain the maximum out of the system. The problem the UK has, of course, is that it is one of the major contributors without achieving the maximum results from the EU. It certainly leaves them vulnerable to attack from those who do not agree with where the process is going.

Reg Empey (UUP, member of the Committee of the Regions) remains adamant that the process of European integration does not have fundamental implications for the structure of the European state system: 'The term "European integration" is very misleading. There is not the remotest prospect of the nation-states fundamentally disposing of their sovereignty' (interview with the author). However, as a party, the UUP appears to be less certain about the prospects for the nation-state in the EU:

> While prepared to play a constructive role in Europe, the Party would seek a wider European relationship than the EC and a reaffirmation of the primacy of national states (UUP, 1992).

Reg Empey believes that the principle of subsidiarity safeguards the interests of nation-states, especially in member states where regional structures are weak. He does not regard subsidiarity as a threat to the sovereignty of nation-states, designed to devolve power to subnational units:

> There is a doctrine now called 'subsidiarity' which is all-pervasive, certainly in every document the Committee of the Regions looks at. That basically means that we try and get the decision-making unit close to the people. In many cases that is a regional authority (which we don't have, unfortunately) but in many others it is the nation-state and the national government. Where there are clearly issues that are supra-border issues, for example, pollution doesn't stop at a customs post, you need to take a wider perspective – we have no problem with that.

Empey points to the actions of some of the EU's net contributors to support his argument that European integration will be contained to a modest degree by the continued dominance of the member states in the decision-making processes of the EU:

> The idea that some people have that there is, at some time, going to be this superstate – I don't believe that is going to happen. There is a reaction against it already. The Germans are fed up paying for all of this and certainly whenever measures come before our committee that involve expenditure, the Germans are the first up . . . they have had it as far as paying in is concerned because they have their own problems. It has been much more costly to unify Germany than they expected and they are running out of money. As far as the British government is concerned, as the next biggest contributor, they have had it as well. So, I believe that the move to have this superstate – while there is a movement on the ground over there, particularly around the Benelux countries – the payers are not for it any more. I

think you can take it so far and no further. While it may have some way to go in dealing with a lot of the issues that transcend national borders my view is that you will not see the sort of integration that some people are talking about in our lifetime.

UUP interviewees reflect the party perception that structural change in the EU will not lead to a fundamental restructuring of the state system in Europe. Jim Nicholson is not convinced that European Monetary Union, the cornerstone of EU structural change, will be achieved. Reg Empey perceives the principle of subsidiarity to be the safeguard for the authority of national governments. Both interviewees perceive a rising tide of anti-integrationist force among member-state governments which is checking the pace of European integration.

DETERMINING STRUCTURAL PARAMETERS FOR NORTHERN IRELAND

An Extraterritorial Context?

Being a part of the United Kingdom is the best possible outcome for everyone in Northern Ireland – it is best in economic terms and in social terms. People are better off for a start. Levels of consumption and standards of living are higher in Northern Ireland than they are in the Republic of Ireland, and Britain is a modern, liberal, multi-cultural, multi-national state, and it is possible for people within the British state to be Scottish and British, to be Welsh and British, to be Ulster and British, and still live within the same entity – even people who voted for nationalist parties. They are operating within a British cultural framework (David Trimble, in *The British People of Northern Ireland – A Short Resumé of Unionism in Ulster*, 1996 p. 11).

The SDLP has maintained a position that rejects entering into a political arrangement that has not secured representation from beyond the boundaries of the UK. Jim Nicholson suggests that there is a middle ground between the SDLP and the UUP positions which would seem to include an extraterritorial element involving the Republic of Ireland:

It depends what level it is at. If John Hume was saying to me we need co-operation with the South on tourism and agriculture, on health matters, on people who are working the black market on both sides of the border, if he is saying that we need it on drainage and a multiplicity of things, I say OK – I don't have any problem with that. However, it is when you try to create what I call 'the third parliament on the island of Ireland' that the Unionist people baulk. It is, once again, a bridge too far. Co-operation to the maximum benefit of both our peoples, with mutual respect to both our peoples, with a mellowing of Articles Two and Three where they cease to be this big hate figure (although Unionists have lived with it for seventy years and it hasn't done them any harm). If John Hume is saying to me: 'Look, we have got to find out a way in which we can co-operate' – as long as we can keep it at executive level, keep it impartial, so that it is not going to be seen by Unionists as the machine trundling Northern Ireland towards a united Ireland then, yes, there can be something worked out.

He recognizes the import of European integration for providing a suitable context for a process of co-operation between Northern Ireland and the Republic of Ireland:

There has to be co-operation, Europe dictates that there has to be co-operation. We have got the INTERREG programme – that's inter-regional, spent on cross-border projects. Europe will no longer fund a programme on Northern Ireland which puts a grand road up to the border at Middletown if there is not going to be a road on the other side of the border to take the people on ahead. Those type of things demand co-operation.

The principle of North-South co-operation in the EU context is accepted. It is the institutionalization of that co-operation and the relationship between the economic and the political that is the cause of concern for Unionists, according to Jim Nicholson:

When it comes down to the level of the political and the constitutional that's when Unionists begin to baulk and say, 'Oh, no way' because it is being sold as more than it may well be and there is no doubt that is a big difficulty for Unionists. At the end of the day, however, those are the sort of problems that politicians are supposed to resolve. If there is goodwill on both sides, if we get the economic regeneration going in this province and this province begins to move forward economically and viably then we become more confident and then we can take on more challenges. So those are the type of things we want to look for as Unionists.

In the aftermath of the AIA the UUP has invested some effort in attempting to wrest the political initiative from John Hume by suggesting a broader arrangement that embraces the whole of the UK and the Republic of Ireland instead of one that takes Northern Ireland as its focus:

> The Agreement [AIA] concentrates exclusively on Northern Ireland and fails to look at the wider relationships throughout these islands. Ulster Unionists wish to see a broader agreement, one which looks at the geographical region as a whole (UUP, 1996).

According to the UUP, it is the 'British Isles' that should be the focus of any extraterritorial arrangement:

> The natural social and economic unit is the British Isles. The human and organisational inter-relationship on the East-West axis between Northern Ireland and the rest of the United Kingdom and also between the Republic of Ireland and Great Britain are greater in relative terms than the North/South inter-relationships between Northern Ireland and the Republic. It is right that these wider relationships should be recognised: that a genuinely British-Irish Agreement should replace the flawed Anglo-Irish one. This would provide a framework within which there could be accommodated an appropriate cross-frontier relationship, based on pragmatic considerations of mutual benefit and not on a political agenda; this relationship would not pose a threat to either jurisdiction and would, unlike the present arrangements, correspond to real needs and enjoy real support (UUP, 1996).

The 'Propositions on Heads of Agreement' document (1998) presented by the two governments to the Multi-Party Talks on 12 January 1998 proposed a replacement of the Anglo-Irish Agreement (1985) with a British-Irish agreement that included an East-West intergovernmental council, favoured by UUP, as well as a North-South Council of Ministers. UUP negotiators appeared confident that the East-West intergovernmental council would act as 'an umbrella' and would, by implication, have supremacy over North-South bodies (*Irish Times*, 13 January 1998). However, while the Multi-Party Agreement (1998) includes a British-Irish (East-West) council, there is no suggestion of a hierarchical relationship between this council and the North-South Council. Indeed it is implied that the North-South Council will have the greater role. The creation of North-South implementation bodies is mandatory, while the establishment of East-West bodies is voluntary. In addition, the Assembly cannot survive without the North-South Council and vice versa. No such provision is made for the East-West Council.

Whatever the complexion of the extraterritorial dimension in the event of a political settlement, Jim Nicholson has not been encouraged by the performance of his own party since 1985:

> Up until now we have been allowing the British government and the Irish government to destroy our affairs in my opinion because we, the Unionists, hadn't the guts to go out and do the decision-making ourselves, we wanted somebody else to do the dirty work for us. Then you have got the Irish government saying, 'Well we are the protector of the Nationalist community'. I happen to have more respect for the Nationalist community. I think John Hume and the SDLP, as the major Nationalist party, have been able to do a very good job for them to date. But they have also been able to use that support of the Irish government to gain certain advantages for them that were not possible for us to attain as Unionists. So the challenge to Unionists now is to be able to stand up on their own two feet and negotiate with whoever. As I see it, that negotiation has got to be between the SDLP and the Ulster Unionists as the two major parties representing seventy per cent of our people.

Although Jim Nicholson recognizes the benefit of an extraterritorial context in terms of co-operating with the Government of the Republic of Ireland on matters of mutual interest, the prospect of the involvement of the Republic of Ireland and UK governments in the creation of harmonizing structures to administer such interests is viewed with trepidation. However, he perceives that economic regeneration in a stable environment will make Ulster Unionists more flexible in their attitude towards the extraterritorial context.

EU Regionalism and UK Devolution

> The concept of regionalism, especially in the European context, is gaining ground and we see in that further justification for our demand for a full return of democratic accountability to our people. The Ulster Unionist Party will continue to press on the Government (of whatever party) the need to implement those ideals which we have so long advocated: a clearly defined Union which demonstrates beyond doubt that the supreme body is presently, and will remain, the Queen in Parliament (UUP, 1992).

By drawing a parallel between the principle of subsidiarity and the desire for devolution that exists within sections of the UUP, Jim Nicholson is attempting to create a vision of the EU that is compatible with Ulster Unionist identities:

> Unionists will always have difficulties with the European context, there is no doubt about that. But then, you see, there is another argument – and to some extent I am also arguing against myself – I happen to believe in a Northern Ireland Assembly with Northern Ireland people administering their own affairs. I am not talking about going back to pre-1973 Stormont or anything like that. I am talking about a partnership operation between ourselves and other democratically elected bodies on the principles of Europe where you get your share of chairmanships and vice-chairmanships according to the strength that the electorate give to you. So, from that point of view, I am quite happy to argue for that but I do not think that weakens the union.

Framing his argument in terms of British subvention, Reg Empey argues that the adoption of a wholesale EU regionalist approach is inappropriate:

> Let's get Europe into perspective. The amount of money that comes to Northern Ireland from Europe, compared to what is spent here, has to be put into perspective. You are talking about two per cent of Northern Ireland public expenditure coming from a European source. If you include the Peace and Reconciliation Initiative it is a bit more, but it is only two-and-a-half per cent over six years. So, you have got to get that into perspective. It is bigger for the Republic because they are a Cohesion Fund country and we are not. Nevertheless, it is a comparatively minor issue as far as we are concerned. The bulk of our money is from

UK tax sources and, therefore, there is no way you can replace that. After 1999, the European money will slow up dramatically and I do not think that we will be the net beneficiaries that we have been. In fact, I suspect that because it will have reached in excess of eighty per cent of average GDP the Republic will become a net contributor.

I think the impact is exaggerated but, on the positive side, where there is clearly a benefit for us at present, one of my objectives is to get as much in here as we can in the short-term. That is not the only reason for being part of the EU but it is certainly a very practical point.

The implications of the 'Europe of the Regions' thesis for Ulster Unionism have received some attention from the unionist academic Norman Porter. He remains sceptical about the strength of the European challenge and the consequences of such a challenge for the Ulster Unionist identity but, nevertheless, considers the argument that it

> undermines the nation-state basis of their thinking, dislodges the issue of sovereignty from the central place unionists accord it in their dispute with nationalists . . . makes secondary the broader question which they regard as primary, and shifts the locus of their political identity (Porter, 1996, p. 38).

UUP interviewees have attempted to draw conceptual parallels between a devolved system of government for Northern Ireland and the concept of EU regionalism in an effort to formulate a means of coping with such a shift. However, Reg Empey reflects the UUP position that a regional government for Northern Ireland should be directly linked to the central authority of the UK, and not with a central authority in the EU. He takes the view that any relationship between such a regional authority and the EU centre should be conducted through the UK government. Empey cites the amount of subvention coming from the respective centres of the UK and the EU to justify the preferred arrangement of the UUP for any prospective regional authority in Northern Ireland.

A Europe of the Regions?

Whilst the Ulster Unionist Party opposed membership of the EC it accepts that the UK is a member and that it is prudent to contribute in a positive sense to the various internal debates within the community institutions. We must ensure that industry, business and agriculture take advantage of the many Community Programmes of financial support. In future we wish to see the development of a Community Programme to combat coastal erosion (UUP, 1992).

Reg Empey perceives there to be no contradiction in his fundamental position as an Ulster Unionist representative and his participation in an integrationist institution like the Committee of the Regions:

We don't see any conflict of interest. We play an active role in our respective assemblies – Jim Nicholson in the Parliament – me in the Committee of the Regions – and we both belong to one of the main political groupings in both of those institutions.

Regions throughout the UK see merit in establishing offices at the EU centre in order to provide better representation for their particular region in Europe. Reg Empey is confident that Northern Ireland can benefit from similar representation:

Denis Haughey (SDLP) and I are directors of the Northern Ireland Centre in Europe and every local authority here contributes towards it. That particular body has been playing a growing role over there and I am one hundred per cent behind the idea of having representation. In fact, while the Irish government had very strong representation, I think some of Southern counties have decided to set up shop as well. The feeling, even in the Republic, was that we needed something more localized. All of the major regions eventually will have offices – this is a trend that you are going to see. I welcome it. It gives us an identity over there.

By advocating such representation Empey implicitly recognizes a shortfall in the representation of Northern Ireland in the EU by the UK government:

We see it as an early warning system because the UK government handles European affairs in a totally different way to most other countries and we tend to be very isolated from it. Agriculture is still our major business but it is not high on the UK government's agenda. There are incompatibilities in objectives so having an outfit out there would be useful.

Despite this, Empey does not entertain the idea that the Government of the Republic of Ireland would be more suited to representing Northern Ireland on such matters in the Council of Ministers. However, his emphasis on cross-border co-operation implies that the regional representation he envisages is not strictly based on the modern territorial alignment of Great Britain and Northern Ireland:

> If we had a regional government I have no doubt it would take that over and expand it and push our own local agenda there because the 'Europe of the Regions' is a concept which allows for cross-border co-operation on a whole range of issues and you are encouraged to have triangular links.

Despite dissatisfaction with the UK government's representation of Northern Ireland's affairs in the EU, the UUP show now signs of withdrawing support for this arrangement. However, Reg Empey suggests that the shortfall might be corrected through some form of direct regional representation to the institutions of the EU.

The Role of 'Humespeak'

The SDLP is a keen exponent of the language of European integration – the concept of a 'Europe of the Regions' is central to its political philosophy. Reg Empey believes that the SDLP's adoption of this discourse in the 1980s was complementary to the political philosophy of European integration but that it had a modern irredentist sub-text:

> It is another way of taking their fundamental objective and packaging it in a way that makes people feel less uncomfortable with it and it happened at that time to be the trend although the trend is not as powerful as it was a couple of years ago. Delors was the driving force at that stage, his loss will probably decelerate the whole process.

When John Hume talks of ' . . . our legitimate calls and efforts to secure for Nationalist people the right to effective political, symbolic and administrative expression of their identity' (Hume, 1996, p. 25), Reg Empey's modernist terms of political reference lead him to interpret such a statement as being incompatible with the principle of consent. This is because the Unionist position maintains that the majority should provide such an expression within a territorial boundary defined by the modern state. Therefore, the witholding of Unionist consent for such an expression by northern Irish Nationalists represents an effective veto on that expression, and on an All-Ireland state, in Reg Empey's interpretation. Empey perceives that the SDLP's objective is still a fundamentally modern nationalist one:

> Going back to the 1970s, their fundamental objective was, in the shorter term, to create a condominium. That was their policy in 1975 and in a variety of forms it re-emerges subsequently. If you use phrases like 'equal political, administrative and symbolic expression', effectively, in order to achieve those, you have to put the Dublin dimension on an equal footing with the London dimension, so effectively you create a condominium. Of course, there is a contradiction in that if you go for the concept of consent and you argue that if you put a proposition separately but concurrently to two separate jurisdictions [as the SDLP do] and they agree to that then it may be that the decision that they want need not necessarily be the one that is agreed to, but I personally feel that is ultimately the objective.

The experience of Northern Ireland is an abject lesson in the reaffirming quality of language. Slogans such as 'No Surrender' and 'Tiochfaidh ar Lá' have dominated the political language in Northern Ireland. With postmodern structural change, John Hume has been keen to pioneer a complementary discourse of 'interdependency', 'consent' and 'agreement' as a means of transcending the dialect of conflict in Northern Ireland. UUP interviewees have shown an interest in applying this dialect to their own context. However, Jim Nicholson perceives that such articulation, aimed at re-contextualizing the political situation in terms of regionalism and community rather than territory and the nation-state, is, of itself, not sufficient to neutralize the Unionist-Nationalist conflict of interest in the short-term. He believes that a political settlement for Northern Ireland cannot wait until the evolution of the state reaches a stage where the equation of the nation and the modern state is less binding:

> I think maybe if you and I were discussing this in ten years time that may well be the case. The problem is what do we do in the interim period. We have got to get something going on. At the

end of the day, we are going to have to sit down and we are going to have to resolve it and there are people who are out there in both communities who have achieved their power from the barrel of a gun who have ultimately got to become politicians – that will take time and it is not going to be easy. But at least as long as the peace holds and nobody is getting killed at least we can look forward maybe to something at the end and it will not be everything I want nor will it be everything that a Nationalist or Catholic will want but at least it will be a nucleus of how we will be able to live together without continually killing each other.

Jim Nicholson agrees that it is the job of politicians not only to reflect the opinions of their constituents but also to influence those opinions. He suggests that the EU, by providing a platform that is not compromised by the constitutional argument, allows Northern Ireland's MEPs to co-operate on the issues upon which they agree. He believes that they are able to reflect and influence opinions through such co-operation without the danger of it becoming politically disabling:

If you look at how closely John Hume, Ian Paisley and myself work together in Europe we have proved that that can be done. The challenge to Unionism is facing up to a Northern Ireland at peace and to develop new arguments that are going to be needed and required for that period and for that time. It is the politician's job to lead the people but it is also his job not to get that far in front of the people that the people don't know where he is going. That has been some of the weaknesses of Unionist politicians in the past and that is one of the strengths that is more abroad at the moment whereby we have been moving substantially but at least where people can see where we are going. It has been easy for John Hume, because he has always had the backing of the Dublin government of whatever political persuasion. I don't think anyone could say the Unionists have the British government in their hip pocket any more. The Ulster Unionists are a very small regional political party with very little financial resources. We don't have any other support and that is one of our major problems. You are taking on the Department of Foreign Affairs in Dublin or the Foreign Office in London or whatever and you have got to be mighty careful when you are dealing with guys like that.

UUP interviewees are tentatively developing an interpretation of structural change and show some signs of adapting to postmodern concepts like 'consent' and 'agreement', with their focus on community rather than on territory. Reg Empey still shares the DUP perception that the 'Euro-speak' pioneered by John Hume is merely a new dialect aimed at achieving a modern nationalist ambition. However, Jim Nicholson admits that an articulation which implies a regional rather than a nation-state context may be a useful contingent in resolving the political conflict in Northern Ireland. Nevertheless, he envisages that more concrete evidence of structural change is required before such a context can be absorbed into the political consciousness of communal identities in Northern Ireland. In the meantime, he is anxious that UUP leaders avoid becoming too far removed from the modernist perceptions of Ulster Unionist identities. It is these modernist perceptions, in turn, that maintain a rejection of major cross-border innovations, especially on the island of Ireland.

Jim Nicholson recognizes that a 'peace process' presents new challenges to Ulster Unionists. However, some political commentators have expressed scepticism about the ability of Ulster Unionist politicians to adopt an innovative and proactive outlook when confronted with opportunities created by the 'peace process' of the 1990s. According to David McKittrick:

> The Unionist psyche is full of dark fears and lurking suspicions. The legacies of history and geography mean that they are subject to an uncertainty that at the best of times borders on the chronic. This means that the average Unionist politician is, naturally enough, opposed to the IRA campaign when the republicans are killing people and doing damage; but is also, paradoxically, suspicious of cease-fires because he sees other dangers there (*The Independent*, 1 September 1994).

STRUCTURAL CHANGE AND UNIONIST IDENTITIES REPRESENTED BY THE UUP

The Economic Resource

Jim Nicholson seems to be amenable to a consideration of ways in which Ulster Unionist identities can be given an EU perspective in terms of their economic resource. Like the DUP interviewees, Nicholson is encouraged by the degree of successful co-operation achieved by the three Northern Ireland MEPs on the European platform:

> One of the things that the three Northern Ireland MEPs were able to do during Jacques Delors' time was to keep EU interest in Northern Ireland confined to economic and agricultural areas and regional policy where they affect everyone and certainly keeping out of the constitutional aspect of things. That has been important for me as Unionist and I presume even more so for Dr Paisley who has even stronger opposing views to Europe than I. I don't think there is a future within Europe whereby the island of Ireland is united or something like that. I think there is a cultural identity amongst the Unionist community that no power on earth can ever remove or change. What we have got to do is, in conjunction with the other people who live in Northern Ireland with us, work out how we are going to live together.

The Territorial Resource

Jim Nicholson candidly admits that there is some incongruity in a Unionist representative going outside the UK's national boundary and attending a supranational parliament that represents a potential threat to the autonomy of the UK: 'There is a fair element of truth in that but this has been the real problem for unionism from the day and hour that the UK joined Europe'. However, he feels justified in his participation because of the current reality of European integration: 'It is there and it is taking on an even greater dynamic approach to things. It is evolving, it is dictating the pace of the political decisions that are happening throughout Europe (interview with the author)'.

This acceptance of the reality of the process moves him to favour interaction with EU institutions:

> We would be very stupid if we were not at least within that trying to get the best for our own region because if you stand in the one place the world passes you by. We can't afford that any more. Modern society dictates that you must be part of whatever is evolving. Now, if you happen to be a minority within that, if you happen to be unable to agree with what is happening or where it is going, you still have the right to have your say and

try to get the best for the people you represent. That, I think, is the Unionist point of view.

The SDLP argues that extraterritorial involvement in a structure of government for Northern Ireland is the best political formula for the representation of Ulster Unionists and northern Irish Nationalist communities. However, Reg Empey remains wary of the motives of political parties that base their politics on 'community' rather than on 'territory'. He questions the 'communal' terms of reference:

What, at the end of the day, does community mean? It can mean a group of people who coalesce around one particular political objective or it can mean a group of people who share a similar religion or race or background or whatever part of the world you happen to be in. The problem is, when push comes to shove, somebody has got to sign the cheques or somebody has got to take a decision on A, B, or C. That is where the concept of 'the state' comes in.

The concept of the state that Empey applies to the quest for political accommodation in Northern Ireland is still rigidly defined by the modern emphasis on sovereign territory:

We have got this overlapping situation [in Northern Ireland] where people see their statehood as being represented by the Irish government and Irish State and others see it being represented by the UK. There are basically three options that you are left with. Either one group concedes to the other or you try and create this condominium.

From our point of view, we have no difficulty with people seeking to pursue whatever legitimate political objectives they wish to pursue by peaceful means. If some people feel themselves to be Irish in the sense of belonging to the island as a single decision-making unit then you cannot take that out of a person – that is how they feel. Equally, if people feel themselves joined to a larger unit you cannot take that out of the person either; that is how they feel; that is what they are; it is their background; it is their culture; it is a variety of different things. But at the end of the day you have to belong to something or other. The difficulty we have is trying to find formulae which do not, on the one hand, conflict with the province being part of the UK in a meaningful sense, and, on the other hand, give those who don't feel comfortable within the UK: (a) a sense of ownership; (b) a feeling that they are not isolated and cut off from the state to which they feel they belong.

Although dismissive of the role of European integration, Reg Empey recognizes that northern Irish Nationalists require, to a greater or lesser extent, the representation of a structure of state other than that of the UK:

> This runs you up against all of the technicalities and legalities of sovereignty and who takes the final decisions etc. My own view is that we are moving to a point where Unionists can acknowledge that there are obvious practical benefits to be gained from what we loosely call 'cross-border co-operation'. But the principal benefit from it is not necessarily the economic benefit, which probably is highly exaggerated but, nevertheless, is there. The principal benefit is that, for those who feel that they wish to belong to a unit that stretches south as opposed to east, if we can create a structure there that allows them to have that feeling then there is a political benefit to be gained. So the question is: how do you design that in such a way that it gives people a sense of belonging to a wider Irish unit without creating effectively the transfer of sovereignty so that Unionists become part of some amorphous country that doesn't quite ... has one leg in, one leg out? That is the art of the solution. As far as I can see, looking at it from a Nationalist perspective, Nationalists will benefit. There will be a net gain in the sense that they will gain by a North-South link. They will not gain as much as they wish to gain but they will have a net gain. From a Unionist point of view, we have got to achieve a net gain out of that as well and I believe that with the practicalities, the economic benefits and the economies of scale, some areas might gain a net benefit from that.

Jim Nicholson believes that it would be a dereliction of duty for the UUP not to support interaction with the extraterritorial structure of the EU. Nevertheless, his desire to maintain a position in the evolving state system, as an MEP, contrasts with his dislike, as a Unionist, for the extraterritorial influence of the EU in the affairs of Northern Ireland and the UK in general. Reg Empey presents a modern diagnosis of the Northern Ireland problem. His assertion that ' ... you have to belong to something or other' indicates that his perception of communal identity cannot envisage a scenario whereby communal identity transcends the territorial bind of the modern state. Reg Empey acknowledges that cross-border structures may provide a key element in achieving political accommodation between Ulster Unionists and northern Irish Nationalists. The art of the solution, he maintains, will be in the formulation of units that do not impinge upon the territorial sovereignty of the UK.

The Cultural Resource

> The Ulster Young Unionist Committee on Culture contends that for too long we have been content to neglect our culture while Gaelic nationalism has made every effort and used every opportunity to propound Irish culture. The end result has been that our side of the cultural argument has not been properly heard . . . for far too many people the term 'Ulster culture' signifies nothing more than Orangemen parading on the 12th of July (Ulster Young Unionist Council, 1986, p. 1).

Shared memories, imbued by religious, social and cultural institutions, practices and values contribute to the cultural resource of Ulster Unionism. These cultural traits are underscored by an essential Protestant-British ethos (Porter, 1996, p. 83). So-called 'liberal' unionists, such as Robert McCartney, MP, subscribe to the British element of this equation which involves placing British institutions, the Act of Union (1801) and the Government of Ireland Act (1920) at the heart of their brand of unionism. They have argued that the overt connection between mainstream Ulster Unionism and Ulster Protestantism detracts from the unionist case by exposing it to the charge of sectarianism (Porter, 1996, p. 73). However, the fact remains that the shared memories of a majority of Ulster Unionists continue to incorporate the historical landmarks of Ulster Protestantism. Ulster Unionist shared memories include: the massacre of Protestants in 1641; the Siege of Derry in 1689; the Battle of the Boyne in 1690; the signing of the Ulster Solemn League and Covenant in 1912; the sacrifice made by the 36th Ulster Division at the Battle of the Somme in 1916; and the Ulster Workers' Council Strike in 1974. The annual Siege of Drumcree (since 1995) is currently being woven into the cultural tapestry of shared memory. For Norman Porter, these essential cultural dates reinforce: (a) a sense of isolation on the island of Ireland in the Ulster Unionist consciousness; (b) their perceived right to uphold the Protestant and British way of life in the North; and (c) the willingness of Ulster Protestants to make sacrifices for the Union and the Ulster Unionist identity (Porter, 1996, p. 87).

With Ulster Protestantism maintaining its position as the cultural core of Ulster Unionism, those Catholics from Northern Ireland who may be pro-union (in the UK context) for economic reasons are presented with a significant stumbling block in subscribing to a unionist position. The chronic nature of this problem was graphically illustrated at the Siege of Drumcree in July 1995 during which David Trimble, MP, negotiated with police to allow an Orange march to pass through a Catholic district of his Upper Bann constituency despite the protests of local constituents. Together with the Reverend Ian Paisley, MP, MEP, he was later awarded a commemorative medal for his leading role in what was perceived to be a 'victory for Protestantism' (*Guardian*, 11 September 1995). The awards ceremony took place on the morning of the UUP leadership election and is thought to have played an influential role in Mr Trimble's unexpected elevation to the leadership of the party (*The Independent*, 11 September 1995). Jim Nicholson concedes that the link between Ulster Protestantism and Ulster Unionism is undeniable:

I don't think there is any point in me starting to deny that Ulster Unionism was born out of Ulster Protestantism – of course it was, just as the twenty-six county state was born out of Catholic nationalism or republicanism. But to a large extent, that was seventy years ago. If you look at the Republic at the moment they have moved towards a much more pluralist society than they ever had or experienced in the past, there have been a lot of changes there although they still have a long way to go of course. There is a lot of folk in the Republic whose only desire in life is to have a better standard of living and a better future for their kids. The difference, as I see it in Northern Ireland is because of, for the lack of better description, 'The Troubles'. They have certainly polarized the communities, where you are encased in a block – whatever church your parents went to. That is something that can only change over a period of time. But you make a point to me that some of us within Unionism are very conscious of because I have met Catholics who have quite openly said to me: 'Look, I am a unionist but to be honest with you I could not join your party at the present moment in time'. I accept that. There is an onus on us, with the process of time, to evolve a party that will be able to take on board the greater number of the people of Northern Ireland.

The Troubles have polarized the two communities – Catholics as well as Protestants – we have got to move away from that but we are still too close to the events of the last twenty-five years to be able to make the quantum leap required and it will take a little bit of time but equally I have got to say to you, you could put that question to John Hume and he would say to you, 'Well I have Protestants who are in my party' but at the end of the day he and I have got to accept one important thing – they are a very small number within our ranks. However, as we move to a more pluralist society these changes will eventually come.

The 1995 UUP annual party conference indicated that a majority of delegates favoured the structural separation of the party from the Protestant Orange Order (*Financial Times*, 23 October 1995). It is possible to interpret such a move as being indicative of the UUP's desire to appeal to those northern Catholics who would perceive their economic interests being best served by maintaining the union. The problem is that when such potential voters see the leader of the UUP appearing to play a co-ordinating role in forcing an Orange march through a Catholic district of his constituency then the UUP lost credibility in presenting itself as a purely political 'pro-union' party able to accommodate those of a pro-union perspective, irrespective of religious affiliation. Reg Empey recognizes this but suggests that practical politics make a disassociation of the party with the symbols and institutions of Ulster Protestantism a perilous task to undertake:

> I understand the point you are making but you have to understand what the other side of that coin is. Our party's supporters, in practice, in the main, at the polls, are up against Paisley. The SDLP are not taking votes from us, Sinn Féin are not taking votes from us. At elections, the main threat is Paisley and that has been the position for many years. Over the past period, with wall-to-wall saturation coverage of Adams and McGuinness making the running – that has created a reaction amongst many of our supporters. They are saying: 'These guys are walking all over us and they are tramping us into the ground' and certain things have happened that appear to be manifestations of the govern-

ment conceding to this, that and the other. So, that is where that sort of thing comes from.

I understand the point you are making and Jim Molyneaux, when he was leader, tried to develop this notion of 'the greater number'. The difficulty for us is that we are not in power of any kind, you cannot implement anything, you cannot do anything. It is very difficult to produce in practice, day-to-day solutions to problems that people could work with and live with. As far as what Trimble was involved in and how that is perceived – I understand, I can see how it is perceived. But, at the end of the day, he is going to have to be measured up in terms of what he actually does and what proposals come forward and are ultimately put to the people for their approval. That, really, is going to be when everybody is going to be called out to put up or shut up. We will see at that point just where we go.

Reg Empey emphasizes his perception that the Irish and British establishments regard Northern Ireland as an alien problem that is best kept isolated:

I do feel that most people, particularly in Dublin (I see a lot of the Irish representatives on the Committee of the Regions) do not want anybody from here messing up their patch. They have got a wee system down there, it is working well, they are happy, they have got the big Mercedes and limousines. In many ways the politicians in the Republic are happy with the Republic – why wouldn't they be? They see us, more or less, as a threat, as a nuisance. We are upsetting their tourist flow and we are costing money for extra security. Ironically, you have this kind of situation where politicians in Dublin and in London share this one common denominator – that we are all a bloody nuisance. At the end of the day, the only people who really care about us – plural – is us.

Unionist representatives present the view that unionism need not necessarily be a signifier of ethnicity, described by the cultural resource of Ulster Protestantism. There is a 'liberal' unionist contingent within the UUP that recognizes Protestantism to be little more than a residual component of British culture and would like to relegate Protestantism in the Ulster Unionist identity accordingly. Nevertheless, UUP interviewees recognize that the cultural cornerstone of Ulster Unionism is Ulster Protestantism, conferring on

Ulster Unionism the status of an ethnic identity. The active participation of the party leader, David Trimble, MP, in the annual 'Siege of Drumcree' was designed to appeal to this cultural resource, underlining the essential Ulster Protestant ethnicity of Ulster Unionists. The alternative cultural expression of Ulster Unionism – 'Britishness' – has eroded with the loss of empire, doubts about the value of the monarchy and the continuing integration of the United Kingdom into the European Union. While such developments have signalled the beginning of a reassertion of nationalities within the United Kingdom, those who continue to identify themselves as 'British' are left with an increasingly bare cultural chest to plunder as they attempt to give meaning to their British 'imagined community'.

10 Dialogue with the Alliance Party of Northern Ireland (APNI)

INTRODUCTION

The APNI was formed in April 1970 and gained support from the pro-O'Neill faction of the Unionist Party. The APNI presents itself as the party of reconciliation, drawing support from Catholics and Protestants in Northern Ireland. The APNI is pro-union with Great Britain, supporting devolution based on a system of power-sharing in that context. During the 1975 Convention election campaign the APNI withdrew its support for the Sunningdale idea of a Council of Ireland (Flackes and Elliott, 1994, p. 78). Thereafter, the APNI consistently opposed the establishment of a formal body to represent a cross-border dimension. However, the party's support for the Framework Documents (1995) and subsequent elaboration by Dr John Alderdice, party leader 1987–98, on the matter in this dialogue indicates that the present position is one of support for a system of 'cross-border structures'.

In its first electoral outing, the 1973 District Council elections, the APNI secured 13.7 per cent of the vote, but the party was squeezed to 3.2 per cent and 6.3 per cent of the vote in the Westminster General elections of February and October 1974 respectively. The vote rallied at 9.8 per cent in the 1975 Convention election and increased to an all-time high of 14.4 per cent in the 1977 District Council elections. Over the past two decades the percentage of the vote gained by the party has fluctuated between 7 per cent and 10 per cent in both General and District Council elections. The APNI's performance in the successive elections to the European Parliament has suffered noticeably from the dominance of Northern Ireland's big political personalities – Ian Paisley and John Hume – in these elections. The party's record in European elections is 6.8 per cent in 1979; 5.0 percent in 1984; 5.2 per cent in 1989; and 4.13 per cent in 1994 (Flackes and Elliott, 1994; *Irish Political Studies*, 1995). In the 1996 Northern Ireland Forum election

179

the APNI received 6.54 per cent of the vote rising to 8 per cent in the 1997 General Election (*Irish News*, 3 May 1997).

The APNI is pro-European integrationist, a position confirmed by the declaration that:

Alliance takes a positive attitude to the European Community. We campaigned successfully for a 'YES' vote in the 1975 referendum on the UK's membership and we continue to believe that Britain should participate wholeheartedly in the Community's institutions (APNI, 1992).

APNI PERCEPTIONS OF STRUCTURAL CHANGE

The enthusiasm of the APNI for structural change based on the EU's regionalist principle was highlighted in a speech by **John Alderdice** before the European Parliament election of 1989:

I want to see a Europe of the Regions where we can proudly maintain our regional heritage but contribute to and be enriched by the interdependence of the whole Community. We do not want to replace Mrs Thatcher's centrism with European centrism, we want to see a united but decentralized Europe, a federal community of free and caring citizens (*Alliance News*, May 1989).

John Alderdice recognizes technological advancement as the catalyst for globalization and has considered its implications for forming and developing transterritorial political relationships:

Some of the folks I'm closest with in working arrangements are people in Washington because of a fax and a 'phone and so on we can communicate backwards and forwards with each other a great deal. I would feel closer then to someone who was liberal say in the United States than I would feel to someone who was a Conservative in Belfast or London (interview with the author).

The APNI's affiliation to the European Liberal, Democratic and Reformist group of parties is the embodiment of such a transterritorial relationship. The APNI asserts that it

. . . is itself well established in Europe. It is one of thirteen member parties of the Federation of the European Liberal, Democratic and Reformist Parties (ELDR) whose representatives are to be found in leading positions in the governments of several member states of the EEC. Alliance supports the Federation's common programme (APNI, 1992).

John Alderdice attended the ELDR's Berlin Congress which was held two months prior to the Maastricht summit. The Congress agreed a set of common resolutions to be proposed at Maastricht on the way ahead for European integration (Greer, 1993, p. 211). The APNI also adopted a common manifesto agreed with its ELDR partners for the 1994 European Election:

> As a member of the ELDR party, the Alliance Party has agreed a common manifesto, 'Building a Citizen's Europe', with its ELDR partners. This manifesto, adopted in December 1993, provides the main planks of our own platform for the elections to the European Parliament in June 1994 (APNI, 1994).

However, Alderdice cautions against a premature translation of this transterritorial political interaction into planning for an effective shift in the balance of power between sub-national, national and supranational structures:

> Well, that is intrinsically a liberal notion, so yes I agree with it but it is the time scale I'm not sure of – is this something that is going to take five years, twenty-five years or a hundred years? I don't know – it's hard to predict how long these things take.

Nevertheless, specific links are developing between the APNI and Liberal Parties in other regions: with the Liberal Democrats in Great Britain, the Progressive Democrats and Fine Gael in the Republic of Ireland, as well as Liberal parties in Europe and further afield. There would therefore appear to be a framework developing for some kind of postmodern political party network that recognizes the incremental shift away from power based at the nation-state centre and is adapting accordingly. He welcomes such a development:

> I would certainly be very pleased to see that happening because while the nation-state has certain values it is not the only way for people in the world to govern themselves by a long stretch. It is a fairly recent phenomenon and it has its big problems and I would like to see us moving away from it. Liberal International has grown enormously in the last ten years so I think you may well be pointing at something that is moving to some kind of international network and whether a United Nations can actually

facilitate that or whether, like the League of Nations, it crumbles away and something else comes into its place I really don't know but I suspect that you are right that we are moving slowly and stumblingly towards another way of operating and certainly if we are that is extremely exciting.

The APNI shares the SDLP's enthusiasm for the process of European integration and agrees that the EU is an endemic feature of structural change in contemporary society. The preferred outcome of structural change for the party also coincides, in many respects, with the SDLP vision of a 'Europe of the Regions'. However, such structural change is viewed as a long-term proposition by John Alderdice and planned for accordingly.

DETERMINING STRUCTURAL PARAMETERS FOR NORTHERN IRELAND

Devolution

The APNI is the principal advocate of a devolved system of government for Northern Ireland (in the UK context) based on a form of power-sharing. It is in this modernist context that the APNI currently gives primary substantive meaning to the concept of regionalism. According to John Alderdice:

> Within Northern Ireland, it is our view that all parties which do not regard violence as a legitimate political instrument have the right to be involved in government in a proportion to the votes they have and the number of assembly people they have. Now, our own proposal as a party, which was published in 1988, suggested that you would need to have a coalition government which could command a minimum of 65 to 70 per cent of the votes in an assembly. No coalition of UUP, DUP and anybody else in this community that did not cross the divisions of this community could ever achieve that sort of level – a weighted majority. So, this is a way of ensuring that right to the very top of any form of government they would have to be drawn from across the community division.
>
> Secondly, that the people of Northern Ireland have the constitutional arrangement which they want, that is to say they remain in the United Kingdom for as long as they want, become part of a united Ireland if they want or whatever it happens to be.

Thirdly, there needs to be some protection for minority rights. We have proposed a Bill of Rights and other protections as well.

The APNI currently upholds the modern delineation of Northern Ireland as the dominant political entity. This position is maintained by the party's consistent support for a devolved form of government for Northern Ireland with a power-sharing executive based on the principle of weighted majority.[1] The APNI's devolutionist proposals indicate that, although the APNI recognizes structural change in the EU and actively participates in extraterritorial party structures pertaining to it, the party continues to perceive the modern state as the structure on which a government for Northern Ireland should be based.

An Extraterritorial Context

The Downing Street Declaration opens the way for the establishment of... an Assembly alongside practical and significant cross-border structures to deal with issues like Animal Health, Tourism, and Environmental Protection. Most importantly, of course, the Declaration is a firm written guarantee that both governments will respect the right of the people of Northern Ireland to determine their own future without coercion (APNI, 1994).

At the beginning of the 1990s the APNI's proposals for a system of government for Northern Ireland adopted an extraterritorial dimension that involved not only strengthening the European dimension but also the development of bodies to facilitate cross-border co-operation where it would be mutually beneficial to North and South, as John Alderdice explains:

We clearly have a relationship with the rest of the island from an economic, social and cultural point of view but because also a minority of people within Northern Ireland look to Dublin rather than to London for their political allegiance – it is important to recognize that. Therefore, the construction of North-South bodies which are accountable and transparent but, nevertheless, significant and recognizing certain economic realities – these are an important matter as well.

In terms of North-South co-operation, we think that there is considerable opportunity for the development of bodies which would have considerable latitude in their own areas as long as they were accountable, constitutionally correct and were able to be transparent to the people so that the people could see what was going on. There are many ways where we co-operate and which have not been exploited. If you look at most professional bodies, most of the main churches – these are all pre-partition organisations that are organized on an All-Ireland basis but there has been little exploitation of that island-wide dimension to many of these things. There is much that can be done at an economic level. There are ways that we can co-operate. There are other ways in which we are in competition and we shouldn't pretend that we are not. I mean Galway is in competition with Dublin too but we are certainly in competition North-South.

Alderdice elaborated on this 'co-operation versus competition' concern and its implication for North-South structures, proposed in the Framework Documents (1995), during a formal contribution to the Forum for Peace and Reconciliation in Dublin on 19 May 1995. He suggested that there were limits to co-operation in the business and industrial sector, such as co-operation between the Industrial Development Agency in the Republic of Ireland and its Northern equivalent, the Industrial Development Board. However, he identified broad areas of interest in agriculture, the environment, energy and transport, alongside specific areas where co-operation would be beneficial, such as, 'high tech' health care, drugs and education (*Irish Times*, 20 May 1995). As well as being intrinsically valuable, Alderdice argues that co-operation may also help alleviate the disaffection of northern Irish Nationalists with the Northern Ireland context: 'There are ways in which we can co-operate and which I think give some sense to Nationalist people that they are not excluded from the political affairs of the island as a whole'.

The APNI supported the Framework Documents (1995) which propose North-South co-operation in aspects of a broad sweep of policy areas – proposals that were rejected outright by both the DUP and the UUP. Previously, agreement between the APNI, the UUP and the DUP on the parameters of a system of governance for Northern Ireland had been reached during the 1991–2 talks. Unionists look to the notion of the sovereignty of the United Kingdom as the fundamental guarantor of their identity. North-South bodies represent a more obvious and immediate threat to the sovereignty of the United Kingdom for them than European integration. However, Alderdice maintains that extraterritorial involvement does not necessarily mean that the sovereignty of the modern state is lost:

> As far as sovereignty is concerned, it is not correct to say that it is lost. Sovereignty is, if you like, the group equivalent of autonomy, and autonomy is not an all-or-nothing phenomenon. One can have degrees of autonomy and one can pool autonomy with other people, they can transfer autonomy when they give other people rights to make decisions about your life. This is what happens at a group level. Now from my point of view the notion of joint authority or joint sovereignty between London and Dublin over Northern Ireland I don't find attractive because I do not think it works practically and, as well as that it is somewhat offensive to a liberal because it means that the people concerned aren't the ones who have the say in their future. What I do find attractive is the notion of people North and South finding ways that they can work together. You can call it sharing autonomy or whatever, I don't really care very much about that. The point is there are certain practical issues on which we can work together and as long as those who represent the North and those who represent the South come to reach agreement with each other on whatever they do together there is no problem about that. You could say that it is shared sovereignty because that term doesn't bother me at all, we do that all the time in Europe.

The APNI appears to be more amenable to the creation of North-South bodies now than in 1975 when it withdrew its support for the Sunningdale idea of a Council of Ireland. However, the APNI adopted a pragmatic approach to its political strategy when it reached agreement with the UUP and DUP on a structure of government for Northern Ireland in the 1991–2 Brooke/Mayhew Talks. The party subsequently endorsed the proposals on North-South links contained in the Framework Documents (1995), proposals vilified by the APNI's erstwhile partners in agreement – the UUP and the DUP.

STRUCTURAL CHANGE AND IDENTITIES REPRESENTED BY THE APNI

'Hybrid' Identities

In the early 1980s, Edward Moxon-Browne detected an attempt by APNI supporters to break the sectarian mould of political allegiance in Northern Ireland. Alliance Protestants were more likely than Protestants in general to consider themselves 'Irish' – 15.7 per cent compared to 6.8 per cent. Alliance Catholics were also more likely than Catholics in general to consider themselves 'British' – 28 per cent compared to 15.7 per cent (Moxon-Browne, 1983, p. 69). However, with 45.9 per cent of Alliance Catholics as opposed to 15.7 per cent of Alliance Protestants considering themselves to be 'Irish' and 57.4 per cent of Alliance Protestants as opposed to 28.2 per cent of Alliance Catholics considering themselves to be 'British', a strong cleavage can be seen to persist. Moxon-Browne concluded that

> on crunch issues affecting the status of Northern Ireland and attempts to subvert it, Protestants and Catholics in the Alliance Party retreat some way, but rarely all the way, towards their traditional 'encampments' (Moxon-Browne, 1983, p. 78).

It has been claimed subsequently that the Catholic vote for the APNI has dissipated because of the growing confidence of northern Irish Nationalists in their identity[2] (in O'Connor, 1993, p. 376). However, a developing system of EU multi-level governance would present an opportunity for the development of 'hybrid' identities in Northern Ireland based on an Irish-British-European axis. The APNI provides a natural conduit for the representation of such identities. As a result, urban, middle-class Catholics could satisfactorily retain an Irish cultural dimension to their identity in such an arrangement, while at the same time, conceivably identify economically with a structural link to Britain. Similarly, though perhaps more fantastically, potential hybrid identities in the Protestant farming community could conceivably maintain a sense of cultural Britishness, defined in terms of Ulster Protestantism, while seeing their economic interests in the EU best served by representation in an Irish regional or border region context. John Alderdice agrees that a movement away from the contextualization of identity by the modern state may be beneficial for identities represented by APNI. He perceives that there is already a postmodernist revival in the complexity of Irish identity incorporating premodern components:

> What I want to take you back to is when you speak about some people seeing themselves as Irish and some people seeing themselves as British: I think what many people here have lost is the fact that pre-partition and the further back you go people didn't see a conflict necessarily between being British and being Irish any more than being Scottish and being British. What is very sad is that the notion of being Irish became, in some people's minds, so exclusive that it became necessarily Gaelic, Catholic etc. whereas there was a breadth and a variety of Irishness which I think, to some extent, has been lost. Now when I say lost, I think it has been increasingly regained over the past twenty-five years but I think there was a time when there was a kind of monotone Irishness. Everything was shades of green rather than a more variegated pattern and so, from my own party's point of view, the notion of being Irish is not a problem in the slightest and some people may feel more or less British and many may feel that they are simply Northern Irish people. That is what is important to them and they will make their judgements on what state they belong to on the basis of what is best for them.

Alderdice also attempts to give these identities a context beyond the modern state by underscoring the value of a European dimension to identity:

> Of course the sharedness of being European is a very valuable thing and I think the more one travels the more one realizes that there is a commonness about our European home and European traditions and music and art and history etc. which is rather valuable and that we can share and the more that we are able to travel in each other's regions and countries and appreciate all of that then that is tremendous.

As a long-term prospect, he is hopeful that identity will centre on a European political axis which is strong on the devolution of power to the regions:

> For me, if you could suddenly magic us forward a hundred years what would be the ideal? I'm quite clear about it – it would be that we would have a united Europe of the Regions and we would like to play up the developments of the Committee of the Regions

rather than the Council of Ministers but I have to say, however, as much as I would like it to be so, that is a long-term objective.

He emphasizes the long-term nature of European integration and its possible influence on communal identity in Northern Ireland when he says that

> the notion of a united Ireland or of a United Kingdom is not going to disappear overnight – I think it will change and it has begun to change but I think it would be unwise to suggest that over the next five or ten years the European ideal is going to transform all these nationalist views and make them irrelevant – I think that is an illusion. These things are much deeper and more profound than that and they won't be magicked away.

The notion of 'hybrid' identities, where the economic, territorial and cultural resources of identity are aligned to different nation-states, is one that the APNI has attempted to accommodate. However, John Alderdice perceives that the development of the structure of power along the supranational-national-subnational axis encourages the emancipation of identity from the nation-state concept. Nevertheless, he also believes that a 'Europe of the Regions' will be slow to evolve and that Nationalist and Unionist identities in Northern Ireland will continue to be defined by the modern nation-state, despite the intimations of postmodernist liberal nationalism in the SDLP discourse.

The Territorial Resource

The APNI opposed the SDLP's 1992 'Commission for Northern Ireland' idea, principally on the grounds that the direct involvement of the European Commission is unrealistic and that it would result in a democratic deficit. It is also possible that the APNI share the suspicion of the Unionist parties that the plan was designed to advance a modern nationalist predilection for irredentism. After all, John Alderdice perceives Nationalist and Unionist positions to be stagnant, determined only by the modern emphasis on territory, even when faced with postmodern structural change. The APNI, on the other hand, claims to eschew the idea that territory should be the determining point of reference for a community:

> The position broadly speaking of Nationalists, it seems to me, has been traditionally that the geographical boundaries of the island should be the natural boundary of the community and,

therefore, any fundamental resolution should involve a united Ireland and, essentially, an independent Ireland. The traditional position of Unionists was that all the people of this archipelago of islands should form one nation – the British nation. Of course, that was sundered in the early part of the century when the twenty-six counties removed themselves from that but the position of Unionists moved to be the retention of all of the rest of the archipelago under one parliament at Westminster.

John Alderdice rejects geographical boundaries as a means of demarcation for a community:

The position that I take is a rather different one in the sense that my view and the view of liberals in general would be that the crucial phenomenon in terms of the establishment of a community is the relationships that a group of people have, not the geographical boundaries. Therefore, if, for example, you take the situation in Ireland, certainly a majority of people on the island would feel that the island is their home but there are many people in the North-East of the island who feel that they are much closer to the people in Scotland than they are to the rest of the people in the island. That's not a new thing and it's not a post-British imperialism thing either.

If you go back long before England was England you have the kingdom of Dalriada where people of the north of Ireland and southern Scotland have a degree of affinity with each other and the reason for that is because the crucial matter of political geography is the communication between peoples and that communication, even in those early days, across the stretch of water was easier than throughout the island as a whole for very obvious transport reasons. So it seems to me, through that, we begin to come to an understanding why people in the North-East of the island have a degree of separateness.

Alderdice points out that it is the ability to communicate which is central to the formation of community. He believes that structural change must be guided by advances in communications that lead to developments in community formation. In postmodern times, Alderdice sees the liberal internationalist approach as the guiding light through community development and structural change:

When we come to the question of Europe the liberal position is quite interesting because, on the one hand, it tends to suggest an approach which is internationalist. In the liberal tradition, we have espoused a world view which is about bringing people together, a free movement of people, of goods and services and trade and so on. However, it is also a notion that says: 'And the relationships we have at a lower level should be based on community, not on nationalism'. Therefore, the thing that would determine the entities in which we are governed (and we like to be governed as close to the people as possible) should be based on relationships established through communication and all those things that make for a community, not a geographical boundary and not a nationalist ideal which says effectively that all the people who are related to us in some kind of an historic way are our people and anyone else is 'the other'. This means that anyone who comes to live in your place is forever a stranger. So the position is that I want to see a United Europe because we have an internationalist commitment, a free Europe where people can travel because of the liberalization of trade and travel but not a Europe of the nation states, not a Europe built on nationalism but on communities of regions.

For John Alderdice, the concept of 'a nation' cannot be equated with the concept of 'a community' because the nation's modernist terms of reference, that differentiate between 'them' and 'us', cannot be transcended. Implicitly, he rejects the notion of liberal nationalism, described by Tamir (1993), which recognizes structural change beyond the nation-state and consequently seeks to create transterritorial alliances between nations based on mutual interest.

The Economic Resource

John Alderdice does not accept that the APNI is a 'unionist' party:

We are not 'unionists' because the word 'unionism' means a whole lot of things. One of the things it means is centralism and in that sense we are not unionists because Home Rule, like devolution, didn't mean independence in the early days. In that sense, we would be home rulers because we were for devolution and we have always been committed to that. However, we are pro-union in the sense that we believe that is in the best current interest now.

Adopting a modern constitutional position on the basis of economic interest alone is not one that is shared by Nationalist and

Unionist identities in Northern Ireland. However, Alderdice believes it to be the correct basis on which to define political identity:

> For me, these cultural matters are important but they are not
> deciding factors in relation to constitution-making and statehood.
> If you travel to most places in central Europe most of the people
> are Germanic. It doesn't matter whether they are in Western
> Poland or Austria or parts of Switzerland or the German state
> proper, they still feel Germanic, their culture is Germanic, there
> is as much difference in the culture of North Germany and South
> Germany as there is between Southern Germany and Austria or
> parts of Switzerland. It doesn't mean that they are in the same
> state. So, from our point of view, we would want to separate out
> nationhood and statehood as we would want to separate church
> from state. It is not that these things are not important but for
> us they are separate matters from citizenship.

Economic concerns are the primary motivating factor in the structure of government favoured by the APNI. John Alderdice believes
there to be no contradiction in the APNI's advocacy of a postmodern
community-based 'Europe of the Regions' and its continued commitment to a modern form of devolution for Northern Ireland within
the UK:

> There is no contradiction at all. We are for the European Union,
> we are for a federal union, we are for a single currency. In terms
> of the position of Northern Ireland constitutionally, in advance
> of that, the question that we have to ask is not what kind of a
> situation do we want in a hundred years or fifty years, that is
> important, but there is also the question what kind of a situation
> do we want now. That question, from our point of view, ought
> to be answered, not on the basis of some doctrinaire national-
> istic notion, whether it's a British nationalism or an Irish nation-
> alism but what do the people believe is in their best current social
> and economic interests.
>
> If we look at that situation and we say to people in Northern
> Ireland: 'What's in your best social and economic interests?' They
> will say that the budget for here is £7 billion. We can raise £3.5
> billion a year in taxation, the other £3.5 billion comes from the
> British Treasury, that is a pretty persuasive argument in terms
> of current economic benefit. However, in twenty or fifty years
> time that may be very different. It might be better for us to be

in a different constitutional situation from our point of view. It is for the people to decide that and if we come to the judgement in twenty or fifty years time or whatever it happens to be that the best social and economic interests of the people of Northern Ireland would be served by being outside the United Kingdom or in a different constitutional arrangement, then we would happily espouse that position. The position of the traditional Unionist or Nationalist would be: it does not matter whether it is in our best social or economic interest or not – 'I hold this because it is what I want'. So in that sense, it is not in any way paradoxical.

While the territorial and cultural resources of northern Irish Nationalist and Ulster Unionist identities have traditionally influenced their nation-state allegiance, Alderdice maintains that the economic resource of identity should be the over-riding factor determining the allegiance of communal identity to a structure of state. The emphasis placed by the APNI on the economic resource of identity determines that such identities support the union of Britain and Northern Ireland. However, that emphasis also determines that the party's position in relation to the structure of state for Northern Ireland will change should the economic advantage of another structural arrangement outweigh the current one.

Conclusion

On the threshold of the next millennium, communal identities in Northern Ireland are experiencing the beginning of a paradigm shift in their political context. The development of the European Union (EU) and the Anglo-Irish political approach to Northern Ireland are the contingencies that are responsible for this shift. In turn, the condition of postmodernity is fundamental to these political changes. Postmodern conditions are responsible for a globalization/localization dynamic in contemporary society. They have impacted upon the modern state boundary and are beginning to usurp the territorial code that has been the linchpin of modern politics. As a result, multiple communal truths are challenging the 'objective' truth of the dominant socio-political group, established in modernity, and are finding expression within related EU and Anglo-Irish political arenas.

The development of the EU polity can be interpreted as a substantive intimation of postmodernity because of the challenge that it presents to the nation-state centre. Interconnecting intimations of postmodernity in political processes affecting Ulster Unionist and northern Irish Nationalist communal identities have flowed from EU initiatives, as well as those taken jointly by the Government of the United Kingdom and the Government of the Republic of Ireland. There is some evidence of a corresponding postmodernist influence on these communal identities. To a greater or lesser degree, the perception of structural change is evident in dialogues with communal representatives from the main political parties in Northern Ireland. However, reactions to such change range from the broadly positive, in the case of the SDLP and the APNI, to the broadly negative, in the case of the UUP, the DUP and Sinn Féin. What is clear is that each representative has been forced to consider the implications of postmodern pressures on the economic, territorial and cultural resources of communal identity, be that identity essentially Ulster Unionist or northern Irish Nationalist in character.

The conceptual tools for studying the relationship between politics and society in the EU and Anglo-Irish contexts also require reassessment in light of postmodern changes. Undoubtedly, the very mention of the word 'postmodernism' can raise whoops of derision and guffaws of laughter on the academic scene (Callinicos, 1989, 1995; Eagleton, 1986). There is an understandable perception that postmodernism is a conceptual lens through which little that is tangible can be seen because of its obsessive critique of modernity and reputation for obfuscation. However, by mobilizing a 'postmodernism of resistance', this book has attempted to demonstrate how postmodernism can provide a useful perspective on contemporary conditions and even be employed in a constructive conceptual approach. The representation of difference is a core value of resistance postmodernism. The representation of difference is encouraged by expanding communications networks that have increased the opportunity of marginalized groups to access a political platform and articulate their particularist culture-bound truth. This beginning of a shift away from attempting to assert a dominant truth within a territorially defined society to a recognition and accommodation of the multiple truths that exist in a multi-level polity has repercussions for academics wedded to the modernist task of uncovering a truth and establishing objectivity. As a result, the authoritative readings of the intellectual-as-legislator appear to be at odds with the core values of postmodern polity. It is suggested that in this highly complex, interdependent and changing postmodern world a more useful role for 'the author' is as an interpreter of the multiple truths that exist.

Transcending Territory

The territorial integrity of Northern Ireland as part of the United Kingdom has come under considerable pressure from a number of directions during the past 30 years. Prime Minister Terence O'Neill's failed attempt at redressing employment and housing imbalances between the two communities in Northern Ireland initiated the mass mobilization of a civil-rights movement, drawn mainly from the northern Irish Nationalist community, towards the end of the 1960s. What developed was a violent conflict involving Republican and Loyalist paramilitaries and the security forces of the UK state. Political pressure on the territorial integrity of Northern Ireland was confirmed by the prorogation of the Stormont Assembly in 1972 and the establishment of a power-sharing executive, incorporating the nationalist SDLP, that was to include an extraterritorial 'Irish dimension'. Although the executive was brought down by the

Ulster Workers' Strike in May 1974, subsequent political initiatives aimed at reasserting the territorial integrity of Northern Ireland have also foundered.

In terms of substantive change to structural arrangements established by the Government of Ireland Act (1920), the Anglo-Irish Agreement (AIA) of 1985 is widely perceived to be a significant milestone. The Agreement recognized the right of the Government of the Republic of Ireland to make representations to the Government of the United Kingdom with regard to the future governance of Northern Ireland. Furthermore, a secretariat was established which included civil servants from the Republic of Ireland. Its remit was to liaise with government departments in Northern Ireland on matters of concern to the northern Irish Nationalist community.

The development of the Anglo-Irish intergovernmental approach to policy-making in Northern Ireland was pursued in the Downing Street Declaration of 1993. The Declaration used language which favoured the due recognition of political and cultural differences, a recognition that suggested the creation of North-South institutions, some with executive power. The Framework Documents of 1995 included such proposals for the creation of powerful North-South bodies. The Framework Documents were intended as a guideline for future multi-party discussion on the governance of Northern Ireland but they were fiercely denounced as a threat to the territorial integrity of Northern Ireland by the Ulster Unionist parties. A 'Propositions on Heads of Agreement' document presented by the two governments to the Multi-Party Talks on 12 January 1998 proved more acceptable to the main Ulster Unionist party, the UUP and to the Loyalist fringe parties, the PUP and the UDP. The creation of a North-South ministerial council was proposed but the UUP maintained that this would be 'under the umbrella' of their preferred extraterritorial model – the intergovernmental council (with representation from the two governments and the devolved administrations of Northern Ireland, Wales and Scotland) also proposed in the document (the *Irish Times*, 13 January 1998). However, the Taoiseach Bertie Ahern insisted that the North-South body would be a stand alone 'executive implementation body' (*Financial Times*, 15 January 1998). In the end, the Multi-Party Agreement (1998) provided for all-Ireland and cross-border 'implementation' bodies, a term which is synonymous with 'executive'.

Academic and media analysis of political developments affecting the territorial integrity of Northern Ireland as part of the United

Kingdom has naturally centred on the initiatives, declarations and propositions of the two governments; the protracted nature of the Multi-Party Talks (1996–8); the reaction of violent paramilitaries; the Multi-Party Agreement and the realization of its provisions. Much less interest has been shown in the potentially paradigmatic implications for state development and communal identity of the steady evolution of multi-level governance within the EU. This book has attempted to redress this imbalance and highlight the way that EU developments, as well as Anglo-Irish processes have been promoted by the condition of postmodernity and underscored by concepts associated with the discourse of postmodernism. Using evidence gained from dialogues with communal representatives and other primary sources, the book has sought to refute the commonly held perception that communal identities in Northern Ireland are hopelessly locked into an inter-communal conflict with (premodern) cultural and (modern) territorial traits.

Intimations of Postmodernity

Modernity was founded on the tenets of objectivity, truth, coherency, and the domination of the nation-state centre in order to meet the demands of the structural changes required by modern revolutions. To this end, the state centre was charged with the task of converting intimate ethnic groups into an overarching modern social order where communication between strangers was possible. Although modern state bureaucracy offered some of the structure required by the old social order – through terminology, symbols and strict relationships – such a system was inadequate when it came to meeting the demands of modern capitalism. The replacement of a highly structured society with one that was socially and occupationally mobile and where communication could be spontaneous and unique was required. To achieve this goal the state established a standardized education system aimed at promoting cultural uniformity (Gellner, 1983, pp. 35–8). Thus order and control based on a single 'high' culture and a strong state centre were the means by which the nation-state aimed to fulfil the conceptual tenets of modernity. Adherence to such principles were thought to offer the path to progress desired by the philosophers of the Enlightenment.

   The condition of postmodernity in the European state system arises from developments in technology, transnational communica-

arrangements with intimations of postmodernity. Political gridlock is the most obvious danger for such inclusive arrangements.

Despite the difficulties, substantive and conceptual intimations of postmodernity in the politics of EU and Northern Ireland make it increasingly difficult to countenance an alternative structural dynamic in the short to medium term. While it is possible that a future Eurosceptic government might contemplate withdrawal from the EU in a vain attempt at reasserting the territorial integrity of the nation-state, the economic risks of going it alone would make this a momentous decision. In the absence of such a drastic measure, the continued infusion of postmodernity into the fabric of the European state system has major implications for the exercise of state power and the resources of communal identities in Northern Ireland.

Political scientists continue to highlight the pre-eminence of the UK government in the political affairs of Northern Ireland in order to give multi-level governance its proper perspective. They point out that Northern Ireland receives a subvention of over £3bn per annum from the UK public exchequer. However, while EU subvention to Northern Ireland is likely to decrease after the millennium, it has been substantial in the past. The tranche of Structural Funds from 1994–9 amounts to £1020m which, although modest compared to UK subvention, nevertheless represents a toehold of around 3 per cent of public expenditure – a not insignificant substantive intimation of postmodernity in the structure of the state in the EU. The EU's INTERREG II and Peace and Reconciliation programmes are further evidence of substantive postmodernity in the structural development of the state in the EU because they are aimed (in whole or in part) at development that transcends the territorial boundary of the modern state. Cross-border partnerships are offered single-package funding aimed at creating 'live' micro-level sites of postmodernity through the active promotion of alliances that may have existed prior to the creation of two modern states on the island of Ireland. Similar partnerships exist on other nation-state borders within the EU.[4] More fundamentally, EU integration culminating in economic and political union remains the macro-level dynamic behind the positive discrimination of EU funds that are enjoyed by local communities on the island of Ireland. European integration combined with the EU's deployment of resources to local communities, mostly via national governments, points to the postmodernist development of a fledgling multi-level form of governance within the EU that can claim to be distinct from intergovernmentalist and integrationist interpretations of the development of the EU (Marks, 1993, pp. 401–2).

Ulster unionism and Irish nationalism, and the identities that coalesce around these twin pillars of Northern Ireland politics, have been definitively shaped by the context of the modern state. However, the fluidity of structural arrangements for the accommodation of Ulster Unionist and Irish Nationalist identities and the encroachment made by the EU on the nature of the state in Europe makes the EU an important consideration for the resources of these communal identities. Consequently, Ulster Unionist and northern Irish Nationalists will be required to reassess the implications of EU developments for the economic, territorial and cultural resources of their respective communal identities. INTERREG II and the Special Support Programme for Peace and Reconciliation are micro-level EU programmes directed and structured to reinvigorate local communities and recontextualize the economic and territorial resources of communal identity. An expansion of EU citizenship rights, post-Maastricht, as well as an enduring European reconstructivist dynamic, are developing macro-level contingencies that may further influence the alignment of these resources of communal identity in the long term.

'Post-'ing Communal Identity

Critics of the 'postmodern Europe' thesis maintain that the hold of modern nationalism on the cultural resource of communal identity ensures that the nation-state remains the persuasive form of polity in the EU. However, such criticism, focused as it is on the notion of a 'European super-state' superseding the modern nation-state arrangement, fails to consider substantive developments in the EU. The evidence (discussed in chapters 4 and 5) points to the development of a much more fluid and multi-tiered arrangement within the EU. The extension of policy-making to include private interest groups is also occurring in 'social partnerships' within the EU sphere of influence. As such, predictions about the replication of modern polity-building on a larger scale in the postmodern era are displaced by the reality of a hotch-potch EU multi-level system of governance that encourages intersubjectivity, interactive decision-making and the *ad hoc* formation of alliances across modern boundaries by government and non-government agencies. While the nation-state undoubtedly remains a going concern, postmodern structural change has promoted the salience of supranational and subnational entities in an interactive EU polity arena. Such change is of consequence to the development and expression of nationalism in the EU. However, postmodern structural change need not necessarily be understood as the signifier of a postnationalist era, as suggested by John Hume (1996) and Richard Kearney (1997).

The concept of 'postnationalism' is arrived at through a discussion of the development of nationalism and the nation in terms of revolutionary transition (Gellner, 1964, 1983). However, a focus on the development of nationalism and the nation in the Irish context facilitates the elaboration of an alternative interpretation whereby history is presented as a collage painted by a particular culture-bound imagined community. The role played by communications media in such development is pivotal in this alternative, postmodernist interpretation. Irish newspapers exploited the negative power of grievance in the formation and mobilization of the Irish nation while, at the same time, regurgitating shared memories, embellishing historical facts and propagating myths in order to provide a buffer to the process of modernization. These narratives became directly responsible for the fortunes of the Irish imagined community.

Contemporary communal identities in Northern Ireland continue to be affected by a complex network of factors including diverse ethnic origins, territorial intermingling, and often mutually exclusive culture-bound interpretations. The structural fault line for these communities was greatly exacerbated by the process of nationalizing ethnic communities in modernity. Different experiences of modern socio-economic development and impoverishment and, more importantly, the bonding of the cultural resource of identity to modern nationalism have provided the fundamental building blocks of contemporary northern Irish Nationalists and Ulster Unionist identities (Walker, 1989, p. 256). Newspapers, television, and the cinema are the vital media for these conflicting imagined communities. However, the development of the nation during the modern era supports the contention that the development of the Irish nation in postmodern times will continue to be determined by the ability of competing nationalist élites to adapt their nationalist ethos to structural change and subsequently to influence the Irish national consciousness through the media. In postmodernity, such a nationalist ethos need no longer be defined in terms of hegemonic control and territorial sovereignty. According to Yael Tamir, it is possible for the nationalist ethos to become liberal and postmodernist in light of contemporary structural change (Tamir, 1993).

In modernity, national identities relied on nationalism in order to secure a strong political expression with the formation of their own nation-state. This modern political differentiation often produced xenophobia. However, a reassessment of the intentions of nationalism and the constitution of national identities that exist within the EU might be made in light of postmodernity. In this postmodernist interpretation, Northern Irish Nationalist identities can legitimately seek to invest the resources of their identity in an EU multi-level polity that incorporates other European nations and ethnic groups, including Ulster Unionists. It follows that Irish Nationalist identities can become 'postmodern' if they forgo their hegemonic content, align the resources of their identities to appropriate subnational, national, and supranational levels, and forge alliances in the common pursuit of economic, cultural and social interests. Such a replacement of modern nationalism with a liberal and postmodernist nationalism, denoted by the anti-hegemonic terms 'consent' 'agreement' and 'accommodation', is central to the discourse of SDLP interviewees. As such, the adoption of liberal nationalism in a climate of postmodern structural change enables a nationalist identity to recreate itself in a way that allows it to play an active role in the intersubjectivity that resistance postmodernism suggests is best able to fulfil the demands of the democratic principle.

Postmodernism is a critique of modern nationalism, that is, the dynamic for national identity to secure a nation-state, because the efforts of modern nationalism to differentiate politically between 'them' and 'us' confirms its hegemonic content. The announcement of a European citizenship in the Maastricht Treaty is a signal of the intention to eliminate the political distinction between 'them' and 'us' within the EU. Although the Maastricht Treaty's version of European citizenship is little more than rhetoric, future substantive development offers the possibility of freeing individuals from the context of the modern state through an extension of the extraterritorial 'right to options' (Urwin and Rokkan, 1983, p. 115). The EU's desire to become a community of nations and its rejection of the modern nation-state's aim of shaping a homogeneous cultural community also indicates that an EU system of multi-level governance has the potential to secure the 'right to roots' of communal identities in the postmodern EU polity. Consequently, anti-hegemonic communal identities are legitimate identities in the context of postmodernity because they are part of the spectrum of diversity that constitutes a multi-cultural identity structure in a postmodern Europe.

Ideas of modern territorial sovereignty and the design of an All-Ireland nation-state are incompatible with a society adapting to the condition of postmodernity. Evidence from the Sinn Féin dialogue suggests Sinn Féin interviewees are beginning to recognize the reconstruction that is taking place in the EU state system. However, they also maintain a state of denial about these developments. The interviewees have followed the party line and incorporated liberal nationalist terms such as 'consent' and 'accommodation' into their political discourse. However, Sinn Féin nationalism retains over-arching hegemonic features, most notably the emphasis on the territory of the nation-state and the failure to accept Ulster Unionist identities as anything other than cultural in nature.

Ulster Unionists argue that maintaining the territorial sovereignty of the United Kingdom of Great Britain and Northern Ireland offers Unionists a secure identity in economic, territorial and cultural terms. The catalyst for Unionist political action is anything that would threaten that union. Therefore, despite the diversity in the character of Ulster Unionist identities (Coulter, 1994), their defining territorial resource of union with Great Britain makes any consideration of a linkage of these identities with emerging postmodern structures of power seemingly impossible. In addition, the cultural core of Ulster Unionism – Ulster Protestantism – has led some Ulster Unionists (most notably those associated with the DUP) to object further to European integration on the grounds that they suspect Catholic influence in EU processes. However, while Norman Porter's exercise in 'rethinking Unionism' (1996) along pragmatic lines remains on the periphery of the Ulster Unionist discourse, UUP interviewees are beginning to consider the implications of European integration for the Ulster Unionist identity. Their strategy thus far, as relayed in the UUP dialogue, has been to formulate a political approach that makes some attempt to define EU regionalism within the context of UK devolution.[5] As far as the APNI is concerned, the primacy of the economic resource in the identity represented by the party dictates that a similar parallel between EU regionalism and UK devolution is made in its 'wait and see' approach to structural change.

Catalysts that have mobilized the resources of (northern) Irish Nationalist and Ulster Unionist communal identities and produced political action include nineteenth-century famine and the Northern Ireland civil-rights campaign of the late 1960s. The third millennium promises a continuation of postmodern conditions and concepts that are initiating change in the structure and operation of the state. In many respects, Northern Ireland has already become a laboratory for postmodern politics – not only by way of EU macro-developments and micro-initiatives but also through the bombardment of Anglo-Irish agreements, declarations, frameworks and propositions. The common postmodernist theme of these developments has been the priority given to diverse communal interests over the will of the territorial majority and the sovereignty of the nation-state. The effectiveness of a postmodern catalyst on the resources of northern Irish Nationalist and Ulster Unionist identities will depend largely on the way in which the European Union and the Anglo-Irish political process evolve; and the success of the internationalized efforts of the UK and the Republic of Ireland in institutionalizing the reality of transterritorialism.

Notes

1. I refer to both the 'national state' and the 'nation-state' simply as the 'nation-state'. Strictly speaking, the state is a 'national state' when its centralized, autonomous and differentiated structures uphold legitimate authority within a boundary which contains multiple regions. However, a nation-state exists only where the citizenry share a common code of national identity expressed in language, religion, myth and custom. The majority of modern European states are quintessentially national states, while only a small minority, ostensibly the Republic of Ireland and Sweden, could satisfactorily qualify as nation-states (Tilly, 1990, pp. 2–3).

2. A proliferation of smaller parties emerged to stand, with modest success, in the 1996 election to the Northern Ireland Forum. These parties recorded the following percentage share of the vote in this election: the UK Unionist Party (UKU), 3.69 per cent; the Progressive Unionist Party (PUP), 3.47 per cent; the Ulster Democratic Party (UDP), 2.22 per cent; the Women's Coalition, 1.03 per cent; and, Labour, 0.85 per cent (*Irish Times*, 1 June 1996). It is appreciated that the fringe parties represent distinct positions in the spectrum of Northern Ireland politics. However, limited space prevents a detailed consideration of these positions.

3. In the 1994 election to the European Parliament the percentage of the vote secured by these five main political parties in Northern Ireland was as follows: DUP, 29.15 per cent; UUP, 23.83 per cent; APNI, 4.13 per cent; SDLP, 28.93 per cent; Sinn Féin, 9.86 per cent – giving a combined total of 95.9 per cent. In the 1997 Westminster General Election, the percentage of the vote secured by the five main political parties in Northern Ireland was as follows: DUP, 13.6 per cent; UUP, 32.7 per cent; APNI, 8 per cent; SDLP, 24.1 per cent; Sinn Féin, 16.1 per cent – giving a combined total of 94.5 per cent.

4. The use of words to signify communal allegiance in Northern Ireland is a subtle art form. Referring to Northern Ireland as either 'Northern Ireland', 'Ulster', 'the North of Ireland', or 'the occupied six counties' can convey communal allegiance. The use of terms in this book are not intended as a personal expression of communal allegiance. However, I am aware that the use of some words for technical reasons, for example 'sub-state' (to denote the federal nature of Northern Ireland between 1921 and 1972), may be interpreted in some quarters as being politically motivated.

1 A POSTMODERNIST APPROACH TO COMMUNAL IDENTITIES IN NORTHERN IRELAND?

1. Agreement between the governments of the Republic of Ireland and the United Kingdom on the content of the Downing Street Declaration (1993) only came after at least 18 drafts had been circulated between officials and ministers of the two governments (Aughey and Morrow, 1996, p. 213).

2. Despite the Commission's wide-ranging consultation, Garvin notes an under-representation of voices from 'hardline east Belfast and Border unionists on the one hand, and hardline nationalists from west Belfast on the other' in the report (Garvin, 1994, p. 123).

3. A subsequent forum called 'Democratic Dialogue' has attempted to emmulate the Commission's achievements in inducing communal self-reflexivity in Northern Ireland. To this end, it holds conferences and publishes reports on a variety of issues related to the Northern Ireland conflict (Democratic Dialogue, 1995; 1996).

2 INTERPRETING THE DEVELOPMENT OF THE NATION, IRISH NATIONALISM AND ULSTER UNIONISM

1. As evidence of this, Unionists have cited what they referred to as the Republic of Ireland's 'illegal, immoral and criminal' constitutional claim on Northern Ireland in Articles 2 and 3 of Bunreacht Na hÉireann/ Constitution of Ireland (Dr Ian Paisley in the *Belfast Telegraph*, 3 July 1996) and the violent campaigns of militant republican groups.

2. John Armstrong is another leading exponent of contextualizing the development of nations within the range of ethnicity. For Armstrong, the development of nations should be seen in terms of the *longue durée* whereby the seeds of ethnic identity, such as symbols and myths of descent, are continually revitalized and reinterpreted in a changing communal identity (Armstrong, 1982, pp. 4–11). Historians such as Hugh Seton-Watson and Suzan Reynolds offer their own contributions to the ethnicist approach. Seton-Watson distinguishes between 'old' and 'new' nations: 'The old are those which had acquired national identity or national consciousness before the formation of the doctrine of nationalism. The new are those for whom two processes developed simultaneously: the formation of national consciousness and the creation of national movements' (Seton-Watson, 1977, p. 6). Suzan Reynolds draws parallels between the features of customs, laws, and myths found in medieval kingdoms in Western Europe and those same features found in modern nations (Reynolds, 1984, pp. 251–6).

3. As well as reformation Protestantism, the settlers brought with them entrepreneurial and industrial skills that corresponded to modern requirements and made Belfast the industrial centre of the island (Ruane and Todd, 1996, p. 27).

4. Joyce had already left Ireland before beginning work on Ulysses. Anderson's concept of 'imagining' (and re-imagining) communal identity would, therefore, have been especially poignant in his case.

5. Hobsbawm defines this invention of tradition as: 'a set of practices, normally governed by overtly or tacitly accepted rules and of a ritual or symbolic nature, which seek to inculcate certain values and norms of behaviour by repetition, which automatically implies continuity with the past' (Hobsbawm, 1983, p. 1).
6. The nationalism of O'Connell focused on Catholic emancipation and the establishment of an Irish parliament ruled by the Catholic majority (Hutchinson, 1994, p. 58).
7. The Social Democratic and Labour Party (SDLP) is the largest 'nationalist' party in Northern Ireland.
8. By John Hume, SDLP, Leader, (Hume, 1996, pp. 118–33); and by Mark Durkan, SDLP, Chairperson (1990–5) and Denis Haughey, SDLP representative in the EU Committee of the Regions, in the dialogues.

3 THE GOVERNANCE OF NORTHERN IRELAND: FROM MODERNITY TO POSTMODERNITY?

1. The Irish Free State government became the 'Government of the Republic of Ireland' after the Government of Ireland Act, 1948.
2. These features are normally associated with the modern state in Western democratic society.
3. The Unionist communal truth continues to repudiate the commonly held perception of widespread discrimination against Catholics during this period.
4. While he was Tánaiste in 1947, Seán Lemass began to consider aloud the idea of a European Customs Union despite the prevailing protectionist ethos of the Irish Free State (Bew and Patterson, 1982, pp. 34–6). This fledgling step signalled the beginning of an extraterritorial context for the economic resource of the Irish Nationalist identity (Bew, 1994, p. 159).
5. Theoretically, non-consociational options for a modern state structure for Northern Ireland include: Assimilation into the UK; assimilation into the Republic of Ireland; joint authority; a UK federation/confederation; Irish federation/confederation; repartition of the island; independence; and majority-rule devolution. Each option would appear to suffer from serious drawbacks when theoretically applied to the political context of Northern Ireland (see McGarry and O'Leary, 1990, for details).
6. A co-signatory of the AIA with Mrs Margaret Thatcher.
7. Although Mrs Thatcher was initially frustrated by the level of security co-operation secured by the AIA (Bew, Gibbon, Patterson, 1995, p. 214).
8. Where the gains made by one community are perceived by the other to have been made at its expense.
9. The right to national self-determination is 'understood as the right of .... members of a nation to preserve their distinct essence, and manage communal life in accordance with their particular way of life' (Tamir, 1993, p. 69).

4 INTIMATIONS OF POSTMODERNITY IN THE DEVELOPMENT OF THE EUROPEAN UNION

1. DG-16, which is responsible for the regional fund, has a staff of 500 managers and field officers (Marks, 1993, p. 397).
2. It must be remembered that representatives coming from nation-states with a strong regional structure, such as Germany and Belgium, already have much more power than MEPs.

5 THE EUROPEAN UNION AND THE RESOURCES OF COMMUNAL IDENTITIES IN NORTHERN IRELAND

1. The Special Support Programme for Peace and Reconciliation was announced in December 1994 from the EU budget for cross-border initiatives.
2. As well as the formation of other regional élites based on policy areas creating maritime, underdeveloped or agricultural regions (*Financial Times*, 6 September 1995).
3. Such as Lisnaskea and Clones Enterprise Development and the Strabane-Lifford Development Commission.
4. With the help of their Conservative allies at Westminster and the abstentionist policy of Sinn Féin.
5. Reaffirmed by David Trimble (UUP, Leader) in the *Financial Times*, 11 September 1995. However, this aspiration appears to have been ditched in the aftermath of devolution for Scotland and Wales.
6. James Anderson and James Goodman have criticized the unionist economist Graham Gudgin of the Cadogan Group for citing British subvention as a 'trump card' against a 'united Ireland'. They argue that this precarious reliance on the British taxpayer, as well as the peripheral location of the island in the EU, actually necessitates the development of economic strategies that includes the creation of North-South institutions (in *Fortnight*, no. 350, May 1996).
7. For Unionists, the preoccupation of Prime Minister Edward Heath with the accession of the UK to the EEC in 1972 was responsible for an ill-considered decision to prorogue the Stormont Assembly in that year. Indeed, Hainsworth believes that this timing influenced Unionist (particularly DUP) hostility to Europe (Hainsworth, 1989, pp. 52–3).
8. In the 1990s, the Progressive Unionist Party (PUP), the political representative of the paramilitary Ulster Volunteer Force (UVF), attempted to adopt a secular liberal approach and develop its Unionist politics in terms of citizenship rights for the individual in Northern Ireland. This caused tension within the UVF and culminated in a decision to disband its semi-autonomous Mid-Ulster unit. The Mid-Ulster UVF (subsequently forming the core of the break-away Loyalist Volunteer Force) had continued to base its thinking in terms of ethnicity, that is, Ulster Protestantism, and had denounced the PUP for aligning itself with the pan-nationalist agenda. One key PUP leader, David Ervine,

was singled out as a traitor to the 'Protestant people' (Steve Bruce in *The Independent*, 6 August 1996).
9. Gaelic football teams from Northern Ireland have won the All-Ireland championship three times in the 1990–7 period.
10. Unless stated otherwise, all extracts in Part Two of this book are from transcripts of interviews with the author, listed in the Bibliography on page 213.

6 DIALOGUE WITH THE SOCIAL DEMOCRATIC AND LABOUR PARTY (SDLP)

1. Indeed, while he was advising London and Dublin to act together, Hume had already embarked on engaging the European dynamic through his appointment as a special adviser to Richard Burke (the Irish EEC Commissioner for Transport) one year ahead of his election as an MEP (White, 1985, p. 202).
2. For an analysis of the defects in the SDLP's Commission model see O'Leary *et al.* 1993.
3. Longley suggests that Hume's emphasis on the Gaeltacht as a region of Ireland, and his assurance that regionalism is not a threat to 'our national destiny' is evidence of his willingness to suppress 'Ulster distinctiveness'. Longley also cites the assessment of Bew and Patterson (contained in Kearney 1988b and also offered by Bew and his associates in the Cadogan Group) that the European discourse of the SDLP is basically a front for an unreconstructed Irish Nationalist identity that clings to aspirations of a modern unitary state to represent the Irish nation (Longley, 1992, p. 18).
4. Kennedy (1994, p. 177) clarifies this by saying that '. . . . the treaty referred to 'the island of Ireland' as a geographical description of the two regions – Ireland (the Republic) and Northern Ireland. This was done, it was speculated at the time, to save the Swedish and other EFTA governments the embarrassment of explicitly promising aid to the UK'.
5. Northern Ireland's Structural Fund allocation of £1,020m for 1994–9 compared with the allocation of £7,300m made to the Republic of Ireland for the same period. Nationalist opinion suggested that if the island as a whole had been treated as an Objective One unit then it was possible that £10,000m could have been secured (Brian Feeney in the *Irish News*, 27 November, 1993). Others maintained that such an approach had potential benefits because the interests that the North and South share, particularly in the agriculture and tourism sectors, are more compatible than the interests of Northern Ireland and the rest of the UK (O'Leary, 1991, p. 163; Attwood, 1995, pp. 24–25; Bradley, 1995, p. 27).
6. A mistake which John Hume continued to make (deliberately) in his joint communiqués with Gerry Adams, the Sinn Féin president.
7. Ruairí Ó'Brádaigh is now leader of Republican Sinn Féin, a republican splinter group.

7 DIALOGUE WITH SINN FÉIN

1. 'Tiochfaidh ar lá' perhaps!
2. Bernadette Devlin-McAliskey was elected as the Unity MP for Mid-Ulster in 1969, and as an Independent between 1970 and 1974 for the same constituency. She helped found the Irish Republican Socialist Party (IRSP) at the end of 1974 (Flackes and Elliott, 1994, pp. 214–6)

10 DIALOGUE WITH THE ALLIANCE PARTY OF NORTHERN IRELAND (APNI)

1. See *Fortnight* (319) 1993, for criticism by the APNI of a power-sharing arrangement for Northern Ireland where Nationalist and Unionist communities have an equal voice.
2. There is evidence to support the assertion that Sinn Féin are disproportionately attracting the votes of a burgeoning Catholic population *vis-à-vis* the SDLP (O'Leary and Evans, 1997, p. 674). However, the static nature of the SDLP's vote and the unprecedented share of the vote secured by Sinn Féin in the 1996 Election to the Northern Ireland Forum and 1997 General Election are shifts in the voting pattern that, at least to some extent, may have been made at the expense of the APNI. It is possible that the fall in the share of the APNI vote in the 1980s and 1990s is due, at least in part, to the attraction of the SDLP's liberal nationalist discourse for those Irish cultural nationalists who reject the territorialism of modern nationalism.

CONCLUSION

1. Over-ruling, for example, the Irish Nationalist perception of the centrality of a British-Irish dimension to the conflict, a dimension that has become recognized in Anglo-Irish intergovernmental initiatives after 1985.
2. For an example of the intellectual-as-legislator see 'Square Circles: Round Tables and the Path to Peace in Northern Ireland' by the Cadogan Group (1996).
3. Unionists argue that an East-West council could oversee a 'totality of relationships'. According to David Trimble (UUP, Leader), priority should be given to Northern Ireland-Great Britain and Great Britain-Republic of Ireland interaction in this framework, rather that a North-South interaction (*Irish Times*, 3 October, 1997).
4. It is beyond the remit of this book to examine the constitutional implications of potential and developing transterritorial structures.
5. Goodman has also drawn attention to the fact that this pragmatic approach of UUP Euro-representatives often contradicts the Eurosceptic approach of UUP MPs and the party at large (Goodman, 1996, p. 301).

Bibliography

INTERVIEWS

John Alderdice (APNI, party leader 1987–98), Belfast, 14 February 1995.
Nigel Dodds (DUP, party secretary), Belfast, 20 March 1995.
Mark Durkan (SDLP, party chairperson 1990–5), Derry, 4 April 1995.
Reg Empey (UUP, member of the Committee of the Regions), Belfast, 19 September 1995.
Denis Haughey (SDLP, member of Committee of the Regions), Cookstown, 27 February 1995.
Mitchel McLaughlin (Sinn Féin, national chairman), Derry, 8 March 1995.
Francie Molloy (Sinn Féin, Councillor), Dungannon, 15 May 1995.
Maurice Morrow (DUP, Councillor), Dungannon, 11 May 1995.
Jim Nicholson (UUP, MEP), Belfast, 31 March 1995.

REFERENCES

Adams, Gerry, 1995. *Free Ireland: Towards a Lasting Peace*. Dingle: Brandon.
Adonis, A. 1991. 'Subsidiarity: Theory of a New Federalism?', pp. 63–74 in Preston King and Andrea Bosco, *A Constitution for Europe: a Comparative Study of Federal Constitution and Plans for the United States of Europe*. London: Lothian Foundation Press.
Alliance Party of Northern Ireland, 1992. *Westminster Election Manifesto*. Belfast: APNI.
Alliance Party of Northern Ireland, 1994. *European Election Manifesto: Our Future Together in Europe*. Belfast: APNI.
Anderson, Benedict, 1991. *Imagined Communities: Reflections on the Origins and Spread of Nationalism*. London: Verso.
Anderson, James and James Goodman, 1994. 'Northern Ireland: Dependency, Class and Cross-border Integration in the European Union', pp. 13–24 in *Capital and Class*, no. 54 (Autumn).
Anderson, Malcolm, Monica den Boer and Gary Millar, 1994. 'European Citizenship and Co-operation in Justice and Home Affairs', pp. 104–22 in Andrew Duff, Jonn Pinder and Roy Pryce (eds), *Maastricht and Beyond*. London: Routledge.
Anderson, Perry, 1983. *In the Tracks of Historical Materialism*. London: Verso.
Armstrong, John, 1982. *Nations Before Nationalism*. Chapel Hill: University of North Carolina Press.
Arthur, Paul, 1984. *The Government and Politics of Northern Ireland*. Essex: Longman.
Arthur, Paul, 1988. 'Initiatives for Consensus: Minority Perceptions', pp. 59–72 in Charles Townshend (ed.), *Consensus in Ireland: Approaches and Recessions*. Oxford: Clarendon.

Arthur, Paul, 1994. 'The Anglo-Irish Joint Declaration: Towards a Lasting Peace?', pp. 218–30 in *Government and Opposition*, vol. 29, no. 2.

Arthur, Paul and Keith Jeffery, 1988. *Northern Ireland Since 1968*. Oxford: Basil Blackwell (2nd ed. 1996).

Attwood, Alex, 1995. 'The Farmers Showing the Way Across the Border', pp. 24–6 in *NI Brief* (Spring). London: Parliamentary Brief.

Aughey, Arthur, 1989a. *Under Siege: Ulster Unionism and the Anglo-Irish Agreement*. Belfast: Blackstaff.

Aughey, Arthur, 1989b. *Northern Ireland and the European Community: an Economic and Political Analysis*. Belfast: Policy Research Institute.

Aughey, Arthur, 1996. 'Unionism', pp. 31–8 in Arthur Aughey and Duncan Morrow (eds), *Northern Ireland Politics*. London: Longman.

Aughey, Arthur and Duncan Morrow, 1996. 'Frameworks and the Future', pp. 213–21 in Arthur Aughey and Duncan Morrow (eds), *Northern Ireland Politics*. London: Longman.

Bardon, Jonathan, 1992. *A History of Ulster*. Belfast: Blackstaff.

Bauman, Zygmunt, 1987. *Legislators and Interpreters*. Cambridge: Polity.

Bauman, Zygmunt, 1991. *Modernity and Ambivalence*. Cambridge: Polity.

Bauman, Zygmunt, 1992. *Intimations of Postmodernity*. London: Routledge.

Bell, Desmond, 1991. 'Cultural Studies in Ireland and the Postmodernist Debate', pp. 83–95 in *Irish Journal of Sociology*, vol. 1.

Berman, Marshall, 1983. *All That is Solid Melts into Air: the Experience of Modernity*. London: Verso.

Bevant, Yann, 1993. 'Some Aspects of the Social and Political Consequences of EC Economic Involvement in Northern Ireland', pp. 93–112 in *Études Irlandaises*, vol. 18.

Bew, Paul, 1994. *Ideology and the Irish Question: Ulster Unionism and Irish Nationalism 1912–1916*. Oxford: Clarendon.

Bew, Paul, 1995. 'Not Yet Passing The Corfu Test', pp. 33–5, in *NI Brief* (Spring). London: Parliamentary Brief.

Bew, Paul and Henry Patterson, 1982. *Seán Lemass and the Making of Modern Ireland 1945–66*. Dublin: Gill and Macmillan.

Bew, Paul and Henry Patterson, 1985. *The British State and the Ulster Crisis: From Wilson to Thatcher*. London: Verso.

Bew, Paul and Henry Patterson, 1990. 'Scenarios For Progress in Northern Ireland', pp. 206–18 in John McGarry and Brendan O'Leary (eds), *The Future of Northern Ireland*. Oxford: Clarendon.

Bew, Paul, Kenneth Darwin and Gordon Gillespie, 1993. *Passion and Prejudice: Nationalist and Unionist Conflict in Ulster in the 1930's and the Founding of the Irish Association*. Belfast: Institute of Irish Studies.

Bew, Paul, Peter Gibbon and Henry Patterson, 1995. *Northern Ireland 1921–1994: Political Forces and Social Classes*. London: Serif.

Bhabha, Homi K. 1990. 'Introduction', pp. 1–7 in Homi Bhabha (ed.), *The Nation and Narration*. London: Routledge.

Boyce, D. George, 1982. *Nationalism in Ireland*. London: Routledge.

Bradley, John, 1995. 'A Peace Dividend for the Economy', pp. 27–8 in *NI Brief* (Spring). London: Parliamentary Brief.

Breuilly, John, 1982. *Nationalism and the State*. Manchester: MUP.

Brown, Terence, 1985. *The Whole Protestant Community – the Making of Historical Myth*. Derry: Field Day.

Bruce, Steve, 1989. *God Save Ulster!: The Religion and Politics of Paisleyism.* Oxford: OUP.

Bruce, Steve, 1994. *The Edge of the Union: the Ulster Loyalist Political Vision.* Oxford: OUP.

Cadogan Group, 1992. *Northern Limits: Boundaries of the Attainable in Northern Ireland.* Belfast: Cadogan Group.

Cadogan Group, 1996. *Square Circles: Round Tables and the Path to Peace in Northern Ireland.* Belfast: Cadogan Group.

Callinicos, Alex, 1989. *Against Postmodernism: a Marxist Critique.* Cambridge: Polity.

Callinicos, Alex, 1995. 'Postmodernism as Normal Science', pp. 734–40 in *The British Journal of Sociology,* vol. 46, no. 4.

Cameron, D.R., 1992. 'The 1992 Initiative: Causes and Consequences', pp. 23–74 in Alberta M. Sbragia (ed.), *Euro-Politics: Institutions and Policymaking in the 'New' European Community.* Washington DC: Brookings Institute.

Camilleri, Joseph A. and Jim Falk, 1992. *The End of Sovereignty? the Politics of a Shrinking and Fragmenting World.* Aldershot: Edward Elgar.

Caporaso, James A., and John T.S. Keeler, 1993. *The European Community and Regional Integration Theory.* Paper Delivered at the Third Biennial International Conference of the European Community Studies Association 27–29 May, 1993, Washington, DC.

Cochrane, Feargal, 1994. 'Any Takers: the Isolation of Northern Ireland', pp. 378–95 in *Political Studies* vol. 42, no. 3.

Cochrane, Feargal, 1995. 'The Isolation of Northern Ireland', pp. 506–8 in *Political Studies,* vol. 43, no. 3.

Cohen, Anthony P. 1994. *Self Consciousness: an Alternative Anthropology of Identity.* London: Routledge.

Conlon, Bernard, 1994. 'Brussels isn't Belfast', p. 21 in *Fortnight,* no. 326.

Connor, Walker, 1978. 'A Nation is a Nation, is a State, is an Ethnic Group, is a . . .', pp. 378–410 in *Ethnic and Racial Studies,* vol. 1, no. 4.

Coogan, Tim Pat, 1995. *The Troubles: Ireland's Ordeal 1966–1995 and the Search for Peace.* London: Hutchinson.

Coulter, Colin, 1994. 'The Character of Unionism', pp. 1–24 in *Irish Political Studies,* no. 9.

Cox, W. Harvey, 1985. 'Who Wants a United Ireland?', pp. 29–47 in *Government and Opposition,* vol. 20, no. 1.

Cunningham, Michael, 1997. 'The Political Language of John Hume', pp. 13–22 in *Irish Political Studies,* vol. 12.

Dallmayr, Fred, 1993. 'Modernity in the Crossfire: Comments on the Postmodern Turn', pp. 39–64 in John Paul Jones, Wolfgang Natter and Theodore R. Schatzki (eds), *Postmodern Contentions.* London: Guilford Press.

de Vries, Pieter, 1992. 'A Research Journey', pp. 47–84 in Norman Long and Ann Long (eds), *Battlefields of Knowledge.* London: Routledge.

Dehousse, Renaud, 1994. 'Community Competencies: Are There Limits to Growth?', pp. 103–25 in Renaud Dehousse (ed.), *Europe After Maastricht: an Ever Closer Union?* London: Sweet and Maxwell.

Delanty, Gerard, 1995. *Inventing Europe: Idea, Identity, Reality.* London: Macmillan.

Delanty, Gerard, 1996. 'Habermas and Post-national Identity: Theoretical Perspectives on the Conflict in Northern Ireland', pp. 20–32 in *Irish Political Studies*, vol. 11.

Democratic Dialogue, 1995. *New Thinking for New Times*. Belfast: Democratic Dialogue.

Democratic Dialogue, 1996. *Reconstructing Politics*. Belfast: Democratic Dialogue.

Democratic Unionist Party, 1992. *The Surrender of Maastricht – What it Means for Ulster*. Belfast: DUP.

Democratic Unionist Party, 1994. *European Election Manifesto*. Belfast: DUP.

Dent, Martin, 1988. 'The Feasibility of Shared Sovereignty (and Shared Authority)', pp. 128–56 in Charles Townshend, *Consensus in Ireland: Approaches and Recessions*. Oxford: Clarendon.

Dixon, Paul, 1995. 'Internationalization and Unionist Isolation: a Response To Feargal Cochrane', pp. 497–505 in *Political Studies*, vol. 43, no. 3.

Docherty, Thomas, 1993. *Postmodernism: a Reader*. London: Harvester Wheatsheaf.

D'Oliveira, Hans Ulrich Jessurun, 1994. 'European Citizenship: Its Meaning, Its Potential', pp. 126–48 in Renaud Dehousse (ed.), *Europe After Maastricht: an Ever Closer Union?* London: Sweet and Maxwell.

Duff, Andrew, 1994. 'The Main Reforms', pp. 19–35 in Andrew Duff, Jonn Pinder and Roy Pryce (eds), *Maastricht and Beyond*. London: Routledge.

Dyson, K., 1987. 'State' in the *Blackwell Encyclopaedia of Political Institutions*. London: Blackwell.

Eagleton, Terry, 1986. 'Capitalism, Modernism and Postmodernism', pp. 131–48 in *Against The Grain: Essays 1975–1985*. London: Verso.

Elliott, Marianne, 1982. *Partners in Revolution: the United Irishmen and France*. London: Yale.

Farrell, Michael, 1976. *Northern Ireland: the Orange State*. London: Pluto.

Flackes, W.D. and Sidney Elliott, 1989. *Northern Ireland: a Political Directory 1968–1988*. Belfast: Blackstaff.

Flackes, W.D. and Sidney Elliott, 1994. *Northern Ireland: a Political Directory 1968–1993*. Belfast: Blackstaff.

Foster, Hal, 1985. 'Postmodernism: a Preface', pp. iv–xvi in Hal Foster (ed.), *Postmodern Culture*. London: Pluto.

Garvin, Tom, 1981. *The Evolution of Irish Nationalist Politics*. Dublin: Gill and Macmillan.

Garvin, Tom, 1987. 'The Politics of Language and Literature in Pre-independence Ireland, pp. 49–64 in *Irish Political Studies*, vol. 2.

Garvin, Tom, 1994. 'Dialogue for the Deaf', pp. 123–5 in *Irish Review*, no. 15.

Gellner, Ernest, 1964. *Thought and Change*. London: Weidenfeld and Nicolson.

Gellner, Ernest, 1983. *Nations and Nationalism*. Oxford: Basil Blackwell.

Gellner, Ernest, 1992. *Postmodernism, Reason and Religion*. London: Routledge.

Geoghegan, Vincent, 1994. 'Socialism, National Identities and Post-Nationalist Citizenship', pp. 61–80 in *Irish Political Studies*, no. 9.

Giddens, Anthony, 1990. *The Consequences of Modernity*. Cambridge: Polity.

Gillespie, Paul, and Rodney Rice 1991. *Political Union*. Dublin: Institute of European Affairs.

Girvin, Brian, 1994. 'Constitutional Nationalism and Northern Ireland', pp. 5–52 in Brian Barton and Patrick J. Roche (eds), *The Northern Ireland Question: Perspectives and Policies*. Aldershot: Avebury.

Goodman, James, 1996. *Nationalism and Transnationalism: the National Conflict in Ireland and European Union Integration*. Aldershot: Avebury.

Gough, Brendan, 1993. *Postmodernism, Social Psychology and Everyday Life*. Belfast: Queen's University (unpublished PhD thesis).

The Government of the United Kingdom and the Government of the Republic of Ireland, 1993. *The Downing Street Declaration*. London and Belfast: HMSO.

The Government of the United Kingdom and the Government of the Republic of Ireland, 1995. *Frameworks for the Future (the Framework Documents)*. London and Belfast: HMSO.

The Government of the United Kingdom and the Government of the Republic of Ireland, 1998. 'Propositions on Heads of Agreement' in the *Guardian* (13 January).

The Government of the United Kingdom and the Government of the Republic of Ireland, 1998. *The Multi-Party Agreement*. London and Belfast: HMSO.

Graham, Elispeth, Joe Doherty and Mo Malek, 1992. 'The Context and Language of Postmodernism', pp. 1–23 in Joe Doherty, Elspeth Graham and Mo Malek (eds), *Postmodernism and the Social Sciences*. Basingstoke: Macmillan.

Greer, Alex, 1993. 'From Maastricht to Dublin and Belfast: the Irish Debate European Union', pp. 197–216 in the *Journal of Social, Political and Economic Studies*, vol. 18, no. 11–14.

Gudgin, Graham, 1990. *The Northern Ireland Economy: Review and Forecasts to 1995*. Belfast: Northern Ireland Economic Research Council.

Guelke, Adrian, 1994. *New Perspectives on the Northern Ireland Conflict*. Aldershot: Avebury.

Guelke, Adrian, 1996. 'Consenting to Consent', pp. 14–15 in *Fortnight*, no. 353.

Habermas, Jürgen, 1985. 'Modernity: the Incomplete Project', pp. 3–15 in Hal Foster (ed.), *Postmodern Culture*. London: Pluto.

Hainsworth, Paul, 1989. 'Political Parties and the European Community', pp. 51–72 in Arthur Aughey, Paul Hainsworth, Martin J. Trimble, *Northern Ireland in the European Community: an Economic and Political Analysis*. Belfast: Policy Research Institute.

Hainsworth, Paul and Duncan Morrow, 1993. 'Northern Ireland: European Region – European Problem', pp. 131–146 in *Études Irlandaises*, vol. 18, no. 2.

Harvey, David, 1989. *The Condition of Postmodernity: an Enquiry into the Origins of Cultural Change*. Oxford: Basil Blackwell.

Hickman, Mary, 1990. *Ireland and the European Community*. London: PNL Press.

Hobsbawm, Eric, 1983. 'Inventing Traditions', pp. 1–14 in Eric Hobsbawm and Terence Ranger (eds), *The Invention of Tradition*. Cambridge: CUP.

Hobsbawm, Eric, 1990. *Nations and Nationalism Since 1780: Programme, Myth and Reality*. Cambridge: CUP.

Holland, Martin, 1993. *European Community Integration*. London: Pinter.

Hollinger, Robert, 1994. *Postmodernism and the Social Sciences – a Thematic Approach*. London: Sage.

Holmes, Michael, 1994. 'Symbols of National Identity and Sport: the Case of the Irish Football Team', pp. 81–98 in *Irish Political Studies*, no. 9.

Hume John, 1979. 'The Irish Question: a British Problem', pp. 300–13 in *Foreign Affairs*, vol. 58, no. 2.

Hume John, 1996. *Personal Views: Politics, Peace and Reconciliation in Ireland*. Dublin: Town House.

Hutchinson, John, 1994. *Modern Nationalism*. London: Fontana.

Irish Political Studies, 1994. 'Election Results', p. 199 in *Irish Political Studies*, vol. 9.

Irish Political Studies, 1995. 'Election Results', p. 273 in *Irish Political Studies*, vol. 10.

Jackson, Alvin, 1994. 'Irish Unionism 1905–21', pp. 35–46 in Peter Collins (ed.) *Nationalism and Unionism: Conflict in Ireland 1884–1921*. Belfast: Institute of Irish Studies.

Jameson Fredrick, 1985. 'Postmodernism and Consumer Society', pp. 111–25 in Hal Foster (ed.), *Postmodern Culture*. London: Pluto.

Jones, John Paul, Wolfgang Natter and Theodore R. Schatzki, 1993. '"Post"-ing Modernity', pp. 1–72 in John Paul Jones, Wolfgang Natter and Theodore R. Schatzki (eds), *Postmodern Contentions*. London: Guilford Press.

Kearney, Richard, 1984. *Myth and Motherland*. Derry: Field Day.

Kearney, Richard, 1988a. *Transitions: Narratives in Modern Irish Culture*. Manchester: MUP.

Kearney, Richard, 1988b. *Across The Frontiers: Ireland in the 1990s*. Dublin: Gill and Macmillan.

Kearney, Richard, 1993. 'Postmodernity, Nationalism and Ireland', pp. 147–55 in *A History of European Ideas*, vol. 13, no. 1–3.

Kearney, Richard, 1997. *Postnationalist Ireland: Politics, Culture, Philosophy*. London: Routledge.

Keating, Michael, and Barry Jones, 1985. *Regions in the European Community*. Oxford: Clarendon.

Keatinge, Patrick, 1992. 'From Community to Union', pp. 2–9 in *Maastricht and Ireland: What the Treaty Means?* Dublin: Institute of European Affairs.

Keatinge, Patrick, 1992(b). 'Towards a Federal Union?', pp. 87–93 in *Maastricht and Ireland: What the Treaty Means?* Dublin: Institute of European Affairs.

Kennedy, Dennis, 1988. *The Widening Gulf: Northern Attitudes to the Independent Irish State*. Belfast: Blackstaff.

Kennedy, Dennis, 1994. 'The European Union and the Northern Irish Question', pp. 166–188 in Brian Barton and Patrick J. Roche (eds), *The Northern Ireland Question: Perspectives and Policies*. Aldershot: Avebury.

Kennedy, Kieran, Thomas Giblin and Deirdre McHugh, 1988. *The Economic Development of Ireland in the Twentieth Century*. London: Routledge.

Laffan, Brigid, 1992a. *Integration and Co-operation in Europe*. London: Routledge.

Laffan, Brigid, 1992b. 'The Treaty: Structures and Themes', pp. 12–17 in *Maastricht and Ireland: What the Treaty Means?* Dublin: Institute of European Affairs.

Laffan, Brigid, 1992c. 'The New Institutional Framework', pp. 22–6 in *Maastricht and Ireland: What the Treaty Means?* Dublin: Institute of European Affairs.

Laffan, Brigid and Edward Moxon-Browne, 1992. 'How Democratic is the Union?', pp. 27–31 in *Maastricht and Ireland: What the Treaty Means?* Dublin: Institute of European Affairs.

Lee, J.J. 1989. *Ireland 1912–1985: Politics and Society*. Cambridge: CUP.

Loftus, Belinda, 1994. *Mirrors: Orange and Green*. Dundrum: Picture Press.

Longley, Edna, 1992. 'Writing, Revisionism and Grass-seed: Literary Mythologies in Ireland', pp. 11–21 in Jean Lundy and Aodán MacPóilin (eds), *Styles of Belonging: the Cultural Identities of Ulster*. Belfast: Lagan Press.

Lyons, F.S.L. 1977. *Charles Stewart Parnell*. London: Fontana.

Lyotard, Jean-Francois, 1984. *The Postmodern Condition: a Report on Knowledge*. Manchester: Manchester University Press.

McAlinden, Gerry, 1995. 'The European Union: a Better Life on the Border', pp. 77–84 in Michael D'Arcy and Tim Dickson (eds), *Border Crossings: Developing Ireland's Island Economy*. Dublin: Gill & Macmillan.

McAllister, Ian, 1977. *The Northern Ireland Social Democratic and Labour Party: Opposition in a Divided Society*. London: Macmillan.

McCall, Cathal, 1994. 'Beyond the Breeze Blocks: Antinationalist Nationalists in Northern Ireland', pp. 18–19 in *Fortnight*, no. 328.

McCall, Cathal, 1995. *Structural Change and Irish Nationalist Identities in Northern Ireland: a Postmodernist Perspective*. Glasgow: University of Strathclyde.

McCall, Cathal, 1998. 'Postmodern Europe and Communal Identities in Northern Ireland' pp. 389–411 in the *European Journal of Political Research*, vol. 33, no. 3.

McCann, Eamonn, 1993. *War and an Irish Town*. London: Pluto.

McGarry, John and Brendan O'Leary, 1990. *The Future of Northern Ireland*. Oxford: Clarendon.

McGarry, John and Brendan O'Leary, 1995. *Explaining Northern Ireland*. Oxford: Blackwell.

McKee, P.G. 1993. *The Discourse of Nationalists in Northern Ireland 1921–1995*. Belfast: Queen's University (unpublished Ph.D thesis).

McKittrick, David, 1989. *Despatches From Belfast*. Belfast: Blackstaff.

McKittrick, David, 1994. *Endgame: the Search For Peace in Northern Ireland*. Belfast: Blackstaff.

Majone, Giandomenico, 1994. 'The Rise of the Regulatory State in Europe', pp. 77–101 in *West European Politics*, vol. 17, no. 3.

Mansergh, Martin, 1996. 'Manufacturing Consent', pp. 13–15 in *Fortnight*, no. 350.

Marks, Gary, 1992. 'Structural Policy in the EC', pp. 192–224 in Alberta M. Sbragia (ed.), *Euro-Politics: Institutions and Policymaking in the 'New' European Community*. Washington DC: Brookings Institute.

Marks, Gary, 1993. 'Structural Policy and Multilevel Governance in the

EC', pp. 391–410 in Alan W. Cafruny and Glenda G. Rosenthal (eds), *the State of The European Community – vol. 2 – The Maastricht Debates and Beyond*. Harlow: Longman.

Meehan, Elisabeth, 1993. 'Citizenship and the European Community', pp. 172–86 in *Political Quarterly*, vol. 64, no. 2.

Millan, Bruce, 1991. *European Integration and the Future of the Regions*. London: Granta.

Mitrany, David, 1970. 'The Functional Approach to World Organisation', pp. 65–76 in Carol Ann Cosgrove and Kenneth J. Twitchett (eds), *The New International Actors: the United Nations and the European Economic Community*. London: Macmillan.

Moran, Michael, 1994. 'The State and the Financial Services Revolution: a Comparative Analysis', pp. 158–77 in *West European Politics*, vol. 17, no. 3.

Moravcsik, Andrew, 1993. 'Preferences and Power in the European Community: a Liberal Intergovernmental Approach' pp. 473–524 in the *Journal of Common Market Studies*, vol. 31. no. 4.

Morrow, Duncan, 1995. 'Warranted Interference? the Republic of Ireland in the Politics of Northern Ireland', pp. 125–48 in *Études Irlandaises*, vol. 20, no. 1.

Moxon-Browne, Edward, 1983. *Nation, Class and Creed in Northern Ireland*. Aldershot: Gower.

Moxon-Browne, Edward, 1991. 'The Legitimacy of the Union', pp. 61–102 in Patrick Keatinge, *Political Union*. Dublin: Institute of European Affairs.

Müller, Wolfgang C. and Vincent Wright, 1994. 'Reshaping the State in Europe: Limits to Retreat', pp. 1–11 in *West European Politics*, vol. 17, no. 3.

Nicoll, William, 1994. 'Representing the States', pp. 190–206 in Andrew Duff, Jonn Pinder and Roy Pryce (eds), *Maastricht and Beyond*. London: Routledge.

Northern Ireland Economic Council (NIEC), 1983. *Additionality of European Community Funds*. Belfast: Northern Ireland Economic Development Office.

Northern Ireland Economic Council (NIEC), 1993. *Economic Assessment (April 1993)*. Belfast: Northern Ireland Economic Development Office.

Northern Ireland Economic Council (NIEC), 1994. *Economic Assessment (April 1994)*. Belfast: Northern Ireland Economic Development Office.

Nugent, Neil, 1994. *Government and Politics of the European Union*. Basingstoke: Macmillan.

O'Connor, Fionnuala, 1993. *In Search of a State: Catholics in Northern Ireland*. Belfast: Blackstaff.

O'Donnell, Rory, 1993. *Ireland and Europe: Challenges for a New Century*. Dublin: Economic and Social Research Institute.

O'Donnell, Rory and Paul Teague, 1993. 'The Potential Limits to North-South Economic Co-operation', pp. 240–70 in Paul Teague (ed.), *The Economy of Northern Ireland: Perspectives for Structural Change*. London: Lawrence and Wishart.

O'Dowd, Liam, 1991a. 'Intellectuals and Political Culture: a Unionist-Nationalist Comparison' in Eamonn Hughes (ed.), *Culture and Politics in Northern Ireland*. Milton Keynes: Open University Press.

O'Dowd, Liam, 1991b. 'The States of Ireland: Some Reflections on Research', pp. 96–106 in *Irish Journal of Sociology*, vol. 1.

O'Dowd, Liam and James Corrigan, 1996. 'Securing the Irish Border in a Europe Without Frontiers', pp. 117–34 in Liam O'Dowd and Thomas M. Wilson (eds), *Border Nations and States*. Aldershot: Avebury.

Ó'Gráda, Cormac and Brendan Walsh, 1994. *Recent Trends in Fertility and Population in Ireland, North and South*. Dublin: University College Dublin.

O'Halloran, Clare, 1987. *Partition and the Limits of Irish Nationalism: an Ideology Under Stress*. Dublin: Gill & Macmillan.

O'Leary, Brendan and Geoffrey Evans, 1997. 'Northern Ireland', pp. 672–80 in *Parliamentary Affairs*, vol. 50, no. 4.

O'Leary, Brendan and John McGarry, 1993. *The Politics of Antagonism: Understanding Northern Ireland*. London: Athlone.

O'Leary, Brendan, Tom Lyne, Jim Marshall and Bob Rowthorn, 1993. *Northern Ireland: Sharing Authority*. London: Institute for Public Policy Research.

O'Leary, Cornelius, 1991. 'Anglo-Irish Relations, the Northern Ireland Problem and the Possible Mediatory Role of the European Community', pp. 155–68, in Preston King and Andrea Bosco, *A Constitution for Europe: a Comparative Study of Federal Constitution and Plans for the United States of Europe*. London: Lothian Press.

O'Malley, Padraig, 1983. *The Uncivil Wars: Ireland Today*. Belfast: Blackstaff.

O'Neill, Terence, 1972. *The Autobiography of Terence O'Neill*. London: Hart-Davis.

Opsahl Report on Northern Ireland, 1993. *A Citizens' Inquiry*. Dublin: Lilliput.

Ó'Tuathaigh, Gearóid, 1994. 'Nationalist Ireland, 1912–22: Aspects of Continuity and Change', pp. 47–74 in Peter Collins (ed.), *Nationalism and Unionism: Conflict in Ireland 1884–1921*. Belfast: Institute of Irish Studies.

Pentland, Charles, 1973. *International Theory and European Integration*. London: Faber.

Phoenix, Eamon, 1994. *Northern Nationalism: Nationalist Politics, Partition and the Catholic Minority in Northern Ireland 1890–1940*. Belfast: UHF.

Pinder, John, 1994. 'Building the Union: Policy, Reform and Constitution', pp. 269–85 in Andrew Duff, Jonn Pinder and Roy Pryce (eds), *Maastricht and Beyond*. London: Routledge.

Poggi, Gianfranco, 1990. *The State: its Nature, Development and Prospects*. Oxford: Polity.

Porter, Norman, 1996. *Rethinking Unionism: an Alternative Vision for Northern Ireland*. Belfast: Blackstaff.

Rabinow, P. 1984. *The Foucault Reader*. New York: Pantheon.

Reynolds, Suzan, 1984. *Kingdoms and Communities in Western Europe (900–1300)*. Oxford: Clarendon.

Robb, Harford, 1995. 'The Border Region: a Case Study', pp. 133–42 in Michael D'Arcy and Tim Dickson (eds), *Border Crossings: Developing Ireland's Island Economy*. Dublin: Gill & Macmillan.

Rose, Richard, 1971. *Governing Without Consensus*. London: Faber and Faber.

Rose, Richard, 1983. *Is the United Kingdom a State?* Glasgow: University of Strathclyde.

Ruane, Joseph, 1994. 'Ireland, European Integration and the Dialectic of Nationalism and Postnationalism', pp. 183–93 in *Études Irlandaises*, vol. 19, no. 1.

Ruane, Joseph and Jennifer Todd, 1989. 'Ireland – North and South – and European Community Integration', pp. 163–92 in Paul Hainsworth (ed.), *Breaking and Preserving the Mould: the Third Direct Elections to the European Parliament (1989) – the Irish Republic and Northern Ireland*. Belfast: Policy Research Institute.

Ruane, Joseph and Jennifer Todd, 1992. 'Diversity, Division, and the Middle Ground in Northern Ireland', pp. 73–98 in *Irish Political Studies*, no. 7.

Ruane, Joseph and Jennifer Todd, 1996. *The Dynamics of Conflict in Northern Ireland: Power, Conflict and Emancipation*. Cambridge: Cambridge University Press.

Ryan, Mark, 1994. *War and Peace in Ireland*. London: Pluto.

Sbragia, Alberta M. 1992. *Euro-Politics: Institutions and Policymaking in the 'New' European Community*. Washington DC: Brookings Institute.

Seton-Watson, H. 1977. *Nations and States*. London: Methuen.

Simons, Herbert W. and Michael Billing, 1994. 'Introduction', pp. 1–11 in Herbert W. Simons and Michael Billing (eds), *After Postmodernism: Reconstructing Ideological Technique*. London: Sage.

Sinn Féin, 1991. *Democracy or Dependency: the Case Against Maastricht*. Dublin: Sinn Féin.

Sinn Féin, 1992. *Towards a Lasting Peace in Ireland*. Dublin: Sinn Féin.

Sinn Féin, 1994a. *Setting the Records Straight: a Record of Communications between Sinn Féin and the British Government, October 1990 – November 1993*. Dublin: Sinn Féin.

Sinn Féin, 1994b. *European Election Manifesto: Peace in Ireland – a European Issue*. Dublin: Sinn Féin.

Smart, Barry, 1990. 'Modernity, Postmodernity and the Present', pp. 14–30 in Bryan S. Turner (ed.), *Theories of Modernity and Postmodernity*. London: Sage.

Smith, Anthony D. 1983. *Theories of Nationalism*. London: Duckworth.

Smith, Anthony D. 1986. *The Ethnic Origins of Nations*. Oxford: Basil Blackwell.

Smith, Anthony D. 1991. *National Identity*. London: Penguin.

Smith, M.L.R. 1995. *Fighting For Ireland?: the Military Strategy of the Irish Republican Movement*. London: Routledge.

Social Democratic and Labour Party, 1992. *Westminster General Election Manifesto*. Derry: SDLP.

Social Democratic and Labour Party, 1994. *European Election Manifesto: Towards a New Century*. Derry: SDLP.

Social Democratic and Labour Party, 1995. *Constitution*. Belfast: Linenhall Library (unpublished).

Soja, Edward, 1989. *Postmodern Geographies: the Reassertion of Space in Critical Social Theory*. London: Verso.

Soja, Edward, 1993. 'Postmodern Geographies and the Critique of Historicism', pp. 113–36 in John Paul Jones, Wolfgang Natter and Theodore R. Schatzki (eds), *Postmodern Contentions*. London: Guilford Press.

Spicker, Paul, 1994. *Concepts of Subsidiarity in the European Community.* Dundee: University of Dundee.

Tamir, Yael, 1993. *Liberal Nationalism.* Princeton: Princeton University Press.

Teague, Paul. 1994. 'Approved Border Road', pp. 31–4 in *Fortnight* no. 332.

Tilly, Charles, 1975. *The Formation of National States in Western Europe.* Princeton: London Princeton University.

Tilly, Charles, 1990. *Coercion, Capital and European States AD 900–1990.* Oxford: Basil Blackwell.

Todd, Jennifer, 1987. 'Two Traditions in Unionist Political Culture', pp. 1–26 in *Irish Political Studies*, no. 2.

Todd, Jennifer, 1990. 'Northern Irish Nationalist Political Culture', pp. 31–44 in *Irish Political Studies*, no. 5.

Trimble, David, 1996. *Speech to the Annual General Meeting of the Ulster Unionist Council.* Belfast: Linenhall Library (Unpublished).

Ulster Unionist Information Institute, 1996. *The British People of Northern Ireland – a Short Resume of Unionism.* Belfast: UUII.

Ulster Unionist Party, 1990. *Signpost to the Future.* Belfast: UUP.

Ulster Unionist Party, 1992. *Westminster General Election Manifesto.* Belfast: UUP.

Ulster Unionist Party, 1994. *European Election Manifesto: Europe – Making it Work for Ulster.* Belfast: UUP.

Ulster Unionist Party, 1996. *Manifesto: Forum Election.* Belfast: UUP.

Ulster Young Unionist Council, 1986. *Cuchulain the Lost Legend: Ulster the Lost Culture.* Belfast: UYUC.

Urwin, Derek and Stein Rokkan, 1983. *Economy, Territory, Identity: Politics of West European Peripheries.* London: Sage.

Walker, Brian M. 1989. *Ulster Politics: the Formative Years 1868–86.* Belfast: UHF.

Walker, Brian M. 1994. 'The 1885 and 1886 General Elections: a Milestone in Irish History', pp. 1–17 in Peter Collins (ed.), *Nationalism and Unionism: Conflicts in Ireland 1885–1921.* Belfast: Institute of Irish Studies.

White, Barry, 1985. *John Hume: Statesman of the Troubles.* Belfast: Blackstaff.

Whyte, John, 1990. *Interpreting Northern Ireland.* Oxford: Clarendon.

Wilson, Thomas M. 1993. 'Frontiers Go but Boundaries Remain: the Irish Border as a Cultural Divide', pp. 167–88 in Thomas M. Wilson and Estellie Smith (eds), *Cultural Change and the New Europe: Perspectives on the European Community.* San Francisco: Westview.

Index

Act of Union (1801), 38, 174
Adams, Gerry, 23, 52–3, 113–4,
    118, 123–4, 176, 211
African National Congress (ANC),
    136
Ahern, Bertie, 195
Alderdice, John, xvi, 13, 179–92
Alliance Party of Northern Ireland
    (APNI), xv, 85, 156, 179–92,
    193, 198, 200, 205, 207, 212
Anderson, Benedict, 19, 26, 29–30
Anderson, James, 115, 210
Anglo-Irish Agreement (1985), 13,
    36, 37, 39, 48–51, 54, 81, 99,
    108, 119, 120, 157, 162, 195–6,
    199, 209
Anglo-Irish political process, xi,
    xvi, 13–14, 18, 49, 90, 193,
    195, 198, 206
Anglo-Irish Treaty (1921), 32
Armstrong, John, 208
Aughey, Arthur, 11
authoritative intellectuals, xiii,
    194, 198

'B' Specials, *see* Ulster Special
    Reserve
Battle of the Boyne, 174
Battle of the Somme, 174
Bauman, Zygmunt, 4, 9, 12, 16, 73
Beckett, Samuel, 24
Belfast, 208
Belfast City Council, 145
Belfast News-Letter, 33
Belfast Telegraph, 33
Berman, Marshall, 4
Bew, Paul, 211
Bloody Sunday, 10
Boundary Commission, 32, 38–9
Bradley, John, 115
Breuilly, John, 20
British subvention, 76–7, 81,
    164–5, 201, 210

British-Irish (East-West) council,
    162–3, 212
Brooke-Mayhew Talks (1991–2),
    46, 47, 51, 99, 103, 141, 144,
    184–5, 199, 200
Bruce, Steve, xv
Bunreacht Na hÉireann/
    Constitution of Ireland (1937),
    39, 50, 54, 208
Burke, Richard, 211

Cadogan Group, 78, 80, 83, 210,
    211, 212
Caporaso, James A. 97
Carron, Owen, 23
citizenship, xvii, 16, 39, 41, 56,
    69–73, 90, 117, 152, 191, 197,
    202, 204
Clinton, Bill, 198
Cohen, A. P. 24
Cohesion Fund, 164
Coleraine, 40
Collins, Michael, 126
Committee of the Regions, xvii,
    56, 67–8, 97, 101, 104–5, 159,
    177, 187
Common Market poll (1975), 56,
    149, 180
community, 88
    see also ethnic identity;
    nation; nationalism
Community Support Frameworks
    (CSFs), 66
Connaught Telegraph, 30
consent, 53, 168, 170, 205
Conservative government, 52, 54
consociationalism, 45–8, 50–1,
    209
Constitutional Convention (1975),
    47
Cooper, Ivan, 95
Cosgrave, W. T. 38
Coulter, Colin, xv

Council of Ireland, 45, 46, 47,
144, 179, 185
Craig, Bill, 46
Craigavon, 40
cross-party talks (1978–9), 47
cultural resource of identity,
86–90, 148–52, 174–8
Currie, Austin, 95

Dalriada, 189
de Valera, Éamon, 38, 109
decentralization, 62, 197
deconstruction, xiii, 62, 64, 73, 197
Dehousse, Renaud, 63, 72
Delors, Jacques, 57, 99, 144, 167,
171
Democratic Dialogue, 208
Democratic Left, 123
Democratic Loyalist Coalition, 138
Democratic Unionist Party (DUP),
xv, 45, 46, 56, 81–2, 99, 120,
138–55, 156, 170, 171, 182,
184–5, 193, 198, 200, 205, 207
Department of Foreign Affairs
(Republic of Ireland), 169
Derrida, Jacques, 8
Derry, 40
Devlin, Paddy, 95
DG-16, 210
dialogue, xvi, 13, 63
discrimination, 39, 40
Dodds, Nigel, xvi, 140–55
Downing Street Declaration
(1993), 14, 39, 51, 55, 108,
126, 155, 183, 195, 200, 208
Dungannon District Council, 125
Durkan, Mark, xvi, 96–122, 209
Dyson, K. 37

economic resource of identity,
76–80, 170–1, 190–2, 205
Education Act (1947), 41
Elliott, Sidney, 139
Empey, Reg, xvi, 67, 108, 158–78
empiricism, xiii
enlightenment, 5, 8–9, 11, 15, 196
Ervine, David, 210
ethnic identity, 19, 20, 27, 30, 35,
88, 177, 203, 208

Euregio, 79
Europe of Nations group, 157
'Europe of the Regions', 64, 83–4,
85, 101–4, 106, 122, 165–7,
180, 182, 187, 188, 191
European Central Bank, 57
European Commission, 47, 48, 57,
59, 60, 64, 65, 66, 68, 97,
99–100, 144, 188, 197, 199
European Community (EC), xi,
49, 56, 82, 96, 157, 159, 165
see also European Union (EU)
European Convention on Human
Rights (ECHR), 70
European Council, 59
European Council of Ministers,
59, 68, 96–8, 116, 167, 188,
199
European Court of Human
Rights, 82
European Court of Justice, 59, 60,
63, 69
European Democratic Group, 157
European Economic Community
(EEC), xi, 82, 99, 130, 140,
180–1
see also European Union (EU)
European integration, xvii, 52,
56–61, 72–3, 78–9, 81–2, 85,
90–1, 98, 115, 117, 120, 121,
124, 137, 140, 145, 149, 152,
158–61, 167, 171, 173, 182,
185, 188, 199, 201, 205
European Liberal, Democratic and
Reformist group, 180–1
European Monetary Union
(EMU), 56, 60, 61, 154, 157,
158, 160, 191
European Parliament, 59, 68, 95,
96–100, 104–5, 123, 132, 134,
138–9, 145, 147–8, 156–7, 166,
179, 181, 199
European Peoples' Party, 157
European Right Group, 157
European Union (EU), xi, xii, xiv,
xvi, xvii, 3, 5–7, 9, 13–14, 16,
18, 47–8, 51–2, 54–5, 56–74,
76–7, 82, 90, 102–3, 105, 107,
112, 114–20, 124, 128–32,

134–7, 139, 141, 143–4, 149,
151–2, 154, 158, 161, 164–7,
169–71, 173, 178, 186, 191,
193, 197–206, 210
'Euro-speak', 66, 107
  see also 'Hume-speak'

Fair Employment Act (1989), 49
famine, 10, 23, 206
Faulkner, Brian, 42, 45–6, 156
Fianna Fáil, 38
Fine Gael, 126, 181
Fitt, Gerry, 95
FitzGerald, Garret, 48, 148
Flackes, W. D. 139
flexible accumulation, 6
Forum for Peace and
  Reconciliation (Dublin), 112,
  184
Foucault, Michel, 8
Framework Documents (1995), 14,
  39, 53, 54, 78, 81, 109, 126–7,
  155, 179, 184–5, 195, 200

Gaelic Athletic Association
  (GAA), 89
Gaelic League, 22, 30
Gaeltacht, 211
Garvin, Tom, 16
Gellner, Ernest, 25–9, 33, 35
Goodman, James, 115, 210, 212
Government of Ireland Act
  (1920), 32, 36, 80, 174, 195
Government of Ireland Bill
  (1920), 32
Government of the Republic of
  Ireland, 13–14, 37, 39, 41, 47,
  48, 49–51, 54–5, 65, 79, 90,
  100, 108, 116, 119, 142, 151,
  152, 155, 163, 167, 169, 172,
  193, 195, 199, 209
Government of the United
  Kingdom, xii, xvii, 13–14, 37,
  41, 43, 46, 49–52, 54–5, 61,
  65, 76–7, 79, 85, 90, 100, 108,
  115–6, 119, 142, 153, 154–5,
  159, 163, 165–7, 169, 193, 195,
  199, 201
Gudgin Graham, 210

Habermas, Jürgen, 4
Hainsworth, Paul, 210
Harvey, David, 4, 6–8, 15, 16, 33,
  62, 197
Haughey, Denis, xiv, xvi, 67,
  97–122, 166, 209
Heath, Edward, 42, 210
'high culture', 25
Hobsbawm, Eric, 26–7, 209
Hollinger, Robert, 4
Hume, John, xi, 47, 52, 86, 95,
  98–9, 101, 103, 104–5, 107,
  108, 111, 113, 116, 118, 132,
  133, 139, 141, 144–6, 148, 156,
  161–3, 167–70, 176, 179,
  198–9, 203, 209, 211
'Hume-Adams' accord, 109, 113–4,
  123, 125–6, 132, 133
'Hume-speak', 107, 145–6, 167–70,
  199
  see also 'Euro-speak'
Hunger Strike (1981), 23
'hybrid identity', 146, 151, 186–8
hyperreality, 9

imagined community, 10, 16, 19,
  29–31, 178, 203, 208
Industrial Development Agency
  (IDA), 184
Industrial Development Board
  (IDB), 184
intergovernmental conference,
  13–14, 48, 50
intergovernmentalism, 57–8
internal-conflict paradigm, xiii, 3,
  198
International Fund for Ireland, 77
interpretation, xiii, 3, 10, 64, 194,
  198
INTERREG, 78–9, 86, 90, 161,
  201–2
intersubjectivity, xiv, 12–14, 73,
  198, 200, 204
Irish Association, 72
'Irish dimension', 45–7, 50, 54, 194
Irish News, 33
Irish Republican Army (IRA), xiv,
  10, 13, 33, 38, 42, 43, 46, 86,
  113–4, 123, 124, 142–3, 151, 170

Irish Republican Socialist Party (IRSP), 212

joint authority, 126–7, 209
Joyce, James, 24, 208
justice, 10, 85, 88

Kearney, Richard, 17, 84, 101, 203, 211
Keeler, John T. S. 97
Kennedy, Dennis, 10, 33, 211
Kerry Sentinel, 30

Labour (Northern Ireland), 53
Labour government, 107
'lateral' ethnic communities, 21
League of Nations, 182
Lemass, Seán, 41, 209
Liberal Democrats, 181
Longley, Edna 101, 211
'low culture', 28
Lyotard, Jean-François, 8, 15

Maastricht Treaty, 52, 57, 59, 60–3, 67, 69–72, 85, 101, 104, 124, 140, 147, 181, 200, 202, 204
Manchester Martyrs, 23
marginalized voices, 7, 15, 50, 64, 75, 194, 200
Marks, Gary, 60
McAlinden, Gerry, 78
McAliskey, Bernadette, 133, 211
McCann, Eamon, 130
McCartney, Robert, 174
McGarry, John, 45
McGuinness, Martin, 176
McKittrick, David, 11, 170
McLaughlin, Mitchel, xvi, 124–37
Meehan, Elizabeth, 69
Mississippi, 7
modern texts, 10
modernity, xiii, xvi, xvii, 3, 4, 7–8, 10, 14–15, 17, 34, 51, 73, 81, 84, 137, 196–7, 203–4
modernization, 4, 8, 22, 34
Molloy, Francie, xvi, 125–37
Molyneaux, Jim, 177
Monnet, Jean, 57–9, 69, 82

Moravcsik, Andrew, 58, 97
Morrison, Danny, 142
Morrow, Maurice, xvi, 141–55
Moxon-Browne, Edward, 70, 186
Müller, Wolfgang C. 59
multilevel governance, xvii, 16–17, 57, 60, 63, 67, 71–3, 77, 79, 90, 128, 186, 194, 196–7, 201–2, 204
Multi-Party Agreement (1998), 39, 47, 53, 55, 78, 128, 155, 162, 195–6
Multi-Party Talks (1996–8), 14, 47, 51, 55, 78, 100, 162, 195–6, 199–200
multiple truths, *see* truth
myth, 9, 22–4, 203, 207

nation, xvii, 19, 20, 21, 25–7, 33, 34, 35, 88, 190, 203, 208
Nation, 30
national self-determination, 12, 52, 113–4, 129, 130, 131, 134–5, 209
nationalism, 4, 17, 20, 21, 26–9, 84, 112, 203–4
    and grievance, 23, 26, 40, 203
    and liberal nationalist, 33–5, 84, 88, 133, 188, 204–5
    and modern nationalist, 34, 202
    and postnationalism, 84, 133, 203
    and 'reactive nationalism', 30
    and traditional nationalist, 41
Nationalist Party, 41
nation-state, xi, xvi, xvii, 3, 4, 5, 7, 10, 17, 26, 35, 57, 58, 83, 96, 98, 102, 105, 111, 140, 145, 159, 170, 190, 196–8, 201–3, 205–6, 207
neo-functionalism, 57–8
New Ireland Forum, 99
newspapers, 29–30, 33–4, 203
Nicholson, Jim, xvi, 86, 105–6, 144, 156, 158–78
Nietzsche, Friedrich, xii
nihilism, 12
'no-go' areas, 43
Northern Ireland Assembly, 47, 53, 100, 164

Northern Ireland Centre in
    Europe, 64, 78, 166
Northern Ireland Civil Rights
    Association (NICRA), 7, 41,
    42
Northern Ireland Constitutional
    proposals (1973), 54
Northern Ireland Office, 76
Northern Whig, 33
North-South Council, 54, 100,
    162–3, 195

objectivity, xiv, 3, 5, 10, 12–14, 42,
    193–4, 196–8
Ó'Brádaigh, Ruairí, 120, 123, 211
O'Connell, Daniel, 30, 209
O'Connor, Fionnuala, 11, 110, 133
O'Donnell, Rory, 87
O'Dowd, Liam, xvi
Official Sinn Féin, 123
Official Unionist Party (OUP), *see*
    Ulster Unionist Party (UUP)
O'Hanlon, Paddy, 95
O'Leary, Brendan, 45, 210
O'Malley, Padraig, 89
O'Neill, Terence, 40–2, 75, 156,
    179, 194
Opsahl Commission, 15, 208
Orange Free State, 136
Orange Order, 23–4, 120, 174, 176
O'Toole, Fintan, 10

Paisley, Ian, 41, 46, 81–2, 86, 138,
    144–5, 148, 156, 157, 169, 171,
    175, 176, 179
'pan-Nationalist front', 124
paradigm shift, xiii, 11, 17, 51, 54,
    193, 198
'parity of esteem', 120–1, 198
Parnell, Charles Stuart, 19–20, 31
Patterson, Henry, 211
Poggi, Gianfranco, 43
political category status, 43
Pope John Paul II, 139
Porter, Norman, xi, 11, 165, 174,
    205
positivism, 8
post-fordism, 6
postmodern paradigm, 14

postmodernism, xii, xiv, 4, 8–9, 12,
    15–16, 18, 19, 50, 194, 196–7,
    204
and 'humpty-dumpty'
    postmodernists, 9, 15
and postmodernism of
    resistance, xiii, xiv, xvi, xviii,
    9, 11, 15, 17, 66, 72–3, 113,
    194, 197–8, 204
and right-leaning
    postmodernists, 9
postmodernity, xii, xvi, xvii, 3, 4,
    8, 34, 45, 50, 51, 54, 66, 68,
    73, 75, 78–9, 80, 84, 86–7,
    90–1, 137, 193, 196–206
Prior, Jim, 47
progress, 5, 8
Progressive Democrats, 181
Progressive Unionist Party (PUP),
    7, 53, 195, 207, 210
'Propositions on Heads of
    Agreement' document, 55, 78,
    128, 155, 162, 195
Protestant Telegraph, 139, 149
Protestant Unionist Party, 138

Reagan, Ronald, 9
reconstruction, xiii, 65–6, 197, 205
Rees, Merlyn, 46
representation of difference, xvi,
    194, 197, 200
Reynolds, Albert, 124
Reynolds, Suzan, 208
Riverdance, 87
Rokkan, Stein, 71, 75
'Rolling Devolution', 47
Royal Ulster Constabulary (RUC),
    38

Sands, Bobby, 23
'Save Ulster from Sodomy'
    campaign, 82
scientific method, 5
Scotland, 134, 210
sectarianism, 90, 151, 174
self-determination,
    see national self-determination
Seton-Weston, Hugh, 208
siege mentality, 23

Siege of Derry (1689), 23, 174–5
Siege of Drumcree (1995–), 174,
    177–8
Single European Act, 56, 61, 78,
    124, 140
Sinn Féin, xiv, 7, 13, 33, 53, 56,
    84–5, 95, 108, 123–37, 142–3,
    153, 176, 193, 198, 200, 205,
    207, 210, 212
Smart, Barry, 3, 4
Smith, Anthony D. 20–5
Social Democratic and Labour
    Party (SDLP), xiv, 33, 37, 47,
    50, 53, 82–4, 95–122, 123–4,
    133, 137, 141, 143, 145, 153,
    160, 163, 167–8, 172, 176, 182,
    188, 193, 194, 198–9, 200, 204,
    207, 209, 212
    and 'Commission for Northern
    Ireland' proposal, 99–100,
    141, 188, 211
social partnership, 66, 79, 202
Soja, Edward, 4, 9, 15, 16
South Africa, 127, 136
sovereignty, 20, 158–9, 185, 198,
    203, 205–6
Soviet Union, 125
Special Support Programme for
    Peace and Reconciliation
    (1995–), 66, 77, 79, 86, 90,
    144, 153, 164, 201–2, 210
'spillover effect', 57–8, 158
state, 20, 37, 42, 70, 174
structural funds, 59, 65, 66, 77,
    125, 153, 201, 211
subsidiarity, xvii, 56, 61–4, 66–8,
    159–60, 164
'sub-state', 207
Sunningdale experiment, 37, 45,
    46, 48–9, 144, 156, 179, 185,
    194

Tamir, Yael, 71, 190, 203
Taylor, John, 89, 156–7
Teague, Paul, 78
television, 7, 12, 203
territorial resource of identity,
    80–6, 133–5, 146–8, 171–4,
    188–90

Thatcher, Margaret, 109, 180,
    209
Third World, 6
Todd, Jennifer, xv
tolerance, 72
'totality of relationships'
    paradigm, 51, 199, 212
transterritorialism, 206, 212
Treaty of Rome (1957), 82, 140,
    149
Treaty of Westphalia (1648), 20
Trimble, David, 89–90, 175, 177–8,
    200, 210, 212
truth, xii, xiii, 7, 10–12, 18, 193–4,
    196, 198, 200, 209

U2, 87
Ulster Convention (1892), 31
Ulster Covenant (1912), 31, 174
Ulster Defence Association
    (UDA), 88
Ulster Democratic Party (UDP),
    7, 53, 195, 207
Ulster Farmers Union, 144
Ulster Special Reserve ('B'
    Specials), 38, 40
Ulster Unionist Council (1905),
    31
Ulster Unionist Party (UUP), xv,
    45, 46, 53, 54, 56, 80–1, 99,
    103, 138, 145, 150, 156–78,
    182, 184–5, 193, 195, 198, 200,
    205, 207, 212
Ulster Volunteer Force (UVF),
    210
Ulster Workers' Council strike, 46,
    98, 174, 195
Ulster Young Unionist Committee
    on Culture, 174
Unionist Party of Northern
    Ireland (UPNI), 156
United Irishmen, 19, 22
United Kingdom Unionist Party
    (UKU), 207
United Nations, 181
United States, 47, 107, 198
United Ulster Unionist Council
    (UUUC), 46, 138, 156
Urwin, Derek, 71, 75

value-neutrality, 8, 198
Vanguard, 45, 156
'vertical' ethnic communities, 21–2

Wales, 134, 210
Whitelaw, William, 43–4
Wilson, Paddy, 95
Wilson, Sammy, 90

Women's Coalition, 53, 200, 207
Workers Party, 123
Wright, Vincent, 59

xenophobia, 204

Yeats, W. B. 24
Young Ireland, 22, 30